Be...

...Coast
...and all three
...e South-West Coast
...t series. On most walks
he's accompanied by Daisy.
Two parts trouble to one part
Parson's Jack Russell, Daisy
has completed ten national
trails as well as the Coast to Coast path and Dales Way.

When not travelling or writing, Henry lives in Battle, East Sussex, editing and also arranging climbs on Africa's highest mountain through his company, Kilimanjaro Experts.

London LOOP

First edition: 2021

Publisher Trailblazer Publications
The Old Manse, Tower Rd, Hindhead, Surrey, GU26 6SU, UK
info@trailblazer-guides.com, ☐ trailblazer-guides.com

British Library Cataloguing in Publication Data
A catalogue record for this book is available from the British Library

ISBN 978-1-912716-21-0

© **Trailblazer** 2021: Text and maps

Editor: Anna Jacomb-Hood   **Proofreading**: Nicky Slade
Cartography: Nick Hill   **Layout & Index**: Anna Jacomb-Hood
Photographs (flora): © Bryn Thomas
All other photographs: © Henry Stedman (unless otherwise indicated)

The maps in this guide were prepared from out-of-Crown-
copyright Ordnance Survey maps amended and updated by Trailblazer.

Acknowledgements

My heartfelt thanks to Anna and Kazuo Udagawa for re-researching the Hogsmill stretch to
make sure that walkers really couldn't follow it all the way to Kingston; and to Ian Bull for
his invaluable help, insights and updates on the trail.
   Thanks are also due to Nick Hill for his usual sterling work designing the maps, and to
Anna Jacomb-Hood once again for her forensic approach to editing and to Roderick Leslie
for insights into birds and trees. Plus, of course, to Bryn Thomas of Trailblazer, for continuing to find projects for me to work on – I'm truly grateful.
   Finally, thanks to Zoe and Henry for making life in between the walking so much fun.

A request

The author and publisher have tried to ensure that this guide is as accurate and up to date
as possible. Nevertheless, things change. If you notice any changes or omissions that should
be included in the next edition of this book, please write to Trailblazer (address above) or
email us at ☐ info@trailblazer-guides.com. A free copy of the next edition will be sent to
persons making a significant contribution.

Warning: long-distance walking can be dangerous

Please read the notes on when to go (pp12-13) and outdoor safety (pp51-3). Every effort
has been made by the author and publisher to ensure that the information contained herein
is as accurate and up to date as possible. However, they are unable to accept responsibility
for any inconvenience, loss or injury sustained by anyone as a result of the advice and information given in this guide.

Updated information will be available on: ☐ **trailblazer-guides.com**

Photos – Front cover and this page: A peaceful stretch of the Grand Union Canal
between Uxbridge and Harefield West.
Previous page: Treading the boards across the saturated ground of Donkey Wood.
Overleaf: The City of London skyline emerges above the trees of Hainault Forest,
on the way to Havering-Atte-Bower.

Printed in China; print production by D'Print (☎ +65-6581 3832), Singapore

London LOOP

LONDON OUTER ORBITAL PATH

48 large-scale walking maps (1:20,000) & route guide
PLANNING – PLACES TO STAY – PLACES TO EAT
includes full public transport information
for day walkers

HENRY STEDMAN

TRAILBLAZER PUBLICATIONS

INTRODUCTION

PART 1: PLANNING YOUR WALK

PART 2: GETTING TO & FROM THE LOOP

PART 3: MINIMUM IMPACT WALKING & OUTDOOR SAFETY

PART 4: THE ENVIRONMENT & NATURE

Contents

PART 5: ROUTE GUIDE AND MAPS

APPENDICES

INDEX 216

OVERVIEW MAPS & PROFILES 221

Contents

This guidebook contains all the information you need. The hard work has been done for you so you can plan your trip without having to consult numerous websites and other books and maps. When you're packed and ready to go, there's comprehensive public transport information to get you to and from the trail and detailed maps (1:20,000) to help you find your way along it. It includes:

● Answers to all your questions: when to go, degree of difficulty, what to pack, and how much the whole walk will cost.
● Walking times and GPS waypoints
● Suggested itineraries
● Accommodation section – for those not living near the LOOP who want to complete the trail over a series of days
● Cafés, pubs, tearooms, takeaways, restaurants along the way – and shops/supermarkets for buying supplies
● Rail, tube, tram and bus information for all places along the path
● Historical, cultural and geographical background information

❑ THIS BOOK AND THE COVID-19 PANDEMIC

This guide book was researched and written during the summer months of 2020, when the country was suffering from the effects of the COVID-19 pandemic. As a result, many of the cafés, restaurants, pubs, museums and other establishments were either closed or operating reduced hours.

Most **accommodation** was back open, albeit with some changes. Some small hotels and guesthouses had reduced the number of rooms that they were letting out at any one time.

The majority of **pubs, restaurants and cafés** were open but they were having to adapt to comply with any restrictions. In general these mean reduced opening hours and a limited menu; booking a table in advance and table service only (though some were only offering takeaway or meals served outdoors). It may still be necessary to wear a face mask when you go into (or move around) a pub, café or restaurant but not when you are sitting down.

Most **train and bus services** were operating to reduced timetables but should now be back to normal. However, it is likely face coverings will still be required on (or in) all forms of public transport.

Museums and galleries may require booking (especially for tours) and also restrict the number of people inside at any one time.

Hopefully, by the time you read this, Coronavirus, lockdowns and other ubiquitous words from 2020 will be nothing but a bad memory of a surreal year. And if that's the case, the operating hours of the establishments en route will be back to 'normal'.

For the latest information visit 🖥 gov.uk/coronavirus.

INTRODUCTION

The LOOP is a **150¾-mile (242.6km) circuit** around the perimeter of England's capital. Its name is derived from the initials of **London Outer Orbital Path**, which is why, in case you're wondering, it's usually written in capitals. It was largely the brainchild of an organisation called the **London Walking Forum**, which was formed in the early 1990s to encourage people to visit and take advantage of the many green spaces in the capital. One of their ideas was to create a walk that followed, roughly, the outskirts of Greater London – and the LOOP was born. The first section (on Farthing Downs, Coulsdon) was opened in May 1996 and the entire route was completed in 2001.

Originally, funding for the trail (and several other walks in the capital) was provided by Transport for London (TfL), but in 2011 the London boroughs assumed responsibility for maintenance. In 2021 Inner London Ramblers (a branch of Ramblers) is taking over the promotion and management of the trail.

One could say that the name of the trail is somewhat misleading. For one thing, the LOOP does not describe a complete loop or circle around the capital: between the official start at Erith and the end at Purfleet-on-Thames there is the small matter of the River Thames, which cannot be crossed easily – at least, not anywhere near there. The ferry that once took passengers from one side of the river to the other near Purfleet has long since ceased and the nearest crossing these days is the Queen Elizabeth II Bridge at Dartford Crossing,

Above: One of the big surprises about the LOOP is how much green space there is on the outskirts of London such as here, near Pyrgo Park (pp184-5).

Introduction

Above – Stage 1: On the Crayford Marshes, between Erith and Bexley, just after setting off.

about four miles (6.5km) away. What's more, pedestrians aren't allowed to walk over the bridge, so you would have to catch a bus across. The only other option is to walk west along the Thames to the Greenwich Tunnel – though at around 15 miles that's a whole day's walk away (not to mention a whole day back again!).

The name is also misleading for another reason: because while it may have London quite literally at its heart, it doesn't stick wholly within the boundaries of the capital but instead regularly calls upon the neighbouring home counties. True, it largely succeeds in avoiding Kent altogether, but the LOOP does indulge in a dalliance with Surrey, flirts with Buckinghamshire, and becomes rather heavily involved with Hertfordshire – before finally settling down for a lasting liaison with Essex. The trail does, however, stay within the M25 – though occasionally you can hear the roar of traffic from it. And by-and-large it likes to stick to the so-called '**Metropolitan Green Belt**' – that buffer zone of green, largely undeveloped land that encircles the city. The first green belt around the capital actually dates back to the Elizabethan age and was designed to stop the spread of the plague. These days, however, the green belt is designed to combat what many see as an equally virulent pestilence – that of the profit-hungry developer looking to build on Britain's diminishing stock of countryside.

In doing so, the designers of the LOOP have made the trail as attractive and tranquil as a walk within the confines of the M25 can be; indeed, the trail is sometimes called the **M25 for walkers**. It means that, scenery-wise, for much of your time you'll be walking through fields, farms and parkland. Indeed, it's only when you look at a satellite image of the walk that you realise you are actu-

Above – Stage 24: The end's in sight! Ambling to Purfleet with the Queen Elizabeth II Bridge looming ahead.

ally always pretty close to civilisation; because, for much of your time on the trail, it simply doesn't feel like it.

That's not to say that your walk around the LOOP will be one continuous 150-mile long rural ramble. London's relentless expansion over the past 200 years has obviously had a deleterious effect on the countryside and on the wildlife that lives within it. There are no hares in Harefield, for example, and no cranes swooping over the Crane River. And if there ever was a moor in Moor Park – well, there's no more moor in Moor Park anymore.

But, having said that I must confess that I saw more wildlife on this walk than on any of my other treks in Britain! I certainly saw more deer – and not just in the parks either, but more often than not running free in the fields and woodland. I also saw more woodpeckers and little owls (yes, really) on this hike than on any other – and certainly more **parakeets**, those relative

> **I saw more wildlife on this walk than on any of my other treks in Britain!**

newcomers to the city that have colonised vast swathes of the capital's greener sections. Nor was that the only foreign interloper on my time on the LOOP, with a **terrapin** also putting in an appearance in the ponds of Foot's Cray meadows.

But it wasn't just the wildlife that was such a pleasant surprise. Some of the **scenery**, too, was really lovely. I am thinking in particular of **Happy Valley**, on the edge of the North Downs, and the open expanse of nearby **Farthing Downs**. Other highlights were the stillness of the former hay meadows at **Totteridge Fields**, and the lovely undulating farmland near **Harefield**, where London abuts Buckinghamshire, and peaceful, unsung **Salmon's Brook** – a river of calm and a lovely spot for a picnic lunch.

In addition to these there are the modern parks that have been carved out of land that formerly belonged to the great country estates. Parks such as **Foots Cray Meadows**, where the 'feel' of the old country estate is perhaps best preserved; **High Elms Country Park**, where the imprint of the destroyed mansion's kitchens can still be seen in the ground; the wonderful **Bushy Park**, my personal favourite (and a favourite of Henry VIII too); **Cranford Country Park**, a lovely oasis of calm beneath the screaming jets of

Above: Fallow deer at Carter's Brook (p186).

Above – Stage 2: Old Bexley Conservation Area (see p73), once a landfill site and quarry but now home to several rare species of plant.

Heathrow; manicured **Trent Park**, a centre of the social whirl of 1920s Britain; and **Forty Hall Park**, one of the few places where the original mansion still stands. These are just half a dozen out of probably twenty or more such parks – all with their own character and charm, and all equally memorable.

Plus, of course, there are the many and varied **nature reserves**, **Sites of Special Scientific Interest (SSSIs)** and other designated 'wild spaces', each created to protect and enhance the local flora and fauna, such as spacious **Oxhey** and **Hainault Woods**, magnificent **Epping Forest** and the mighty **Rainham Marshes RSPB Reserve** near the trail's end.

Nor is it just the natural features of the LOOP that entice. A few of the villages, such as cute **Farnborough** and grand **Monken Hadley**, are delightful, while the town of **Kingston-upon-Thames** is as majestic and handsome as the former site of royal coronations should be. And the LOOP also takes you to places that you may well have heard of, but perhaps never had reason to visit. Places such as the **film and TV Mecca of Elstree**, where so many movie and television programmes are still made; or **Stockley Park**, a name you may well have heard while listening to football commentary (it is where all the VAR decisions are made). Whether you like these places when you visit them on the LOOP is a moot point – but it *is* satisfying to discover where these places are.

And I haven't even mentioned the joy of walking by the **Grand Union Canal**, a vein of calm through the West London clamour.

Not only is the LOOP worth doing, but it's relatively straightforward too. There aren't any serious gradients, few stiles, and the biggest hazard you'll be likely to encounter is a muddy footpath. True, the total length is 150¾ miles (242.6km), which is quite long, but the LOOP has been officially divided into 24 stages, each fairly short, with the longest being only 11 miles, and the shortest fewer than 4 miles. And if you are struggling to complete a stage, that's not a problem either: the route was deliberately designed to skirt by train and tube stations (an average of almost two per stage), and there are bus services in between the stations too.

So that's the LOOP for you; a lengthy but straightforward stroll through some of London's less well-known quarters. It may not feature the grand vistas or unconfined wilderness of some of England's other long-distance trails and, when viewed on a map, it may not appear the most enticing region for a lengthy walk. But don't be put off by any negative preconceptions you may have.

Because the LOOP will, I am pretty sure, surprise you.

How difficult is it?

The LOOP is a very straightforward walk. Yes, there are a few gradients, but ones at which experienced and inexperienced walkers alike will probably scoff. They aren't taxing. The walking is largely conducted on footpaths, though there's plenty of walking on pavements and bridleways too.

The most difficult thing about the LOOP is **finding your way**. This being London, there are a lot of people around and, as a result, the signposts are often knocked down, twisted round, or simply vanish altogether. Indeed, I found that signposts were more useful as confirmation that I was on the right trail – but were not, necessarily, pointing to where I needed to go next. Follow the maps closely in Part 4 and you shouldn't get lost too often, or for too long.

Another potential obstacle is **mud**. The paths can get very, very muddy outside the summer season; wear good boots (or walking shoes) and gaiters, or wellies, to keep the lower half of your trousers clean and you should be OK.

Below – Stage 4: St John the Baptist Church, on the hill above Coney Hall Park (see p91).

How long do you need?

It's a rare walker who attempts the LOOP in one go, staying in B&Bs or hotels along the way and not returning home until they've reached the end. For the vast majority of people, the LOOP is tackled in day trips, using London's extensive public transport network to ferry them to and from the various stages.

With a total length of just over 150 miles, fast, fit walkers willing to spend all day on the trail could complete it in just over a week, though **two weeks or longer** is more usual, relaxing and, for the vast majority of people, more suitable too.

See p36 for some suggested itineraries

When to go

Britain is a notoriously wet country but the South-East is at least its sunniest corner. Given that most people will be tackling it over a series of day walks, it's possible to avoid getting rained on for the entire hike: if rain is forecast you can choose to stay at home that day. For this reason, the LOOP is one of those walks where not only is it feasible, but it's actually quite pleasant to walk at least in part in **winter**. True, the woods you march through may look a little bare and large sections of the path may have turned to mud too; mud can be a real problem so it is worth wearing wellies or having gaiters if you prefer boots. It's true, too, that the amount of daylight available is less at that time so you may not be able to walk so far each day. But the transport links to and from the path are many, providing you with plenty of options for shortening your walk, and a bright, crisp winter's day is a wonderful time to wrap up warm and get on the trail.

Above – Stage 2: The ruins of Scadbury Manor, just off the trail in Park Woods (see p77).

That said, if I had to choose a season for walking the LOOP **springtime** probably wins out. The wild flowers are coming into bloom, lambs are skipping in the meadows, the grass is green and lush and the cafés along the way are yet to get very busy. True, there may be puddles on the path, and stretches will doubtless still be very muddy, particularly as springtime can be such a wet season; but a decent pair of boots or hiking shoes and gaiters should ensure you remain clean, upright and water-tight.

As for **summer**, well of course the weather is more reliably warm at this time – indeed, occasionally it's even a little too warm. But if you're looking to tackle the LOOP in one go, or over a period of consecutive days, you're more likely to find a dry week or so during the summer than at any other time of year. The days are much longer at this time too, of course, and all the facilities and attractions are operating to their maximum extent, so walking the LOOP at this time is slightly more straightforward. It will also be a lot less muddy.

Autumn comes a close second to springtime when it comes to choosing my favourite time to walk; or at least early autumn does, before the leaves have fallen and the summer flowers have wilted. The parks and paths grow quieter now as the children return to school and their parents to work. The days are milder, and while it's still very possible to find a prolonged period of dry weather at this time, the heat should be less furious. That post-summer lull, through September and the first half of October, before the country begins to hunker down against the worsening weather and starts its lengthy, chaotic countdown to Christmas, is one of the loveliest times for a stroll.

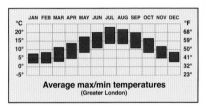

Average max/min temperatures
(Greater London)

While I'm on the subject of when to walk, I have one more piece of advice: **avoid weekends if you can**. A sunny summer weekend is when all of London seems to flock to the parks – many of which the LOOP takes you right through. It depends on how gregarious you are, of course, but personally I prefer my sauntering to be more solitary. Nature tends to thrive away from chaos, and calmness is more conducive for contemplation. If weekends are your only option, maybe think about getting up extra early to avoid the throngs – the extra effort required to drag your body back onto the trail at some Godforsaken hour will be more than amply rewarded.

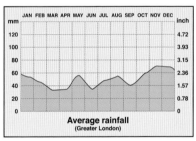

Average rainfall
(Greater London)

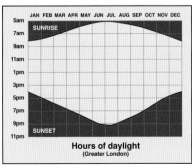

Hours of daylight
(Greater London)

Highlights – the best day walks

The suggestions on the following pages are for those who want to get the best of the LOOP without worrying about accomplishing the whole path. All sections can be walked in either direction and, unless specified, have good public transport services.

❑ **BEST DAY WALKS**
Stage 3: Petts Wood to Coney Hall (8 miles/12.9km + 1km to Hayes station)
As the LOOP brushes against the North Downs there are some proper ascents as well as some decent tracts of woodland – and perhaps the most famous oak tree in the country. All this and Farnborough is one of the loveliest villages on the trail, too. **See pp80-9**

Photos – A glimpse of Holwood House through the trees from Shire Lane (**above**). Tubbenden Meadow (**below**).

❏ **BEST DAY WALKS**
**Stage 5: Hamsey Green
to Coulsdon South
(6½ miles/10.5km)**

There's lots of lovely rural rambling through common and heath to be done on this stage. But it's the wonderful wild-flower meadows of Happy Valley (**shown here**), and the delightful strolling atop Farthing Down, that really steal the show, making this perhaps the most memorable stage on the entire LOOP.

The closest stations to Hamsey Green are Whyteleafe and Upper Warlingham; both are then a bus journey or 40-minute walk to the LOOP.

See pp98-103

❏ **BEST DAY WALKS**
**Stage 6: Coulsdon South
to Banstead Downs
(4¾ miles/7.6km)**

Though bookended by some lengthy pavement plodding at the start, and a rather sterile golf course at the finish, there's still lots to enjoy on this stage, the highlight being Mayfield Lavender Fields, where every summer people flock in their finery to be photographed amongst the flowers.

See pp103-7

❏ BEST DAY WALKS
Stage 8: Ewell (Bourne Hall Park) to Kingston Bridge (7¼ miles/11.7km)
A pleasant and untaxing afternoon can be had strolling along historic but little-known Hogsmill River, a source of inspiration for many artists. At the end, Kingston-upon-Thames is a lively and absorbing place to finish your walk.　　**See pp111-17**

❏ BEST DAY WALKS
Stage 9: Kingston Bridge to Hatton Cross (9½ miles/15.3km)
The highlight of this lengthy stage is undoubtedly the former royal hunting ground of Bushy Park (**below**) and its famous deer herds. But one shouldn't overlook the Crane River or tranquil, historic Hounslow Heath.　　**See pp117-28**

❏ **BEST DAY WALKS**
Stage 11: Hayes & Harlington to Uxbridge (7¼ miles/11.7km)
A stroll along any canal is rarely boring and the Grand Union Canal (**below**, and a bright barge on the Slough arm, **right**) is fascinating and, occasionally, picturesque too. A diversion to the lake of Little Britain (**above**) and a riparian stroll along the Colne make for a great afternoon's walk.

See pp132-8

❏ **BEST DAY WALKS Stage 16: Elstree to Cockfosters (11 miles/17.7km)**
The highlight for many walkers on this, the LOOP's longest stage, is the little-known but mightily impressive Monken Hadley village, (**shown here**) with its gorgeous houses and quaint church. But for me it was the tranquil former hay meadows of Totteridge Fields that stood out – the ideal place for a sun-blessed picnic. **See pp157-65**

❏ **BEST DAY WALKS Stage 18: Enfield Lock to Chingford (4¾ miles/7.6km)**
There are some decent nature reserves on this stage, including Sewardstone Marsh and Sewardstone Hills. But a traipse to the scouting movement's HQ at Gilwell Park brings you to Epping Forest, one of the largest stretches of woodland left in the region.
See pp173-7

GILWELL PARK

❏ **BEST DAY WALKS**
Stage 17: Cockfosters to Enfield Lock
(8½ miles/13.7km)
There's some great walking to be had on this stage, including a leisurely stroll through mani-cured Trent Park (**below**), the isolated splendour of Salmon Brook, and the delightful Tudor parkland of Hilly Fields and Forty Hall (**above**).

See pp165-73

❑ **BEST DAY WALKS**
Stage 23: Upminster
Bridge to Rainham
(4½ miles/7.3km)
It's impressive how the LOOP manages to find so much greenery on its journey, no more so perhaps than here, as you march from two busy urban centres along the Ingrebourne River, before entering the birdwatching haven of Hornchurch Country Park (**shown here**).

See pp191-6

❏ **BEST DAY WALKS**
Stage 20: Chigwell to
Havering-atte-Bower
(7 miles/11.3km)
Much of this stage is spent walking through the surprisingly delightful Hainault Forest (**shown here**, with distant views of London's centre), a mixed landscape of woodland, heath and lake, with the odd timber sculpture dotting the trail too. The walk through an avenue of giant sequoias in Havering Country Park (**left**) provides a suitably grand finale. (Note that the single bus service to/from Havering-atte-Bower operates Monday to Saturday only). **See pp179-84**

❏ BEST DAY WALKS
Stage 24: Rainham to Purfleet (4¾ miles/7.6km)
Though perhaps best known for its march through the marshes, one of the best places to go birdwatching in the South-East, the highlight of this stage for most people is the final stroll along the Thames, with such unusual sights as an armada of concrete barges and a deep-sea diver made out of metal emerging from the mud-flats (**below**). With views of the trail's official start in Erith just across the water (**above**), the final stage of the LOOP ends at Purfleet-on-Thames, conveniently right by a hotel!
See pp196-200

Practical information for the walker

ROUTE FINDING

The LOOP logo shows a hovering kestrel.

At the time of research the hardest part of tackling the LOOP was being able to follow the path. There were **signposts** along the way but, this being a busy part of the country, these signs had often been stolen or, more likely, knocked down or about so they no longer pointed in the right direction. This may still be the case when you do the walk but at the time of writing volunteers from Inner London Ramblers were planning to replace missing signs and ensure all face the correct direction. This may take a while as it depends on support from local councils.

❑ **USING GPS WITH THIS BOOK**

I never carried a compass, preferring to rely on a good sense of direction ... I never bothered to understand how a compass works or what it is supposed to do ... To me a compass is a gadget, and I don't get on well with gadgets of any sort.   **Alfred Wainwright**

While Wainwright's acolytes may scoff, other walkers will accept GPS technology as an inexpensive, well-established if non-essential, navigational aid. To cut a long story short, within a minute of being turned on and with a clear view of the sky, **GPS receivers** will establish your position as well as elevation in a variety of formats, including the British OS grid system, anywhere on earth to an accuracy of within a few metres. These days most **smartphones** have a GPS receiver built in and mapping software available to run on it (see box p40).

The maps in the route guide include numbered waypoints; these correlate to the list on pp201-2, which gives the grid reference as well as a description. You can download the complete list of these waypoints for free as a GPS-readable file (that doesn't include the text descriptions) from the Trailblazer website: 🖥 trailblazer-guides.com.

Bear in mind that the vast majority of people who tackle the LOOP do so perfectly successfully without a GPS unit. Instead of rushing out to invest in one, consider putting the money towards good-quality waterproofs or footwear instead.

That said, with this guidebook in your hand, lots of information online and, usually, plenty of people around to ask, you shouldn't get lost for more than a few minutes.

ACCOMMODATION

Unlike other Trailblazer guides to the long-distance footpaths of Great Britain, the accommodation information in this guide is fairly minimal. There's a good reason for this, of course, in that I think the vast majority of people who will use this book will already be living in London and will return to their home at the end of each day's walking, and will thus not take advantage of the accommodation available en route.

That said, when researching this book I *did* stay at B&Bs and hotels, either en route or, more likely, where they were only a short bus or train ride away. I suppose there may be one or two other hikers who, like me will also be looking to stay by the trail, so for their benefit I have included brief suggestions for accommodation that's convenient for the LOOP but also notes on options for finding a base in London and using that for the duration of the walk.

Note that there aren't many options for **campers** along the trail. Even wild camping is very tricky (and illegal, of course), given the proximity of the path to civilisation. So I would leave the tent at home for this trip. Nor, for that matter, are there any camping barns, or bunkhouses.

The situation is similar when it comes to **hostels**: outside central London there aren't that many and they aren't convenient for the trail. However, the YHA (Youth Hostels Association of England and Wales; ☎ 01629 592700, freephone ☎ 0800 019 1700, 🖥 yha.org.uk) has some hostels in central London which could provide a base for doing the walk. These are: YHA London Central, near Great Portland St & Goodge St; Earls Court; St Pancras; Oxford Street; St Paul's; Thameside (Rotherhithe) and Lee Valley (Cheshunt). Most offer private rooms, many of which are en suite, but because of COVID dorm accommodation wasn't available at the time of writing, nor were any of the shared facilities.

So in the absence of hostels and campsites, hikers are forced to rely on hotels for this walk especially as conventional **B&Bs** are few and far between on the LOOP. However, plenty of properties along the LOOP are advertised on the **AirBnb** website (🖥 airbnb.co.uk) – and these may well form the bulk of your accommodation along the way. In case you're unaware of the whole AirBnb phenomenon, this is where private homes and apartments are opened up to overnight travellers on an informal basis. As always, do check thoroughly what you are getting and the precise location: while the first couple of options listed may be in the area you're after, others may be too far afield for walkers. At its best, this is a great way to meet local people in a relatively unstructured environment, but do be aware that these places are not registered B&Bs, so standards may vary, and prices may not necessarily be any lower than the norm.

Bed & breakfasts and guesthouses

Bed and Breakfasts (B&Bs) are a great British institution! There's nothing mysterious about them; as the name suggests, they provide you with a bed in a private room and a (usually cooked) breakfast, though they range in style enormously. The difference between a B&B and a guesthouse is minimal, though some of the better guesthouses are more like hotels, offering evening meals and a lounge for guests. If not, there's nearly always a pub or restaurant nearby.

There are few B&Bs/guesthouses actually on the LOOP but there are plenty in and around London.

Pubs and inns

Pubs and inns also offer B&B-style accommodation and prices are no more than in a regular B&B. Rates usually include breakfast, but not always. However, very few pubs on the LOOP offer accommodation.

Hotels

Hotels generally cost more, however, and some can be a little irritated with a bunch of smelly hikers turning up and treading mud into their carpet.

Walkers on a budget should perhaps look at **chain hotels**, such as Travelodge and Premier Inn. Travelodge (🖳 travelodge.co.uk) has hotels at several places that are convenient for the trail. The Premier Inn (🖳 premierinn.com) chain also has a pretty good network of hotels serving the trail and in many of the same places as Travelodge. Both chains regularly have special offers, so it's worth joining their mailing lists if you're looking to walk the LOOP in one go; by taking advantage of a 2-for-1 offer, for example, I was able to stay for six nights with Travelodge on one research trip, yet had to pay for only three.

Other chains offering good-value accommodation in and around London are: easyHotel (🖳 easyhotel.com); Holiday Inn Express (🖳 ihg.com/holidayinn express); ibis (🖳 ibis.accor.com); and Jurys Inn (🖳 www.jurysinns.com).

PLANNING YOUR WALK

❏ ACCOMMODATION RATES

B&Bs in London start as low as £30pp in a twin/double room. Solo trekkers should take note: single rooms are not so easy to find so if you are on your own you will often end up occupying a double/twin room, for which you'll usually have to pay a single occupancy (sgl occ) rate, often amounting to the room rate minus the cost of one breakfast (usually £10-15). Some places are more generous towards solo travellers, though, and will let you stay for closer to the per-person rate. Rates are sometimes discounted for stays of two or more nights.

Do also check out the nationwide chains such as Travelodge and Premier Inn (see above) – you'll often find it cheaper to stay with them. Room rates start at about £44 as long as you pay at the time of booking though these are generally non refundable. Flexible rates (pay when you check in at the hotel) are from about £75; the advantage of these is that you can usually cancel with no penalty up to 24 hours before checking in. And of course there are plenty of upmarket hotels in and around London where the tariff is much higher but even they sometimes offer special deals.

Other options

In the summer holiday period (July-August) some university **halls of residence** are available for let as self-catering and/or serviced apartments; for suggestions see 💻 www.visitlondon.com/where-to-stay.

Aparthotels are a good option for people happy to self-cater. Providers in London include: Citadines (💻 citadines.com); Staycity (💻 staycity.com); and SACO (Serviced Apartment Company; 💻 sacoapartments.com).

❏ INFORMATION FOR FOREIGN VISITORS

● **Currency** The British pound (£) comes in notes of £50, £20, £10 and £5, and coins of £2 and £1. The pound is divided into 100 pence (usually referred to as 'p', pronounced 'pee') which come in 'silver' coins of 50p, 20p, 10p and 5p, and 'copper' coins of 2p and 1p. Debit/credit cards are accepted in many places but it is always worth having some cash.

Up-to-date currency **exchange rates** can be found on 💻 xe.com/currencyconverter, at some post offices, and at most banks and travel agents.

● **Business hours** Most **grocery shops** are open Monday to Saturday 9am-5pm, though some (especially convenience stores) open as early as 7.30/8am; many also open on Sundays. **Supermarkets** are open daily 8am-8pm (often longer), though on Sundays main branches are restricted to six hours so generally open 10am-4pm or 11am-5pm.

Main **post offices** generally open Monday to Friday 9am-5pm and Saturday 9am-12.30pm; **banks** typically open at 9.30/10am Monday to Friday and close at 3.30/4pm.

ATMs (cash machines) located outside a bank, shop, post office or petrol station are open all the time, but any that are inside will be accessible only when that place is open. However, ones that charge, such as Link machines (💻 link.co.uk/consumers/locator), may not accept foreign-issued cards.

Pub hours are less predictable as each pub may have different opening hours. However, most pubs on the LOOP open daily 11am-11pm (some close at 10.30pm on Sunday) but some may close in the afternoon.

The last entry time to most **museums and galleries** is usually half an hour, or an hour, before the official closing time.

● **Public (bank) holidays** Most businesses are shut on 1 January, Good Friday (March/April), Easter Monday (March/April), the first and last Monday in May, the last Monday in August, 25 December and 26 December.

● **School holidays** School holiday periods in England are generally: a one-week break late October, two weeks around Christmas/New Year, a week in mid February, two weeks around Easter, a week in late May/early June (to coincide with the bank holiday on the last Monday in May), and six weeks from late July to early September. Private-school holidays fall at the same time, but tend to be slightly longer.

● **Travel/medical insurance** Until the UK left the EU the **European Health Insurance Card** (EHIC) entitled EU nationals (on production of an EHIC card) to necessary medical treatment under the UK's National Health Service (NHS) while on a temporary visit here. This is unlikely to be the case for EU nationals once their EHIC card has expired. The latest information can be found at 💻 myhealth.london.nhs.uk/help (click on advice for 'Overseas visitors to London'), or 💻 nhs.uk/nhs-services (click on: 'Visiting-or-moving-to-England') before arrival in the UK.

OTHER SERVICES

Pretty much every café and pub has **wi-fi** now. There's also no shortage of **grocery/convenience stores** and **supermarkets**, usually one of the main chains (Tesco, Co-op etc). **Post offices** are numerous too, as are **pharmacies/chemists**.

There are **outdoor equipment shops** near the trail or the link path to the station in both Kingston and Uxbridge.

But the EHIC card was never a substitute for proper medical cover on your travel insurance for unforeseen bills and for getting you home should that be necessary. Also consider getting cover for loss or theft of personal belongings, especially if you're staying in hostels, as there may be times when you'll have to leave your luggage unattended.

● **Documents** If you are a member of a National Trust organisation in your country bring your membership card as you should be entitled to free entry to National Trust properties and sites in the UK and there are a couple on the LOOP; see box on p55.

● **Weights and measures** Milk in Britain is still sometimes sold in pints (1 pint = 568ml), as is beer in pubs, though most other **liquids** including petrol (gasoline) and diesel are sold in litres.

Road **distances** are given in miles (1 mile = 1.6km) rather than kilometres, and yards (1yd = 0.9m) rather than metres. The population remains divided between those who still use inches (1 inch = 2.5cm) and feet (1ft = 0.3m) and those who are happy with centimetres and millimetres; you'll often be told that 'it's only a hundred yards or so' to somewhere, rather than a hundred metres or so.

Most **food** is sold in metric weights (g and kg) but the imperial weights of pounds (lb: 1lb = 453g) and ounces (oz: 1oz = 28g) are often displayed too.

The **weather** – a frequent topic of conversation – is also an issue: while most forecasts predict temperatures in °C, some people continue to think in terms of °F (see temperature chart on p13 for conversions).

● **Time** During the winter the whole of Britain is on Greenwich Mean Time (GMT). The clocks move one hour forward on the last Sunday in March, remaining on British Summer Time (BST) until the last Sunday in October.

● **Smoking** Smoking in enclosed public places is banned. The ban relates not only to pubs and restaurants, but also to B&Bs, hostels and hotels. These latter have the right to designate one or more bedrooms where the occupants can smoke, but the ban is in force in all enclosed areas open to the public – even in a private home such as a B&B. Should you be foolhardy enough to light up in a no-smoking area, which includes pretty well any indoor public place, you could be fined £50, but it's the owners of the premises who suffer most if they fail to stop you, with a potential fine of £2500.

● **Telephones** The international access code for Britain is ☎ 44, followed by the area code minus the first 0, and then the number you require. If you're using a **mobile (cell) phone** that is registered overseas, consider buying a local SIM card to keep costs down. Also remember to bring a universal adaptor so you can charge your phone. Mobile phone reception is generally good on and around the LOOP.

● **Emergency services** For police, ambulance and/or fire dial ☎ 999, or the EU standard number ☎ 112.

Budgeting

London is a notoriously expensive part of the world and, though you aren't in its very centre, you'll still find that bargains are few even this far away from its extortionate heart. That said, walking is one of the few things in London that is still free. Furthermore, if you're already in possession of a Travelcard, your transport costs will be lower (depending on what zones your card is valid for) or free/almost free if you are entitled to a Freedom Pass or Oyster 60+ card and travel after 9.30am for rail services – and after 9am, from 15 June 2021, for other services – on weekdays though at any time at the weekend or on bank holidays.

Your accommodation costs will be zero too unless you choose to stay somewhere to save travelling to and fro. Forego the pleasures of the pubs and cafés en route by packing your own drink and picnic you already have and it's entirely possible that you can compete the LOOP without spending any money at all! In other words, the LOOP may actually be one of the few long-distance trails in Britain – and very possibly the only one – where it's cheaper to be on it, than not be on it, and you may spend *less* money tackling it than you would if you were just carrying on your day-to-day existence.

Of course, that doesn't really apply if you don't have a Travelcard, and/or if you are staying in hotels/B&Bs along the way and are buying your food and drink as you go. In this situation you'll be spending nearer **£25-40 per day plus accommodation**, as these two samples of my overall budget illustrate.

The first lesson to draw from these budgets is just how quickly things add up – though that's something I find in every aspect of life, and not just when I'm on the trail. The second lesson is that, even when living on a relatively tight budget, buying lunch from supermarkets etc, it's still difficult to keep the daily budget down below £20. Add accommodation onto this (I was staying for a couple of nights at Clapham Travelodge) and the budget rises above £50.

Of course, as I've already mentioned, if you already have a Travelcard that covers the LOOP, take a packed lunch and get home in time for dinner, it's possible that your budget will be zero, or close to it.

PLANNING YOUR WALK

❏ TWO SAMPLE DAILY BUDGETS	
Day 1	
Ticket (Clapham Junction to Kingston)	£ 4.60
Lunch (Tesco)	£ 3.25
Swan & Bottle drink	£ 4.13
Ticket (Uxbridge to Cricklewood)	£ 2.80
Supper	£ 9.00
	£23.78*
Day 2	
Ticket (Cricklewood to Uxbridge)	£ 4.60
Lunch (from Moor Park shop)	£ 4.10
Ticket (Borehamwood to Cricklewood)	£ 3.20
Supper	£11.43
	£23.33*
* plus a minimum of £25-40 per day for hotel	

Itineraries

Part 4 of this book has been organised in a clockwise direction, though there is of course nothing to stop you from tackling the LOOP in the opposite direction, ie anti-clockwise; the timings on the maps cover both directions and the route descriptions are arranged so it is easy to use them for either direction.

To help you plan see pp14-24 in the colour pages at the front of the book for the highlights of the LOOP if you are aiming just to do day trips. If you want to complete the LOOP in one go (or over time) see the box on p38 for some **suggested itineraries** and at the back of the book there are **distance charts** as well as colour maps with **altitude profiles** and an overview **planning map**.

The **table of village/town facilities** (pp32-5) gives a run-down on the essential information you will need for each of the places en route, with particular regard to transport connections and services. The **public transport map** is on pp42-3; details of **rail services** are in the box on pp46-8 and information about Tramlink in the box on p49. A list of **bus services** relevant for the LOOP is on pp203-7. When planning your day's walking you will have to factor in the travel time to reach your starting point and then of course getting back at the end of the day; crossing London west to east can take two hours or more.

Once you have an idea of your approach turn to Part 4 for information on services in each place en route. Also in Part 4 you will find summaries of the route to accompany the detailed trail maps.

WHICH DIRECTION?

The Inner London Ramblers (and TfL) websites as well as the only other LOOP guidebook start their walk in Erith and head **clockwise** around the LOOP to finish at Purfleet-on-Thames. To avoid confusion, this guide sticks with this same direction and breaks the walk into the identical stages as Ramblers/TfL. There is no decisive rationale for doing so, of course, and you can just as easily start in Purfleet-on-Thames and head anti-clockwise if you prefer. However, if you want to make things simple, at least when it comes to following this book, heading clockwise from Erith is the most straightforward option.

Of course, with it being a near-circular route **you don't even have to start at Erith or Purfleet-on-Thames**. No matter where you join it, as long as you end up back there eventually you will have completed the trail; and it is possible to complete the LOOP by taking buses between Erith and Purfleet (see p200 for details). Personally, I think it's best to start at Erith and end at Purfleet if you can; it's the one place where the 'circle' around London is broken, so makes for a natural beginning/end to your hike. I also think that there's something suitably majestic about finishing your odyssey by the Thames. But you may have far more practical reasons for starting somewhere else on the LOOP that outweigh these considerations.

VILLAGE AND

Place name **Bold**=end/start of stage (text in brackets)= place is not within 300m of the trail	Distance from previous place approx miles§	 km§	Restaurants, cafés, pubs & takeaways ✔=1 ✔✔=2 ✔✔✔=3+	Food store	Post office	Chemist
Erith			✔✔✔	✔	✔	✔
Crayford	5¾	**9.3**	✔✔✔	✔	✔	
(for Crayford station)	[¼	0.5]				
Bexley	2½	**4.0**	✔✔✔	✔	✔	
Petts Wood/	7¼	**11.7**	✔✔✔	✔	✔	✔
Jubilee Country Park						
(for Petts Wood station)	[½	0.8]				
Farnborough	3	**4.9**	✔✔✔		✔	✔
Keston	3¾	**6**	✔✔	✔	✔	
Coney Hall	1¼	**2**	✔✔✔	✔		
(for Hayes/Hayes station)	[¾	1.1]		✔		
Shirley	3¼	**5.3**	✔	✔		
Hamsey Green	5½	**8.8**	✔✔✔	✔	✔	
Godstone Road	1½	**2.4**		✔		
(for Whyteleafe & Upper Warlingham stations)	[¾	1.1]				
Coulsdon South station	5	**8.1**				
(Coulsdon)	[¼	0.4]	✔✔✔	✔		✔
Clock House village	1¼	**2**	✔	✔	✔	
Banstead Downs	3½	**5.6**				
(for Banstead station)	[½	0.8]		✔	✔	✔
Ewell	3½	**5.6**	✔✔✔	✔	✔	✔
(for Ewell West station)	[¼	0.4]				
Link	3¾	**6.1**				
(for Malden Manor station)	[¼	0.4]				
Berrylands	1½	**2.4**	✔	✔		
Kingston-upon-Thames	2	**3.2**	✔✔✔	✔	✔	✔
(for Kingston station)	¼	0.5				
Fulwell High St	3½	**5.6**				
(for Fulwell station)	[¼	0.4]				
A30	6	**9.7**				
(for Hatton Cross station)	[¾	1.2]	✔			
Cranford	¾	**1.2**	✔	✔		
Hayes & Harlington	2¾	**4.4**	✔✔	✔	✔	✔
West Drayton/Yiewsley	3	**4.8**	✔✔	✔		✔
Uxbridge	4¼	**6.9**	✔			
(for Uxbridge station)	[½	0.8]	✔✔✔	✔	✔	✔
West Harefield	5	**8**	✔✔✔			

§ Distances in square brackets are the distances off the path *but not necessarily
from the previous place mentioned.*

(cont'd on p34)

PLANNING YOUR WALK

TOWN FACILITIES

Railway terminal/ station(s) in London # See below	Underground (tube) line	Fare zone	Place name Bold=end/start of stage (text in brackets)= place is not within 300m of the trail
CCross, CStreet, WEast & LBridge#		6	**Erith**
			Crayford
CCross & CStreet#		6	(for Crayford station)
CCross & CStreet#		6	**Bexley**
			Petts Wood/Jubilee Country Park
CCross#, CStreet# & Victoria		5	(for Petts Wood station)
		6	Farnborough
		6	Keston
			Coney Hall
CCross, CStreet, WEast & LBridge#		5	(for Hayes/Hayes station)
		5	Shirley
		6	**Hamsey Green**
			Godstone Road
LBridge# (Whyteleafe)		6	(for Whyteleafe &
Victoria & C Junction# (Upper Warlingham)		6	Upper Warlingham stations)
Victoria & LBridge#		6	**Coulsdon South station**
LBridge# (Coulsdon Town)			(Coulsdon)
		6	Clock House village
			Banstead Downs
Victoria & C Junction#		6	(for Banstead station)
			Ewell
Waterloo & C Junction#		6	(for Ewell West station)
			Link (for
Waterloo & C Junction#		4	Malden Manor station)
Waterloo & C Junction#		5	Berrylands
			Kingston-upon-Thames
Waterloo & C Junction#		6	(for Kingston station)
			Fulwell High St
Waterloo & C Junction#		6	(for Fulwell station)
			A30
	Piccadilly	6	(for Hatton Cross station)
		5	Cranford
Paddington		5	**Hayes & Harlington**
Paddington		6	West Drayton & Yiewsley
			Uxbridge
	Metropolitan & Piccadilly	6	(for Uxbridge station)
		–	**West Harefield**

CCross = Charing Cross; CStreet = Cannon Street; C Junction = Clapham Junction; L Bridge = London Bridge; St Pancras Intl = St Pancras International; WEast = Waterloo East

(cont'd on p35)

PLANNING YOUR WALK

(cont'd from p32)

VILLAGE AND

Place name **Bold**=end/start of stage (brackets)= place is not within 300m of the trail	Distance from previous place approx miles§ km§		Restaurants, cafés, pubs & takeaways ✔=1 𝑾=2 𝑾𝑾=3+	Food store	Post office	Chemist
Moor Park	4¾	7.6				
(for Moor Park station)	[¾	1.2]		✔	✔	
Hatch End	3¾	6				
(for Hatch End station)	[¾	1.2]	𝑾𝑾	✔	✔	✔
Spring Pond	4¾	7.6				
(for Stanmore station)	[1	1.6]				
Elstree & Borehamwood	4	6.5	𝑾𝑾	✔		✔
Great North Road	7½	12.1				
(for High Barnet station)	[¼	0.4]	𝑾			
& New Barnet	[¼	0/4]	✔	✔		
Cockfosters	3½	5.6	𝑾	✔	✔	
Turkey Street	7¾	12.5				
Enfield Wash	¼	0.4	𝑾𝑾	✔		✔
Enfield Lock	½	0.8				
Chingford	4¾	7.6	𝑾𝑾	✔	✔	
Chigwell	4	6.4	𝑾	✔	✔	✔
Havering-Atte-Bower	7	11.3				
Harold Wood	5¼	8.5	𝑾	✔	✔	
Upminster Bridge	4¼	6.8	𝑾𝑾	✔	✔	✔
Rainham	4½	7.3	𝑾𝑾	✔		
Purfleet-on-Thames	4¾	7.6	✔			

§ Distances in square brackets are the distances off the path *but not necessarily from the previous place mentioned.*

TAKING DOGS ALONG THE LOOP

As long as your dog is fit, there's no reason why you can't take him/her with you on the LOOP. That said, it may not be the most enjoyable walk for him or her, purely because for much of the time you'll have to keep your dog on a lead for their own safety due to the proximity of the path to busy roads.

Note that **dogs *are* allowed on the underground network, as well as on all buses and trains serving London**. However, they must always be on a lead on any public transport and kept in control.

If you're planning on staying in B&Bs or hotels along the way, do check that your dog can stay with you. The Travelodge chain **allows dogs** (though for a stiff £20 *per stay* fee); some hotels in other chains accept dogs but almost always have a fee. However, Premier Inn and Jurys Inn hotels do not allow dogs. Some cafés and pubs accept dogs but generally they will need to be on a lead and in pubs they are often only allowed in the bar area.

TOWN FACILITIES

(cont'd from p33)

Railway terminal/ station(s) in London # See below	Underground (tube) line	Fare zone	Place name **Bold**=end/start of stage (brackets)= place is not within 300m of the trail
			Moor Park
	Metropolitan	6/7	(for Moor Park station)
			Hatch End
Euston		6	(for Hatch End station)
			Spring Pond
	Jubilee	5	for Stanmore station)
St Pancras Intl & Blackfriars#		6	**Elstree & Borehamwood**
			Great North Road
	Northern	5	(for High Barnet station)
			& New Barnet
	Piccadilly	5	**Cockfosters**
Liverpool Street		6	Turkey Street
		6	Enfield Wash
Liverpool Street & Stratford		6	**Enfield Lock**
Liverpool Street		5	**Chingford**
	Central	4	**Chigwell**
		6	**Havering-Atte-Bower**
Liverpool Street		6	**Harold Wood**
	District	6	**Upminster Bridge**
Fenchurch Street		6	**Rainham**
Fenchurch Street		6	**Purfleet-on-Thames**

\# St Pancras Intl = St Pancras International

PLANNING YOUR WALK

Other considerations? Well, you have to ask – and be honest with – yourself: can your dog really cope with walking several miles a day? And just as importantly, will he or she actually enjoy it? If you think the answer is yes to both, you can start preparing accordingly.

❑ SUGGESTED ITINERARIES

The itineraries below show how you can complete the LOOP and are also useful for planning day walks as both start and end points have good transport (rail/tube) connections.

Places with accommodation on (or very near) the LOOP are noted for those walking the LOOP in one go. A bus, train or tube ride will also provide access to many other accommodation options. More details are provided in Part 4 (the route guide).

Itinerary for fast walkers

Day	Route	Approx miles	km	Accommodation on LOOP
1	Erith ←→ Petts Wood	15½	25	Bexley, Sidcup
2	Petts Wood ←→ Hayes (Kent)	8	12.9	(off LOOP options)
3	Hayes ←→ Coulsdon South	15¼	24.6	(off LOOP options)
4	Coulsdon South ←→ Kingston-upon-Thames	15½	25	Kingston-upon-Thames
5	Kingston-upon-Thames ←→ Hayes & Harlington	13	20.9	Hampton Wick, Fulwell, Hatton Cross, Cranford
6	Hayes & Harlington ←→ Moor Park	17	27.3	Stockley Park, Uxbridge
7	Moor Park ←→ Elstree & Borehamwood	12½	20.1	Northwood, Old Redding
8	Elstree & Borehamwood ←→ Cockfosters	11	17.7	(off LOOP options)
9	Cockfosters ←→ Chingford	13¼	21.3	Chingford
10	Chingford ←→ Harold Wood	16¼	26.2	Chigwell
11	Harold Wood ←→ Purfleet-on-Thames	13½	21.7	Purfleet-on-Thames

Itinerary for steady walkers

Day	Route	Approx miles	km	Accommodation on LOOP
1	Erith ←→ Petts Wood	15½	25	Bexley, Sidcup
2	Petts Wood ←→ Hayes (Kent)	8	12.9	(off LOOP options)
3	Hayes ←→ Coulsdon South	15¼	24.6	(off LOOP options)
4	Coulsdon South ←→ Ewell	8¼	13.2	(off LOOP options)
5	Ewell ←→ Kingston-upon-Thames	7¼	11.7	Kingston-upon-Thames
6	Kingston ←→ Hayes & Harlington	13	20.9	Hampton Wick, Fulwell, Hatton Cross, Cranford
7	Hayes & Harlington ←→ Uxbridge	7¼	11.7	Stockley Park, Uxbridge
8	Uxbridge ←→ Moor Park	9¾	15.6	(off LOOP options)
9	Moor Park ←→ Elstree & Borehamwood	12½	20.1	Northwood, Old Redding
10	Elstree & Borehamwood ←→ Cockfosters	11	17.7	(off LOOP options)
11	Cockfosters ←→ Chingford	13¼	21.3	Chingford
12	Chingford ←→ Chigwell	4	6.4	Chigwell
13	Chigwell ←→ Harold Wood	12¼	19.8	(off LOOP options)
14	Harold Wood ←→ Purfleet-on-Thames	13½	21.7	Purfleet-on-Thames

PLANNING YOUR WALK

What to wear, what to take & how to take it

It feels strange to write this – as someone who has written several guides on the long-distance footpaths of Britain, and who is used to advising people to pack for all weathers and terrains – but, assuming that you're one of the majority who are 'doing' the LOOP in a series of day walks, you can, I suppose, set off on the trail with little more than **this guide book, a smartphone, your wallet/purse and your house key.**

Water, snacks, a **waterproof jacket**, **sun-screen**, **sun hat**, **headphones**, a **camera**, plus something to put them all in (ie **a small daypack of 20-30 litres**) could all be considered, too, I suppose. Some people like using **walking poles**, though again they are far from essential and you may feel a bit silly 'trekking' up the various high streets with them.

Other non-essential but potentially useful items include **sunglasses, smartphone/ipod** (or similar) and **headphones, binoculars** and a **flask**.

However, the reality is that in every guidebook I advise readers to *keep luggage light* – and on the LOOP you really can obey this mantra to the maximum – but if planning to walk it in one go see box on p38.

WHAT TO WEAR ON THE TRAIL

Footwear
I left my hiking boots at home for this trail and instead walked in **hiking shoes**. Of course you can wear boots, but I thought they would be too heavy and too sweaty. I prefer still to wear a shoe that is designed for walking, as the grip is slightly better and the chance of getting blisters is less (as long as they are broken-in properly). But I also recognise that many wear comfy trainers on the LOOP and don't seem to suffer unduly because of that. In the winter months wellies are a good option as the path can be very muddy. In short, as long as your footwear is comfortable, durable and waterproof, it doesn't really matter what you wear. If you haven't got a pair of the modern hi-tech walking **socks** the old system of wearing a thin liner sock under a thicker wool sock is just as good.

Clothing
Some hikers find trekking trousers an unnecessary investment and any light, quick-drying trousers should suffice. Jeans are not usually recommended for hiking – they're heavy and dry slowly – but if you're walking the LOOP in day trips and you find them comfortable, then why not? On really hot sunny days you'll be glad you brought your shorts.

One item that is very useful is a good pair of **gaiters**, as many of the trails can get extremely muddy after rain, even during the summer months.

Modern hi-tech outdoor clothes come with a range of fancy names and brands but they all still follow the basic two- or three-layer principle, with an inner base layer to transport sweat away from your skin, a mid-layer for warmth and an outer layer to protect you from the wind and rain.

A thin lightweight **thermal top** of a synthetic material is ideal as the base layer as it draws moisture (ie sweat) away from your body. Cool in hot weather and warm when worn under other clothes in the cold so pack at least one thermal top. Over the top in cold weather a mid-weight **polyester fleece** should suffice. Fleeces are light, more water-resistant than the alternatives (such as a woolly jumper), remain warm even when wet and pack down small in rucksacks; they are thus ideal trekking gear.

Over the top of all this a **waterproof jacket** is essential. 'Breathable' jackets cost a small fortune (though prices are falling all the time) but they do prevent the build-up of condensation.

In winter you may like to consider a woolly **hat** and **gloves**, though do bear in mind that while you may be cold when you step outside the front door, after a mile or two of walking you may find yourself removing layers.

A pair of **waterproof trousers** is useful if rain is forecast and thermal **long johns** take up little room in the bag if you're tackling the LOOP in one go.

> ### ❏ IF YOU'RE TACKLING THE LOOP IN ONE GO
>
> If you're planning on completing the LOOP without returning back to base at the end of each day, you will need to put a bit more thought towards what you should pack, and how you are going to carry it. Nevertheless, the golden rule is the same: **keep it light**. Remember, the enjoyment of any walk is inversely proportional to the amount carried, so take only the bare essentials, while at the same time ensuring you have all the equipment necessary to make the trip safe and comfortable.
>
> Given that camping is not really practical on the LOOP, you should be able to get by with a **40- to 60-litre rucksack**. When choosing a rucksack, make sure it has a stiffened back and can be adjusted to fit your own back comfortably. Make sure the hip belt and chest strap (if there is one) are fastened tightly as this helps distribute the weight more comfortably with most of it being carried on the hips. Some people carry a small daypack inside the rucksack, as this will be useful to carry things in when leaving the main pack at your accommodation.
>
> Don't forget to bring a **waterproof rucksack cover**. Most rucksacks these days have them 'built in' to the sack, but you can also buy them separately for less than a tenner. Lining your bag with a strong **bin liner** is another sensible, cut-price idea. Finally, it's also a good idea to keep everything wrapped in plastic bags inside the rucksack; that way, even if it does pour with rain, everything should remain dry.
>
> Items to pack include four to five changes of **underwear**; any more is excessive, any less unhygienic. A change of legwear and several tops will also be necessary, in addition to the waterproof outer layer. Bring a few pairs of socks too; you certainly don't want to start any day of hiking in socks that are anything other than clean and bone dry. Because backpacks can cause bra straps to dig painfully into the skin, women may find a sports bra more comfortable.
>
> For **toiletries** you will probably want to bring toothpaste and toothbrush, deodorant, razors and tampons/sanitary towels. Finally, don't forget your **phone charger**.
>
> Remember, too, that it's not the end of the world if you forget anything: the LOOP passes through or close to several towns so it won't be difficult to buy a replacement.

❏ ONLINE INFORMATION

innerlondonramblers.org.uk/loop The 'official' guide to the trail was originally on 🖥 tfl.gov.uk/modes/walking/loop-walk but at the time of writing volunteers from Inner London Ramblers were updating both the maps and the route descriptions. They hope the new website will be live in 2021 and a link to it will be set up from the TfL website. Short-term disruptions are already noted on the Inner London Ramblers website and will continue to be added. See also Ramblers below.

tfl.gov.uk The website of **Transport for London** is jam-packed with honest, useful information. Their journey planner is a thing of joy: just let it know where you want to go, and where from, and it will tell you the easiest/quickest way of travelling between the two on public transport (as well as providing times and route suggestions for cyclists and walkers).

🖥 **desdemoor.blogspot.com/p/london-loop_44.html** Incredibly thorough, frequently updated and wholly admirable description of the trail by walker, beer nut and seemingly inveterate blogger, Des de Moor. Well worth a look.

🖥 **gojauntly.com/london-loop** Online guide with photos that is designed for you to take along on the trail using their smartphone app.

🖥 **toptiplondon.com** Not particularly useful for the trail itself, but great as a general guide to the capital (particularly the centre) and if you want to visit relatively cheaply.

🖥 **visitlondon.com** The official guide to the capital, though outer London receives little attention.

Organisations for walkers

● **Ramblers** (🖥 ramblers.org.uk) Looks after the interests of walkers throughout Britain. They publish a large amount of useful information including their quarterly *Walk* magazine, also available in pdf and audio format. Members can choose a local branch to be assigned to and will be kept informed of walks in that area. The Inner London Ramblers branch (see above) is driving the effort to promote the LOOP (and the Capital Ring, see box p159) despite the fact that the LOOP is nowhere near Inner London. Annual membership costs from £36.60, £49 for two people.

● **The Long Distance Walkers' Association** (🖥 ldwa.org.uk) An association of people with the common interest of long-distance walking. Membership includes a journal, *Strider*, three times per year giving details of challenge events and local group walks as well as articles on the subject. Individual membership is £18 a year (£26, for non-UK residents) with discounts for direct debit payments.

OTHER EQUIPMENT

I've mentioned bringing your **smartphone** already, but it really is useful for several reasons: for playing the **radio/music/podcasts** to entertain you while you're walking; to use the **GPS** facility to help you find out where you are if you're lost; to check on your progress/step count using a **fitness app**; to use the **internet** to check on weather forecasts and also bus and train timetables etc; or, even to use it as a regular **phone** to contact someone in an emergency, book a table for dinner etc. As such, it can be a pretty invaluable tool to have on the trail, though do keep it fully charged (and maybe bring a power-pack to make sure it stays charged).

You could consider a **first-aid kit** that includes items such as: aspirin or paracetamol; plasters for minor cuts; blister plasters, an elasticated joint support for supporting a sprained ankle or a weak knee; antiseptic wipes; antiseptic cream; safety pins; tweezers; and scissors. Remember, however, that you're never far from a high street where all these things are available.

MONEY AND DOCUMENTS

ATMs (cash machines) are plentiful along the LOOP, or at least a short walk from it, and given that most places accept credit and debit cards now, there's no need to carry too much cash with you. If you are a member of the **National Trust** (see box on p55), your **membership card** will be useful if you plan to visit Hall Place Park in Crayford (where you'll get a discount) and Rainham Hall (which is free for National Trust members).

MAPS

The hand-drawn maps in this book cover the trail at a scale of 1:20,000. This large scale, combined with the notes and tips written on the maps, *should* be enough to stop you losing your way. Nevertheless, some people like to have a separate map of the region to help identify local features and landmarks and for devising possible side trips. **Ordnance Survey** (🖳 ordnancesurvey.co.uk) maps cover the whole trail over a series of nine maps. Explorer OL162, OL161, OL160 (briefly), OL172, OL173, OL174 and OL175. Buying the paper versions of those maps individually will set you back about £63 so you may want to buy the smartphone versions instead, where the maps are downloaded onto your phone; currently this service is £2.99 for one month, £23.99 for the year.

Alternatively, if you insist on the paper versions, members of Ramblers' (see box p39) can make use of their library which allows them to borrow up to ten maps for up to six weeks free of charge. UK residents may also be able to borrow them from their local public library.

❏ DIGITAL MAPPING

There are several software packages that provide Ordnance Survey maps for a PC or smartphone. Maps are usually supplied by direct download over the internet. They are then loaded into an application, also available by download, from where you can view them, print them and create routes on them. Additionally, the route can be viewed directly on a smartphone or uploaded to a GPS device. If your smartphone has a GPS chip, you will be able to see your position overlaid onto the digital map on your phone.

Many websites now have free routes you can download for the more popular digital mapping products; anything from day walks to complete Long Distance Paths. It is important to ensure any digital mapping software on your smartphone uses predownloaded maps, stored on your device, and doesn't need to download them on-the-fly, as this may be expensive and will be impossible without a signal.

Smartphones and GPS devices should complement, not replace, the traditional method of navigation (a map and compass) as any electronic device is susceptible to failure and, particularly, battery failure. Remember that battery life will be significantly reduced, compared to normal usage, when you are using the built-in GPS and running the screen for long periods.   **Stuart Greig**

GETTING TO AND FROM THE LOOP

I assume that the vast majority of people tackling the LOOP will be Londoners, and they'll be doing it as day walks. But there may also be some people looking to circumnavigate the capital who *don't* live within its borders – who may not even live in Britain – and the information on pp49-50 is for you.

LONDON TRANSPORT AND THE LOOP

For most of your time on the LOOP you'll probably be relying on London Transport's extensive network of buses and trains as well as the underground system to ferry you to the start of your walk, and back again at the end of the day. Those who live in London will be very used to how the transport system works and the various tickets, cards and payment options that are available. But for those who don't the following is a quick guide:

Transport for London (TfL)

All of London's public transport comes under the aegis of Transport for London (🖥 tfl.gov.uk). They run the day-to-day operation of the capital's public transport network and look after London's main roads too. Their website, by the way, is a mine of useful information, with maps and journey planners. It's also refreshingly honest ('*Public transport in London is not cheap*' is just one quote I found on their website.) Also worth getting is their **app**: Tfl Go (🖥 tfl.gov .uk/maps_/tfl-go), available for both IoS and Android devices.

Above: The LOOP crosses the Thames at Kingston. However, on the east side there's no link between the start at Erith and the finish at Purfleet so you'll need to use public transport if you wish to get between the two.

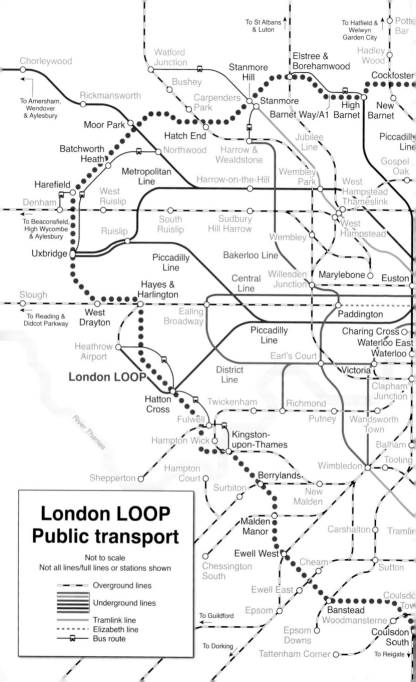

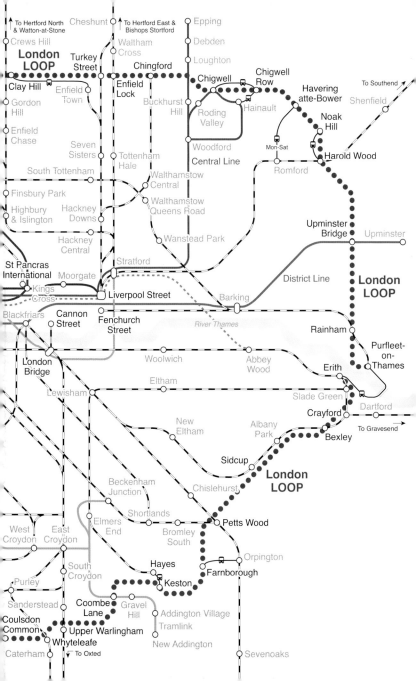

Fares

London is divided into **9 fare zones**. However, Zones 7, 8 and 9 cover just a small corner of north-west London, so it's probably easier to think of there being just 6 fare zones. (Though note that Zone 7 does include Rickmansworth, which is close to the LOOP). These zones roughly form a series of concentric circles, with Zone 1 the most central and Zone 6 the outermost zone. Note that this zone system applies only to tube and train fares; **buses** and **trams** (see below for both) have a separate, simpler system.

For much of your time on the LOOP you will be walking in the furthest reaches of the capital, ie in Zones 5-6. (That said, there are in fact two places the LOOP skirts into Zone 4: at Malden Manor (see p114), near Kingston, and at Chigwell, p179; and in a few places you aren't within the TfL network at all.)

As you'd expect, the more zones your journey covers, the greater the fare. It should also be noted that fares are **Fares are cheaper outside the** cheaper outside the rush hours, or **rush hours, or peak times** peak times. **Rush hour is Monday to Friday 6.30-9.30am and 4-7pm.** For example, a single fare from Zone 1 (Piccadilly Circus) to Zone 6 (Uxbridge) using an Oyster card or contactless credit/debit card is £3.30 off-peak and £5.30 at peak times.

There are daily caps: Zones 1-6 £13.50 anytime and off peak; Zones 1 to 7/8/9 £14.70/17.40/19.30 anytime and £13.60 off peak. The equivalent weekly caps are £67.70/73.70/87/96.50. Caps for Zones 1-6 for paper tickets are £19.60/13.90. Caps are valid over 24 hours from 04.30am-04.29am.

Bus and tram fares The zone system does not apply to the bus or tram (see box on p49) network: **You can travel by bus all over the capital, in zones 1-6, with any Travelcard regardless of what zone it covers.** If you don't have a Travelcard, fares are £1.55 for up to an hour's journey if you're using a contactless card or Oyster card (once again, just tap it on the yellow reader on entering the bus); this is called a 'hopper fare'.

If you're using buses a lot in one day, the maximum that TfL will deduct from your card is £4.65 and over a week the cap is £21.90. Anyone with a Freedom Pass or an 'English National Concessionary Travel Scheme bus pass' can travel for free on all buses except between 4.30am and 9am on weekdays, though at anytime at weekends and on public holidays.

How to pay

The fare you pay depends to a large degree on the method of payment you use. The different methods of payment are as follows:

Visitor Oyster Cards These smart cards cost £5 each, though this one-off cost is refundable if you return the card. You can buy them from underground station ticket machines, overground railway stations, newsagents etc. You need to add money to your card (ie top it up) before you begin travelling and it then works like a pay-as-you-go mobile, where the balance on the card is reduced every time you use it (ie every time you take a journey on public transport). Oyster cards can be used on buses, trains and the underground – you simply need to tap your card on the yellow reader at the ticket barriers (or when entering the bus), and tap it again when you arrive at your destination. (Don't forget to tap out or you'll end up paying a lot more.)

The big advantage with an Oyster card is that the fares are less than for a paper ticket, though you can get the *same* fares if you pay with a….

Debit or credit card If you don't have an Oyster card you can obtain the same cut-price fares by simply tapping your credit/debit card on the yellow readers in the same way that you would an Oyster card. The advantage of using your own credit/debit card is that you don't need to top it up all the time; as long as you have enough money in your account to pay for the journey, you should be fine. But do remember to tap in and out **with the same debit or credit card** or, again, you'll pay a lot more for your journey than you should. At first your card will be charged 10p to check it is working/valid; the actual fare will only be charged at the end of the day.

Travelcards Travelcards are passes that allow you unlimited travel for a one-off payment and are valid for a day, week, month or even up to a year. You can buy one that's off-peak only, or one that allows you to travel anytime; and one for all zones or one that is limited to certain zones only. You can get either a bus-only ticket, which is cheaper, or a 'regular' Travelcard that covers all modes of transport (the tube, Overground and national rail trains in London, buses, trams and the Docklands Light Railway). The big advantage with a Travelcard is that, once you've bought one, you can travel without additional cost – assuming you obey the limitations of your ticket, of course.

The Travelcard system is too complex to go into great detail here, but do visit the TfL website or one of TfL's visitor centres (though the centres were closed during the COVID-19 pandemic) for advice on which version is best for you. But here are a couple of points that people regularly ask about Travelcards:

Firstly, what if you already have a Travelcard but your destination is in a zone that is not covered by it? Then you just need to pay what they call an **excess (or extension) fare**. For example, let's assume that you already have a Travelcard that covers Zones 1 & 2, but your destination is Chigwell on the LOOP in Zone 4. In this instance you'll need to pay an excess/extension fare to travel in Zones 3 & 4, which will cost £1.70 off peak or £2.50 in peak hours assuming you use the cheaper contactless method of payment (see above).

Secondly, if you have a Travelcard that covers Zones 3 & 4, and you start and end your journey in those zones but travel via Zones 1 & 2 to get to your destination, you will need to pay an extra fare.

Buying a paper ticket Paper tickets can be bought from either an underground/train station ticket machine, or a TfL ticket office, using either cash or a debit/credit card. Note that you can't buy paper tickets for bus or tram services.

If you adopt this method you'll pay the full fare for your journey, and as the TfL website says, '**You should never pay the full fare for tickets on any form of transport in London**'. In other words, don't use this method unless you are happy to pay more for your journey than you could have done. Given this, it's quite surprising that there are still facilities that enable you to buy tickets at the station – presumably they're for those who don't have a credit/debit card, and don't want to purchase either an Oyster card or a Travelcard.

Transport outside of London

Just occasionally the LOOP enters an area that is outside the TfL remit. Ewell West and Purfleet are two such places that spring to mind. In this case your Oyster cards and Travelcards won't be valid. However, if you have a Travelcard that covers, for example, travel within Zones 1-6, you can purchase a ticket from whichever station is the first station in Zone 6 and use your Oyster card/Travelcard to cover the rest of the journey. And if travelling out of London you will need to pay an excess fare (see p45).

GETTING AROUND

Most LOOP walkers will need to take a train and/or tube (and in some cases a bus) to reach the start point of their day's walk and to return at the end of the day. The map on pp42-3 shows the main rail, tube and Tramlink routes and will help with planning your journey. The table on these pages and p48 lists the main rail operators and the services they provide that are relevant for the walk as well as the frequency. See box on p49 for details of the Tramlink network. Details of useful bus services are provided in the relevant places in the route guide and the maps show the location of bus stops near the LOOP and states which services stop there. See pp203-7 for a full list of the most relevant bus services.

❏ RAIL SERVICES FOR THE LOOP

The list below includes services to places on the LOOP (in bold text) as well as stations nearby. It also lists other lines that are useful for crossing London but do not actually go to anywhere on the LOOP.
Note: not all stops are listed.

Chiltern Railways (🖳 chilternrailways.co.uk)
● London Marylebone ↔ Aylesbury via Wembley, Sudbury Hill Harrow, South Ruislip, West Ruislip, Denham, Beaconsfield & High Wycombe, daily 1-2/hr

C2C (🖳 c2c-online.co.uk)
● London Fenchurch Street ↔ Grays via Barking, **Rainham** & **Purfleet**, daily 2/hr

Greater Anglia (🖳 greateranglia.co.uk)
● London Liverpool Street ↔ Hertford East via Tottenham Hale, **Enfield Lock**, Waltham Cross, Cheshunt & Broxbourne, Mon-Sat 1-2/hr
● Stratford ↔ Bishops Stortford via Tottenham Hale, **Enfield Lock**, Cheshunt, Broxbourne & Hertford East, Mon-Sat 1-2/hr, Sun 2/hr Stratford ↔ Hertford East
● London Liverpool Street ↔ Southend Victoria via Stratford, Romford, Shenfield & Southend Airport, daily 2-3/hr

Great Northern Railway (🖳 greatnorthernrail.com)
● Moorgate ↔ Welwyn Garden City via Highbury & Islington, Finsbury Park, New Barnet, Hadley Wood, Potters Bar & Hatfield, Mon-Fri 4/hr, Sat & Sun 2/hr

Great Northern Railway *(cont'd)*
● Moorgate ←→ Watton-at-Stone via Finsbury Park, Enfield Chase, Gordon Hill, Crews Hill & Hertford North, Mon-Fri 2/hr (+ 2/hr to/from Hertford North), Sat & Sun 1/hr +1/hr London Kings Cross ←→ Stevenage

GWR (🖥 gwr.com)
● London Paddington ←→ Didcot Parkway via Ealing Broadway, **Hayes & Harlington** & Slough, daily 1-2/hr

London Overground (🖥 tfl.gov.uk/modes/london-overground)
● London Euston ←→ Watford Junction via Willesden Junction, Harrow & Wealdstone, **Hatch End**, Carpenders Park, Bushey & Watford High Street, daily 3-4/hr
● Liverpool Street ←→ Cheshunt via Hackney Downs, Seven Sisters & **Turkey Street**, daily 1-2/hr
● Liverpool Street ←→ **Chingford** via Hackney Downs & Walthamstow Central, daily 2-3/hr
● Liverpool Street ←→ **Enfield Town** via Hackney Downs & Seven Sisters, daily 2/hr
● Clapham Junction ←→ Stratford via Willesden Junction, West Hampstead, Finchley Road & Frognal, Gospel Oak, Camden Road, Caledonian Road & Barnsbury, Highbury & Islington, & Hackney Central, daily 3-4/hr
● Gospel Oak ←→ Barking via Upper Holloway, South Tottenham (for Seven Sisters to Enfield Town), Walthamstow Queen's Road (for Walthamstow Central to Chingford) & Wanstead Park, daily 3-4/hr

Southeastern (🖥 southeasternrailway.co.uk)
● London Charing Cross ←→ Dartford via Waterloo East, London Bridge, Woolwich & **Erith**, daily 2/hr
● London Cannon Street ←→ Deptford via London Bridge, Lewisham, Eltham, Slade Green & **Erith**, daily 1-2/hr
● London Cannon Street circular route via London Bridge, Deptford, Woolwich Dockyard & Arsenal, Slade Green, **Crayford**, **Bexley**, Albany Park, Sidcup, New Eltham & Lewisham, daily 1-2/hr
● London Charing Cross ←→ Gravesend via Waterloo East, London Bridge, New Eltham, Sidcup, Albany Park, **Bexley**, **Crayford** & Dartford, Mon-Sat 2/hr
● London Charing Cross ←→ Dartford via Waterloo East, London Bridge, New Eltham, Sidcup, Albany Park, **Bexley** & **Crayford**, daily 2/hr
● London Victoria ←→ Orpington via Beckenham Junction, Shortlands, Bromley South & **Petts Wood**, daily 2/hr
● London Cannon Street ←→ Orpington via London Bridge, Lewisham, Chislehurst & **Petts Wood**, Mon-Sat 1-2/hr
● London Charing Cross ←→ Sevenoaks via Waterloo East, London Bridge, Chislehurst, **Petts Wood** & Orpington, daily 1-2/hr
● London Cannon Street ←→ **Hayes** via London Bridge, Lewisham & Elmers End, daily 2/hr
● London Charing Cross ←→ **Hayes** via Waterloo East, London Bridge & Elmers End, Mon-Sat 2/hr

Southern (🖥 southernrailway.com)
● London Victoria ←→ East Grinstead via Clapham Junction, East Croydon, **Upper Warlingham** & Oxted, daily 2/hr (change at Oxted for services to/from Uckfield)
● London Victoria ←→ **Coulsdon South** via East Croydon & Purley, daily 2/hr

(cont'd overleaf)

❏ RAIL SERVICES FOR THE LOOP *(cont'd from p47)*

● London Victoria ↔ Reigate via Clapham Junction, East Croydon, Purley, **Coulsdon South** & Redhill, daily 1-2/hr
● London Victoria ↔ Epsom Downs via Clapham Junction, Balham, West Croydon, Sutton & **Banstead**, daily 2/hr
● London Victoria ↔ Epsom via Clapham Junction, Carshalton, Sutton, Cheam & **Ewell East**, daily 4/hr
● London Bridge ↔ Tattenham Corner via East Croydon, South Croydon, Purley, **Coulsdon Town** & Woodmansterne, daily 2/hr
● London Bridge ↔ Caterham via South Croydon, Purley & **Whyteleafe**, daily 2-3/hr
● London Bridge ↔ Horsham via East Croydon, **Coulsdon South**, Redhill & Gatwick Airport, daily 1-2/hr

SouthWestern Railway (🖳 southwesternrailway.com)
● London Waterloo ↔ Guildford via Clapham Junction, Wimbledon, **Ewell West** & Epsom, daily 1/hr
● London Waterloo ↔ Chessington South via Clapham Junction, Wimbledon & **Malden Manor**, daily 1-2/hr
● London Waterloo ↔ Dorking via Clapham Junction, Wimbledon, **Ewell West** & Epsom, daily 1/hr
● London Waterloo ↔ Hampton Court via Clapham Junction, Wimbledon, New Malden, **Berrylands**, Surbiton & Thames Ditton, daily 1-2/hr
● London Waterloo circular route via Clapham Junction, Wimbledon, New Malden, **Kingston-on-Thames**, **Hampton Wick**, Twickenham, Richmond, Putney & Wandsworth Town, daily 1-2/hr
● London Waterloo ↔ Shepperton via Clapham Junction, Wimbledon, New Malden, **Kingston-on-Thames**, **Hampton Wick** & **Fulwell**, daily 1-2/hr

Thameslink (🖳 thameslinkrailway.com)
● London Bridge ↔ **Coulsdon South** via East Croydon, Mon-Sat 2/hr, Sun 1/hr
● Luton ↔ Orpington via St Albans, West Hampstead Thameslink, London St Pancras International, London Blackfriars, Shortlands, Bromley South & **Petts Wood** (Mon-Fri 6-9am & 5.30-7.30pm 1-2/hr plus London St Pancras International to Orpington, Mon-Fri 2/hr)
● London Blackfriars ↔ Sevenoaks via Shortlands & Bromley South, daily 2/hr
● St Albans ↔ Sutton via **Elstree & Borehamwood**, West Hampstead Thameslink, London St Pancras International, London Blackfriars, Tooting & Wimbledon, daily 2/hr
● Horsham ↔ Peterborough via Gatwick Airport, Redhill, **Coulsdon South**, East Croydon, London Bridge, Blackfriars & London St Pancras International, daily 1-2/hr

Tfl Rail (🖳 tfl.gov.uk/modes/tfl-rail)
● London Paddington ↔ Reading via Ealing Broadway, **Hayes & Harlington**, **West Drayton**, Slough & Maidenhead, daily 1-3/hr
● London Paddington ↔ Heathrow Airport via Ealing Broadway, **Hayes & Harlington**, daily 2-4/hr
● London Liverpool Street ↔ Shenfield via Stratford, Romford & **Harold Wood**, daily 4-6/hr
Note: When the Elizabeth Line opens (latest estimate at the time of writing is 2022) services will go from Reading to Shenfield and Heathrow Airport to Abbey Wood (via Woolwich), though it is possible there won't be direct services for the full routes so you may have to change in central London.

❑ **TRAMLINK**

Tramlink (🖳 tfl.gov.uk/modes/trams) is a light rail system that operates across south-ern London from Wimbledon to Beckenham Junction, Elmers End and New Addington. It is part of the TfL network and it offers connections to the tube, London overground, national rail and bus services.

● Wimbledon ←→ Elmers End via East Croydon station, daily 2-6/hr
● Wimbledon ←→ New Addington via East Croydon station, **Coombe Lane**, Gravel Hill & Addington Village, daily 2-6/hr
● East Croydon ←→ Beckenham Junction, daily 2-6/hr.

GETTING TO AND FROM LONDON

London is the transport hub of the UK and beyond. If you're coming from out-side London you may well have to go into the centre first, then 'bounce' out to the trail itself.

By train

You can get to London from pretty much anywhere with a railway station in mainland Britain. Sure, it might involve a change of trains – but with London the terminus of almost all British railway lines, it shouldn't be too difficult to find your way to the capital.

National Rail Enquiries (☎ 03457-484950 – operates 24hrs, 🖳 national rail.co.uk) or The Trainline (🖳 thetrainline.com) are both very good at helping you plan your journey; you can either get tickets from the train companies themselves, or at any rail station in the UK, or from The Trainline.

Getting cheaper train tickets You probably already know that the **earlier you buy your train ticket, the cheaper it will be**. But did you also know you could save money by '**splitting your ticket**? Because of Britain's complex rail system, it can often be cheaper to buy two separate tickets that cover your whole journey rather than pay just one single fare. For example, if you're travelling from A to C, rather than just buying a single ticket for the journey it might be cheaper to buy two separate tickets, one from A to B, which is one of the stops en route, and then from B to C. Note that paying two separate fares in this way doesn't make any difference to the actual journey. Just because you have two tickets for the journey doesn't mean you have to change trains. But the savings can be large. The rail companies say that there are plans afoot to alter the price structure of rail fares to ensure that there is no financial advantage to fare split-ting – but it's still worthwhile investigating the possibility as that may take them a while to do.

For further information the website 🖳 moneysavingexpert.com has a good article on fare splitting, and there are websites that help you find the cheapest price for your journey – sites such as 🖳 mytrainpal.com and 🖳 traintickets .com. Note that none of these is ideal – the sites don't always find the best fare, or are slow, or charge commission – but they will at least point you in the right direction to help you split the fare yourself.

By coach

The principal coach (long-distance bus) operator in Britain is **National Express** (💻 nationalexpress.com). Coach travel is generally cheaper (though with the excellent advance-booking train fares and special deals offered by the train companies, that is not always the case now) but the journey time is longer than if travelling by train. National Express's main coach station in London is London Victoria but there are also coach stations at Heathrow Airport, Stratford and Golders Green and for many services you can get off at stops in outer London such as Marble Arch, Mitcham and Vauxhall.

Megabus (💻 uk.megabus.com), a low-cost coach company, operates services between London and various cities in Britain.

By car

This is the worst way to get to London. Not only is it the most polluting, but given the price of fuel, the parking charges in London and the fact that, if you drive into the centre, you'll have to pay the congestion charge, it's simply not worth it. And I haven't even mentioned the traffic yet. Do yourself and everyone else a favour and leave your car behind for this adventure.

❏ GETTING TO BRITAIN

● **By air** Heathrow and Gatwick International Airports are the main airports serving London; indeed, at one point the LOOP runs alongside the fenced perimeter of Heathrow. Stansted and Luton also serve the capital, as does the smaller London City Airport on the eastern side of London. There are excellent train and/or underground connections to each airport.

● **From Europe by train** Eurostar (💻 eurostar.com) operates the high-speed passenger service via the Channel Tunnel between Paris/Brussels/Amsterdam and London. The terminal in London is St Pancras International.

For more information about rail services from Europe, contact your national rail provider or Railteam (💻 www.railteam.eu).

● **From Europe by coach** Eurolines (💻 eurolines.com) have a huge network of long-distance coach services connecting over 500 cities throughout Europe to London. Check carefully: often, once expenses such as food for the journey are taken into consideration, it doesn't work out much cheaper than flying, particularly when compared to the prices of some of the budget airlines.

● **From Europe by ferry (with or without a car)** There are numerous ferries plying routes between ports around the UK and those in Ireland and continental Europe. Dover–Calais is the busiest route with the most frequent crossings, and from Dover there are trains to London Victoria, Charing Cross and London St Pancras.

A useful website for further information is 💻 directferries.com.

● **From Europe by car** Eurotunnel (💻 eurotunnel.com) operates '**le shuttle**' (the shuttle) train service for vehicles via the Channel Tunnel between Calais and Folkestone taking just 35 minutes. Remember, though, that if you drive into the centre of London you're liable to pay a congestion charge.

MINIMUM IMPACT & OUTDOOR SAFETY

Minimum impact walking

Though the LOOP passes through less countryside than your average long-distance trail, the rules of behaviour remain the same and are neatly summarised in the **Countryside Code**. First drawn up in the 1950s and originally called the 'Country Code', it has been revised and relaunched several times, most recently in 2021 to include considerations regarding COVID-19, though its central message remains the same: **When you visit rural parts of the UK, have some consideration for those who make their living there**. If you manage to obey that simple rule, you won't be going too far wrong.

An adapted version of the 2021 Code, launched under the logo 'Respect. Protect. Enjoy.' is reprinted here (see box on p52).

Outdoor safety

SAFETY ON THE LOOP

The biggest danger for hikers on the LOOP are the many busy **roads** that cut across the trail. If you remember your Green Cross Code negotiating these will not be a problem, but just keep your wits about you as you emerge back into civilisation after strolling through the countryside for a while. Don't try to cross a road where it clearly isn't meant to be crossed. If you need to climb over barriers to get to the other side, you shouldn't be crossing there at all. Follow the instructions in Part 4 of this book which points out the correct place to cross.

Other dangers? Well the South-East of England is the hottest part of the country, and **it can get very hot** – so do take some water and wear (high-factor) suncream and a sunhat.

Carrying a torch may be a good idea (you've probably got one on your phone) in case you're walking late in the day and it's starting to get dark.

It is very possible (indeed, probable) that you'll get lost, too, so do keep this book with you – hopefully the instructions provided on the maps in Part 4 will enable you to keep to the trail.

❏ THE COUNTRYSIDE CODE

Respect everyone

● **Be considerate to those living in, working in and enjoying the countryside** If, for example, farm animals are being moved or gathered keep out of the way and follow the farmer's directions. Being courteous and friendly to those you meet will ensure a healthy future for all based on partnership and co-operation.

● **Leave gates and property as you find them** A farmer normally closes gates to keep farm animals in, but may sometimes leave them open so the animals can reach food and water. Leave gates as you find them or follow instructions on signs. When in a group, make sure the last person knows how to leave the gates. Use gates or gaps in field boundaries if you can – climbing over walls, hedges and fences can damage them and increase the risk of farm animals escaping. If you have to climb over a gate because you can't open it always do so at the hinged end. Leave machinery and farm animals alone – if you think an animal is in distress alert the farmer. Give wild animals, livestock and horses plenty of space; their behaviour can be unpredictable, especially when they are with their young. Also do not feed livestock, horses or wild animals.

● **Take special care on roads without pavements** To be safe, walk facing the oncoming traffic and carry a torch or wear highly visible clothing when it's getting dark.

● **Share the space** Cyclists and horse riders should respect walkers' safety, but walkers should also take care not to obstruct or endanger them.

● **Follow local signs and keep to marked paths, even if they're muddy, unless wider access is available** Follow paths unless wider access is available, such as on open country or registered common land (known as 'open access land'). However, stick to the official path across arable/pasture land; minimise erosion by not cutting corners or widening the path. Give way to others when the path is narrow. Get to know the signs and symbols used in the countryside.

Protect the environment

● **Take all your litter home – leave no trace of your visit** Litter and leftover food spoil the beauty of the countryside and can be dangerous to wildlife and farm animals.

● **Take care with BBQs and do not light fires** Fires can be as devastating to wildlife/habitats as they are to people and property; be careful with naked flames & cigarettes.

● **Always keep dogs under control and in sight** This means that you should keep your dog on a lead or in sight at all times, be aware of what it's doing and be confident it will return to you promptly on command. Across farmland dogs should always be kept on a short lead. During lambing time they should not be taken with you at all. Always clean up after your dog and get rid of the mess responsibly – 'bag it and bin it'.

● **Care for nature – do not cause damage or disturbance** Take special care not to damage, destroy or remove features such as rocks, plants and trees. Also be careful not to disturb ruins and historic sites. Help keep all water clean; going to the toilet near a water source can pollute people's water supplies.

Enjoy the outdoors

● **Check your route and local conditions; plan your walk so you know what to expect and what you can do** You're responsible for your own safety: be prepared for natural hazards, changes in the weather and other events.

● **Make no unnecessary noise** Enjoy the peace and solitude of the outdoors by staying in small groups and acting unobtrusively.

● **Follow advice and local signs** In some areas temporary diversions are in place; take notice of these and other local trail advice. Walking on the LOOP is pretty much hazard free but ensure you follow the simple guidelines outlined in this section.

Abide by the following rules, however, to minimise any risks:
● Avoid walking on your own if possible.
● Make sure that somebody knows your plans for every day you are on the trail. This could be a friend or relative whom you have promised to call every night. That way, if you fail to turn up or call, they can raise the alarm.
● Use footwear with good grip and consider having ankle support.
● Be extra vigilant with children.
● For information on walking safely with dogs, see pp34-5 and pp208-9.

Dealing with an accident
● Use basic first aid to treat the injury to the best of your ability.
● In an emergency dial ☎ 999 or ☎ 112. Before you call work out exactly where you are; on the app What3words (🖥 what3words.com) the world is divided into three-metre squares and each has its own three-word geocode so it makes it easy to tell people where you are.

WEATHER FORECASTS

It's a good idea to try to find out what the weather is going to be like before you set off for the day. You can get an online forecast through 🖥 bbc.co.uk/weather or 🖥 metoffice.gov.uk. Pay close attention to it and alter your plans for the day accordingly (or abandon them altogether).

You can also install the BBC Weather app on your smartphone; just type in the name of the place for which you want information. Dark Sky (🖥 darksky .net/app) is another popular weather app, but is for iOS only.

BLISTERS

It is important to break in new footwear before embarking on a walk. Make sure your boots or shoes are comfortable and try to avoid getting them wet on the inside. Air your feet at lunchtime, keep them clean and change your socks regularly. If you feel any hot spots, stop immediately and apply a blister plaster (Compeed is the best-known brand, at least in the UK) and leave on until it is pain free or it starts to come off. If you have left it too late and a blister has developed you should make sure the wound is thoroughly clean (preferably apply some sort of antiseptic cream too) before applying a plaster.

HEAT EXHAUSTION & SUNBURN

Symptoms of **heat exhaustion** include thirst, fatigue, giddiness, a rapid pulse, raised body temperature, low urine output and, if not treated, delirium and finally a coma. **Sunburn** can happen, even on overcast days. The way to avoid it is to stay wrapped up but that's not really an option if it's really sweltering. What you must do, therefore, is to wear a hat and smother yourself in sunscreen (with a minimum factor of 30); apply it regularly throughout the day.

Don't forget your lips, nose, the back of your neck and even under your chin to protect yourself against rays reflected from the ground.

THE ENVIRONMENT & NATURE

Conservation

GOVERNMENT AGENCIES AND SCHEMES

Natural England

Natural England (🖳 gov.uk/government/organisations/natural-eng land) is the single body responsible for identifying, establishing and managing: National Parks, Areas of Outstanding Natural Beauty, National Nature Reserves and Sites of Special Scientific Interest. Local authorities also designate areas of land for protection (see below).

The highest level of landscape protection is the designation of land as a **national park** (🖳 nationalparksengland.org.uk). At the time of writing there were 10 national parks in England, though none particularly near the LOOP. The second level of protection is **Area of Outstanding Natural Beauty** (**AONB**; 🖳 landscapesforlife.org .uk), of which there are 33 wholly in England (plus the Wye Valley which straddles the English–Welsh border) covering some 15% of England and Wales. The only AONB near the trail is Surrey Hills AONB (🖳 surreyhills.org), which the LOOP comes very close to without ever entering. The primary objective of all AONBs is conservation of the natural beauty of a landscape.

There are no National Nature Reserves on the route of the LOOP but there are **Sites of Special Scientific Interest** (**SSSIs**). These range in size from little pockets protecting wild flower meadows, important nesting sites or special geological features, to vast swathes of upland, moorland and wetland. On the trail there are several, including Crayford Marshes (see p68), Happy Valley (see p99 & p102) and Farthing Downs (see p102), Banstead Downs (p107), Bentley Priory (p152) and Hainault Forest (p182).

Local Landscape designations

Associated with AONBs, but designated by local authorities, are several **Areas of Great Landscape Value** (**AGLV**), though these are also called Special Landscape Area or Area of Special Landscape Importance. AGLVs on the LOOP include Happy Valley (see p99 & p102) and Farthing Downs (see p102).

❑ CAMPAIGNING AND CONSERVATION BODIES/ORGANISATIONS

● **English Heritage** (🖳 english-heritage.org.uk) English Heritage looks after, champions and advises the government on historic buildings and places. However, in April 2015 it was divided into a new charitable trust that retains the name English Heritage and a non-departmental public body, Historic England (see below).

● **Historic England** (🖳 historicengland.org.uk) Created in April 2015 as a result of dividing the work done by English Heritage. Historic England is the government department responsible for looking after and promoting England's historic environment and is in charge of the listing system, giving grants and dealing with planning matters.

● **National Trust** (NT; 🖳 nationaltrust.org.uk) A charity that aims to protect, through ownership, threatened coastline, countryside, historic houses, castles and gardens, and archaeological remains for everybody to enjoy. In particular the National Trust cares for about 775 miles of the British coastline, over 250,000 hectares of countryside and 300 historic buildings, monuments, parks, gardens and reserves, including Rainham Hall (see p194) and sections of the woodland near Petts Wood (see p78).

● **Royal Society for the Protection of Birds** (RSPB; 🖳 rspb.org.uk) The largest voluntary conservation body in Europe focusing on providing a healthy environment for birds and wildlife and with over 200 reserves in the UK – including the fantastic Rainham Marshes (see box on p194) – and more than a million members.

● The umbrella organisation for the 46 wildlife trusts in the UK is **The Wildlife Trusts** (🖳 wildlifetrusts.org). Those relevant to the LOOP are **Kent Wildlife Trust** (🖳 kentwildlifetrust.org.uk), **Surrey Wildlife Trust** (🖳 surreywildlifetrust.org.uk), **Berks, Bucks and Oxon Wildlife Trust** (🖳 bbowt.org.uk), **Herts & Middlesex Wildlife Trust** (🖳 hertswildlifetrust.org.uk), **Essex Wildlife Trust** (🖳 essexwt.org .uk) and **London Wildlife Trust** (🖳 wildlondon.org.uk).

● **Forestry Commission** (🖳 www.gov.uk/government/organisations/forestry-commission) A non ministerial government body whose role is to 'increase the value of woodlands to society and the environment' and which works with Forest Research and **Forestry England** (🖳 forestryengland.uk). Ingrebourne Hill (see p194) is managed by Forestry England.

● **Woodland Trust** (🖳 woodlandtrust.org.uk) The trust aims to conserve, restore and re-establish native woodlands throughout the UK. The trust owns Devilsden Woods (see p102) and Warren Farm (see p108).

THE ENVIRONMENT AND NATURE

There are also some **Local Nature Reserves** (**LNRs**) on the route, including Foots Cray (p73), Darrick & Newstead Woods Nature Reserve (p82), Selsdon Wood (p95), Hogsmill (p112), Denham Quarry & Frays Valley (p139), Oxhey Woods (p148), Scratchwood (pp158-9), Totteridge Fields (p161), Sewardstone Marsh (p174), Roding Valley Meadows (p178), Chigwell Row Wood (p181) and Ingrebourne Valley (p193).

Flora and fauna

As mentioned in the introduction, one of the unexpected pleasures of the LOOP is the amount of wildlife the average walker can see. There are two reasons for this, I think. Firstly, the wildlife that does live around London's perimeter has doubtless become more accustomed to the the presence of humans, and thus, as a result, less shy. Secondly, those same creatures are forced to share an ever-diminishing supply of their natural habitat – and the LOOP goes through that same habitat. You are more likely to see a herd of deer if they have just a couple of acres to inhabit, rather than if that same herd of deer was free to roam over hundreds of acres.

Nevertheless, it's still a lovely surprise to see so much fauna on the trail. The following is not in any way a comprehensive guide, but merely a brief run-down of the more commonly seen animals on the trail, together with some of the rarer and more spectacular species.

For identifying obscure plants and peculiar-looking beasties as you walk, Collins and New Holland publish a pocket-sized range to Britain's natural riches. The Collins Gem series are tough little books; current titles include guides to *Trees*, *Birds*, *Mushrooms*, *Wild Flowers*, *Wild Animals*, *Insects* and *Butterflies*.

MAMMALS

One creature you will definitely see along the walk is the **rabbit** (*Oryctolagus cuniculus*). It was actually the Romans who brought the first rabbits to Britain. Timid by nature, most of the time you'll have to make do with nothing more than a brief and distant glimpse of their white tails as they race for the nearest warren at the sound of your footfall. Because they are so numerous, however, the laws of probability dictate that you will at some stage during your walk get close enough to observe them without being spotted; trying to take a decent photo of one of them is a different matter.

One of the rare creatures on the LOOP is the **water vole** (scientifically known as *Arvicola terrestris*, but better known as 'Ratty' from Kenneth Grahame's classic children's story *Wind in the Willows*). Poor Ratty has had a hard time of it over the past few decades, largely because of an alien invader, the **mink** from North America (*Mustela vison*) which has successfully adapted to the British countryside after escaping from local fur farms. Unfortunately, the mink not only hunts water voles but is small enough to slip inside their burrows. Thus, with the voles afforded no protection, the mink is able to wipe out an entire riverbank's population in a matter of months. It's highly unlikely you'll see either water vole or its nemesis, the mink, but three places where voles are said to thrive on the LOOP are the River Crane, Sewardstone Marsh and Rainham Marshes.

Other creatures that you have a greater chance of seeing include the ubiquitous **fox** (*Vulpes vulpes*), now just as at home in the city as it is in the country. While generally considered nocturnal, it's not unusual to encounter a fox during the day too, often lounging in the sun near its den. One creature you will probably not see in daylight – though *occasionally* they might emerge in the afternoon – is the **badger** (*Meles meles*). Relatively common throughout the British Isles, these sociable mammals with their distinctive black-and-white striped muzzles live in large underground burrows called setts, appearing around sunset to root for worms and slugs.

One creature that is strictly nocturnal, however, is the **bat**, of which there are 17 species in Britain, all protected by law. Your best chance of spotting one is at dusk while there's still enough light in the sky to make out their flitting forms as they fly along hedgerows, over rivers and streams and around street lamps in their quest for moths and insects. The commonest species in Britain is the **pipistrelle** (*Pipistrellus pipistrellus*).

In addition to the above, keep a look out for other fairly common but little-seen species such as the carnivorous **stoat** (*Mustela erminea*), its diminutive cousin the **weasel** (*Mustela nivalis*), the **hedgehog** (*Erinaceus europaeus*) – these days, alas, most commonly seen as roadkill – and any number of species of **voles**, **mice** and **shrews**.

Finally, pretty much every hiker will encounter deer on their walk. Most of these encounters will be in Bushy Park, where there's a resident population of semi-tame (though do not go near them – they do attack if they feel threatened!) red and fallow deer. The **red deer** (*Cervus elaphus*) is actually Britain's largest native land mammal. Outside of Bushy, you're most likely to spot **roe deer** (*Capreolus capreolus*), a small native woodland species, though it can also be seen grazing in fields. Selsdon Wood, by Carter's Brook in Harold Hill and Scratchwood are just some of the places where they seem to thrive. As with most creatures, your best chance of seeing one is very early in the morning.

REPTILES

The **adder** is the only poisonous snake of the three species in Britain. They pose very little risk to walkers – indeed, you should consider yourself extremely fortunate to see one, providing you're a safe distance away. They bite only when provoked, preferring to hide instead. The venom is designed to kill small mammals such as mice, voles and shrews, so deaths in humans are very rare but a bite can be extremely unpleasant and occasionally dangerous to children or the elderly. You are most likely to encounter them in spring when they come out of hibernation and during the summer when pregnant females warm themselves in the sun. They are easily identified by the striking zigzag pattern on their back. Should you be lucky enough to encounter one, enjoy it but leave it undisturbed.

The other species you're likely to see is the harmless green and yellow **grass snake** (*Natrix helvetica*), Britain's longest snake, with adults sometimes reaching 1.5m.

THE ENVIRONMENT AND NATURE

BUTTERFLIES

Butterfly-lovers will have a field day on the LOOP – literally. All the nature reserves along the way are home to several species some of which are actually quite rare. Indeed, over half of Britain's native butterfly species are said to thrive at Happy Valley (see p102). Even such minor patches of greenery as Carshalton Road Pastures (see p106) boasts that over 18 species can be found on its land, including the **small blue** and **brown hairstreak butterflies**.

The rarest species on the LOOP, however, is probably the **purple emperor** (*Apatura iris*), which lives in Bishop's Wood (see p144). Sightings of this butterfly are rare, not only because there simply aren't many of them but also because they like to make their home in the treetops, descending to the ground only occasionally to feed on animal dung.

Butterflies that you probably *will* see on the LOOP include the **meadow brown** (*Maniola jurtina*), a very common species, dusty brown in colour with a rusty orange streak and dark, false eyes. They can be seen in meadows all along the trail. The small **gatekeeper** (*Pyronia tithonus*) likes a similar habitat and is also widespread throughout the LOOP. They are identified by their deep orange and chocolate-brown markings.

The **peacock** (*Inachis io*) is perhaps Britain's most beautiful butterfly; it's quite common around the fringes of London. The markings on the wings are said to mimic the eyes of an animal to frighten off predators. Also common is the impressive **red admiral** (*Vanessa atalanta*). Owing to climate change it is now starting to overwinter in Britain and appears to be thriving.

The **brimstone** (*Gonepteryx rhamni*) is also widespread, and easy to spot when in flight thanks to its vibrant yellow wings. However, at rest it's well camouflaged as the underside of those wings looks like leaves.

The **white admiral** (*Limenitis camilla*) is declining in numbers but may still be seen in some woodland sites such as Bishop's Wood, where it lives alongside the purple emperor (see above) and the equally rare **silver-washed fritillary** (*Argynnis paphia*).

Although it has also recently been in decline in other parts of the country, the **small tortoiseshell** (*Aglais urticae*) is still widespread here around the LOOP. Other very common butterflies include the **small white** (*Pieris/Artogeia rapae*) and the **large white** (*Pieris brassicae*); both can travel large distances, some migrating from continental Europe each year.

Along many of the country lanes and tracks the **speckled wood** (*Pararge aegeria*) can be seen basking on hedgerows. It is a small dark butterfly with a few white spots and six small false eyes at the rear.

The **holly blue** (*Celastrina argiolus*) and **chalkhill blue** (*Polyommatus/Lysandra coridon*) are both similar in appearance, being very small and pale blue in colour, although the chalkhill blue has a dark strip on the edge of each wing. The latter can be seen on Riddlesdown Common (see p98).

FLOWERS

Spring is the time to come and see the spectacular displays of colour on the LOOP, when most of the flowers are in bloom.

Woodland, hedgerows and riverbanks

From March to May **bluebells** (*Hyacinthoides non-scripta*) proliferate in some of the woods along the trail, providing a wonderful spectacle. The white **wood anemone** (*Anemone nemorosa*) – wide open flowers when sunny, closed and drooping when the weather's dull – and the yellow **primrose** (*Primula vulgaris*) also flower early in spring.

Red campion (*Silene dioica*), which flowers from late April, can be found in hedgebanks along with **rosebay willowherb** (*Epilobium angustifolium*) which also has the name fireweed due to its habit of colonising burnt areas.

In scrubland and on woodland edges you will find **bramble** (*Rubus fruticosus*), a common vigorous shrub responsible for many a ripped jacket thanks to the sharp thorns and prickles. **Blackberry** fruits ripen from late summer to autumn.

Fairly common in scrubland and on woodland edges is the **dog rose** (*Rosa canina*) which has a large pink flower, the fruits of which are used to make rosehip syrup.

In streams or rivers look out for the white-flowered **water crow-foot** (*Ranunculus penicillatus pseudofluitans*) which, because it needs unpolluted, flowing water, is a good indicator of the cleanliness of the stream.

Other flowering plants to look for in wooded areas and in hedgerows include the tall **foxglove** (*Digitalis purpurea*) with its trumpet-like flowers, **forget-me-not** (*Myosotis arvensis*) with tiny, delicate blue flowers, and **cow parsley** (*Anthriscus sylvestris*), a tall member of the carrot family with a large globe of white flowers which often covers roadside verges and hedgebanks.

Perhaps the most ubiquitous plant on the trail, however, is none of the above – nor is it even a British native. **Himalayan balsam** (*Impatiens glandulifera*) is a tall plant that can reach to well over head height and produces pink flowers with pods that 'explode' when squeezed, scattering their seeds. Introduced in 1839, it particularly enjoys riverbanks where it thrives, often suffocating out any other plant.

Grassland

There is much overlap between the hedge/woodland-edge habitat and that of pastures and meadows. You will come across **common birdsfoot-trefoil** (*Lotus corniculatus*), **Germander speedwell** (*Veronica chamaedrys*), **tufted** and **bush vetch** (*Vicia cracca* and *V. sepium*) and **meadow vetchling** (*Lathyrus pratensis*) in both. Often the only species you will see in heavily grazed pastures are the most resilient.

Of the thistles, in late summer you should come across the **melancholy thistle** (*Cirsium helenoides*) drooping sadly on roadside verges and hay meadows. Unusually, it has no prickles on its stem.

THE ENVIRONMENT AND NATURE

The **yellow rattle** is aptly named, for the dry seedpods rattle in the wind, a good indication for farmers that it is time to harvest the hay.

Other widespread grassland species include **harebell** (*Campanula rotundifolia*) and **devil's-bit scabious** (*Succisa pratensis*). Also keep an eye out for orchids such as the **fragrant orchid** (*Gymnadenia conopsea*), **early purple orchid** (*Orchis mascula*) and the **bee orchid** (*Ophrys apifera*) whose flowers are shaped like bees.

BIRDS

The LOOP is something of a birdwatcher's paradise. There is, after all, no shortage of different habitats for birds along the LOOP – and as a consequence, there's a great variety of species. River, lake, pond, stream, meadow, marsh, woodland, farmland, hedgerow, suburb, town centre – each of these provides a

THE ENVIRONMENT & NATURE

❑ THE PARAKEETS OF LONDON

Whether you have an interest in bird-spotting or not, you can't fail to be struck by the beautiful, alien rose-ringed parakeets (*Psittacula krameri*). It's arguable that they are now the most popular bird on the LOOP, but even if they're not, they are almost certainly the most visible, thanks to their bright green plumage, and definitely the most voluble.

Parakeet sightings are actually nothing new, with stories of them appearing in Norfolk, Dulwich and Brixton in the 19th century. But the fact they've managed to establish not just a viable population, but one that is thriving to such an extent that they've colonised pretty much every piece of woodland and parkland in London and beyond, is certainly new.

There are several urban myths about their introduction to the UK. The most popular one is that the movie industry was to blame: that they were brought over as 'extras' on the Humphrey Bogart and Lauren Bacall classic *The African Queen*. It's said that a pair escaped, survived the harsh London winter – and their offspring have been thriving ever since. Another legend states that Jimi Hendrix released a pair in the epicentre of Swinging London in the 1960s, Carnaby Street. Or that they escaped from aviaries that were damaged or destroyed by the Great Storm of 1987 – a theory that sounds plausible, until you realise that there was already a population of over 500 London parakeets by 1983. The more prosaic explanation for their presence over here is that they simply escaped from aviaries in the late 1960s or early 1970s, and despite the very different climate to the one they were used to in their native African or Indian subcontinent, they have managed to flourish.

Though London is their base in England, they are spreading throughout the South-East (there's a large population around Margate, Ramsgate and Broadstairs now, on the East Kent coast). Many of the other great cities of England, including Liverpool, Manchester, Birmingham, Oxford, have all reported populations of parakeets living in their parks, and the birds have now even crossed the border into Scotland, with both Glasgow and Edinburgh reporting sightings.

As beautiful as the birds undoubtedly are, there are concerns about their environmental impact, particularly on the native British birdlife. Indeed, in 2009 Natural England added parakeets to the 'general license', meaning they can be hunted and culled without fear of prosecution or the need for special permission.

Peacock
Inachis io

Butterflies – see p58

Small
Tortoiseshell
Aglais urticae

Large White
Pieris brassicae

Chalkhill Blue
Lysandra coridon

Brimstone
*Gonepteryx
rhamni*

Red
Admiral
Vanessa atalanta

Painted Lady
Cynthia cadui

Small White
*Artogeia
rapae*

White
Admiral
*Limenitis
camilla*

Silver-washed Fritillary
Argynnis paphia

Common Ragwort
Senecio jacobaea

Cowslip
Primula veris

Yarrow
Achillea millefolium

Foxglove
Digitalis purpurea

Bird's-foot trefoil
Lotus corniculatus

Meadow Buttercup
Ranunculis acris

Marsh Marigold
(Kingcup)
Caltha palustris

Yellow Rattle
Rhinanthus minor

Primrose
Primula vulgaris

St John's Wort
*Hypericum
perforatum*

Tormentil
Potentilla erecta

Honeysuckle
*Lonicera
periclymemum*

Ox-eye Daisy
Leucanthemum vulgare

Old Man's Beard
Clematis vitalba

Common Vetch
Vicia sativa

Common Knapweed
Centaurea nigra

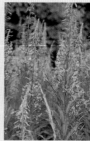

ba palumbus), that famously thrive in Central London,
tions of their number one enemy, the **sparrowhawk**

land on the LOOP. Oak woodland is probably the most
habitat that's not exclusively made up of oak. Other trees
lude **downy birch** (*Betula pubescens*), its relative the **sil-**
ndula), **holly** (*Ilex aquifolium*) and **hazel** (*Corylus avella-*
ionally been used for coppicing (the periodic cutting of
sting).

celsior) also dominates many of the woods along the trail,
n (*Ulmus glabra*), **sycamore** (*Acer pseudoplatanus*) and
ccata). The **hawthorn** (*Crataegus monogyna*) also grows
lly in isolated pockets on pasture, or, more commonly, as
d/or a field boundary. These species are known as 'pioneer
ay a vital role in the ecosystem by improving the soil.
from man, these pioneers – the hawthorn and its compan-
us aucuparia) – would eventually be succeeded by longer-
the oak.

areas and along rivers and streams you are more likely to
utinosa). There's also the **juniper** (*Juniperus communis*),
ive British species of conifer, the blue berries of which are

s that does well in some of the woodland that you cross is
ee (*Sorbus torminalis*), also known as the 'chequers' or
cies that is part of the same family as the mountain ash, it
ark, though distinctively it flakes away to reveal a darker
ardwood, and the wood is valuable. The tree requires a lot
out-competed by other trees. Its presence usually indicates
s ancient. Bishops Wood (see p144) is one place where it

that indicates that the woodland is ancient is the **field**
stre). On the LOOP you can find it in Churchfield Woods
n Crofton & Darrick Woods.

Harebell
Campanula rotundifolia

Rosebay Willowherb
Epilobium angustifolium

Himalayan Balsam
Impatiens glandulifera

Early Purple Orchid
Orchis mascula

Rowan (tree)
Sorbus aucuparia

Dog Rose
Rosa canina

Forget-me-not
Myosotis arvensis

Red Campion
Silene dioica

Scarlet Pimpernel
Anagallis arvensis

Bluebell
Hyacinthoides non-scripta

Germander Speedwell
Veronica chamaedrys

Herb-Robert
Geranium robertianum

Ramsons (Wild Garlic)
Allium ursinum

Meadow Cranesbill
Geranium pratense

Common Dog Violet
Viola riviniana

Common Centaury
Centaurium erythraea

Above, clockwise from top left: Grey heron in Bushy Park (© Anna Udagawa), mallard, Egyptian geese, Canada goose, mute swan, greylag goose (all © HS), black-headed gull (© BT).

home for several species of bir
Marshes, perhaps the most fam
home to a state-of-the-art visit

For waterfowl, you'll defi
well as the large, grey, prehis
egret (*Egretta garzetta*) and **lit**

Of the several species of
(*Branta canadensis*). Introduc
mately 300 years ago, the pop
most common goose in souther
able with their dramatic black
contrast to their wild congenit
of the continent in huge flock
aggresive, they can even threat
an outstretched neck and hissin
able bird on the LOOP, along w

You may also see (and hea
birds found here seem to have
parts of the UK are still migran
each spring.

If you're very lucky you m
(*Porzana porzana*) and **bitte**
Country Park or Rainham Mars
(*Tyto alba*) and **short-eared ow**

At home either by marshes
LOOP **lapwings** (*Vanellus vane*
of Hornchurch Country Park. Bl
the lapwing is approximately th
characteristic, however, is the m
when disturbed, believed to be
to distract predators from its ne

Woodland birds that you m
the **treecreeper** (*Corthia familia*
species: **great spotted** (*Dendr*
minor) and **green** (*Picus viridis*)
trees by hopping up them (thou
method). They share the woods
communis), **cuckoo** (*Cuculus ca*
call is often heard, though their n
ticular the **tawny** (*Strix aluco*) a
is a great place to see most of th

In the suburbs it's the usual
(*Parus major*), **coal tit** (*Parus*
(*Turdus merula*), **mistle thrush**
rubecula). The most numerous

woodpigeon (*Colu*
despite the depred
(*Accipiter nisus*).

TREES

There's lots of woo
prevalent, a diverse
that flourish here in
ver birch (*Betula p*
na) which has trad
small trees for harve

Ash (*Fraxinus*
along with **wych e**
some **yew** (*Taxus b*
along the path, usu
part of a hedgerow
species' and they
Without interferen
ion the **rowan** (*Sor*
lived species such a

In wet, marshy
find **alder** (*Alnus*
one of only three na
used to flavour gin

One rare speci
the **wild service t**
'checker' tree. A sp
has a smooth grey
brown layer. It's a
of light but is ofte
that the woodland
thrives.

Another speci
maple (*Acer camp*
before Bexley and

THE ENVIRONMENT & NATURE

Using this guide

In this guide the trail is divided into 24 stages, as described on the Inner London Ramblers/TfL websites (see box on p39). These stages vary in length from 3½ miles (5.6km) up to 11 miles (17.7km). Do not, however, assume that this is the only way to plan your trek. There are so many options for catching public transport along the trail that you can pretty much divide up your hike however you want.

On p36 are tables to help you plan an itinerary. To provide further help, practical information is presented on the trail maps, including: walking times; shops where you can buy supplies; eateries and accommodation options; bus stops (with service numbers) as well as tube/railway/tram stations where relevant. Further service details are given in the text under the entry for each settlement. See also the colour maps and profile charts at the back of the book.

TRAIL MAPS   [see map key p202]

Direction
(See p31 for a discussion of the pros and cons of walking clockwise versus anti-clockwise.) This guide has been ordered in a clockwise direction, beginning at Erith and ending at Purfleet-on-Thames, so you will find it easier to follow if you head in the same clockwise direction. But there's nothing to stop you using this guide 'in reverse' and heading round the trail in an anti-clockwise direction, and hopefully you'll still find the route descriptions and maps useful.

Scale and walking times
The trail maps are to a scale of 1:20,000 (1cm = 200m; 3⅛ inches = one mile). Walking times are given along the side of each map and the arrow shows the direction to which the time refers. The black triangles indicate the points between which the times have been taken. **See box on walking times below**.

❏ **IMPORTANT NOTE – WALKING TIMES**

Unless otherwise specified, **all times in this book refer only to the time spent walking**. You should add 20-30% to allow for rests, photos, checking the map, drinking water etc, not to mention time simply to stop and stare. When planning the day's hike count on 5-7 hours' actual walking.

The time-bars are a tool and are not there to judge your walking ability. There are so many variables that affect walking speed, from the weather conditions to the weight you're carrying, the state of your feet and how many beers you drank the previous evening. After the first hour or two of walking you will be able to see how your speed relates to the timings on the maps.

Up or down?
The trail is shown as a red dotted line. An arrow across the trail indicates the slope; two arrows show that it is steep. Note that the arrow points towards the higher part of the trail. If, for example, you are walking from A (at 80m) to B (at 200m) and the trail between the two is short and steep, it would be shown thus: A – – – – >> – – – – B. Reversed arrow heads indicate a downward gradient.

Other features
Features are marked on the map when pertinent to navigation. In order to avoid cluttering the maps and making them unusable not all features have been marked each time they occur.

The route guide

If you're doing this walk in a **clockwise direction** (**C**, ie starting in Erith and ending at Purfleet) follow the maps below in an ascending order (from 1 to 48) and the text as below.

If you're walking in an **anti-clockwise direction** (A/C, Purfleet to Erith), follow the maps in a descending order (from 48 to 1). Turn to p199 to start your walk in this direction.

ERITH   [Map 1, pp66-7]
Erith fulfils its role as the starting point for a long-distance trail quite admirably. Not only does it have plenty of shops selling provisions for your walk, but it's also a place that most people are glad to leave. Few people will consider this amalgamation of scrap-metal dealers, bus depots, supermarkets and shopping malls to be picturesque, but the industrial landscape you see today is, perhaps, a reflection that man has been living in and around the area for a long time – and thus has had centuries to despoil it.

There's been a village here since at least the Anglo-Saxons of the 5th century, when it was called *Ærre hyðe*, meaning 'old haven'. The town enjoyed a brief heyday as a **riverside resort** for Victorian Londoners taking advantage of the newly built railway for a day-trip out of the 'Big Smoke'; but for most of the last 200 years the town has survived on the profits of heavy industry, whether it be as a small port or as a manufacturer of guns and ammunition.

Erith became part of the London Borough of Bexley in the 1960s, having

---

SYMBOLS USED IN TEXT
🐕 Dogs allowed; see pp34-5 for more information
fb signifies places that have a Facebook page (for latest opening hours)
C = walking clockwise A/C = walking anti-clockwise

previously been part of the county of Kent. Unfortunately, little of the capital's prosperity has trickled down to the residents of the town, as a result of which it now feels like it belongs neither to the capital nor the 'Garden of England'. The house prices reflect this, being the third lowest of any ward in London (only Barking and Dagenham have lower).

The one 'sight' in the town is **Deep Water Wharf**, otherwise known as **Erith Pier**, a 360m-long L-shaped landing once used to unload cargo but now a pleasant place for a promenade; it's really rather nice, though whether you want to add 720m to your walk is another matter.

Services

Erith's aesthetic drawbacks are at least partially compensated by its facilities. There's a **post office** (Mon-Sat 9am-6pm) with **ATM** very close to the trail, a **bus station** (stops on the road side) next to it, and a **shopping mall**, Erith Riverside Shopping Centre (🖳 erith-riverside.co.uk), behind that, where you'll find a **chemist**, JG Harrisons (Mon-Fri 9am-6pm, Sat to 5pm).

There's a Morrisons **supermarket** (with **toilets** and **ATM**) adjacent to the path, with a smaller Premier Stores (Mon-Sat 6am-9pm, Sun 8am-7pm) right on the trail.

The **shopping centre** has several *cafés* and *restaurants* but, if you've been walking the LOOP in anti-clockwise direction and you're looking for somewhere to celebrate *finishing* your walk without leaving the trail, ***Running Horses*** (☎ 01322-348097; 🐾 on lead; bar 11.30am-10pm) is the closest option to the station (and thus the finish line). At the time of writing they were only serving food on Sundays (noon-3pm) but they hope to serve daily in 2021.

Transport   [see map pp42-3]

Most people will arrive by **train**, That is useful, of course, because the railway station is also where the LOOP begins (though you'll see no sign of this). Erith is connected by regular Southeastern trains to both London Cannon Street (approx 45 mins) and also to Charing Cross (approx 60 mins); in the other direction services go to Dartford and Crayford, Bexley & Sidcup. See p47 for more details.

For **buses**, the No 99 (Woolwich to Bexleyheath via Slade Green & Barnehurst; daily 2-5/hr), 229 (Thamesmead to Sidcup via Bexleyheath & Bexley; daily 4-6/hr), and the 469 (to Woolwich; Mon-Sat 8/hr, Sun 4/hr) call here. The No 428 (to Bluewater via Dartford & Crayford; daily 2-4/hr) stops near the shopping centre.

STAGE 1: ERITH TO BEXLEY   [MAPS 1-2]

Given the variety of scenery encountered on the LOOP, it's fair to say that there is no such thing as a typical day's walking. But the first part of this **8¼-mile section (13.3km; C & A/C 3¼ to 4¼hrs)**, is, perhaps, even less typical than normal. At one time, around 2000 years ago, when the land around the Thames was swampy as far as central London, the topography on the first half of this stage would not have seemed unusual. But with the draining of the land, a process that started way back in medieval times, this waterlogged terrain began to disappear. Now, only the little pocket of wilderness outside Erith, which today is called **Crayford Marshes**, its neighbour, Dartford Marshes, and its twin across the Thames in Rainham, are all that is left of this ancient landscape.

It is in the Marshes that you join and follow **Darent River**, a muddy waterway which in turn brings you to the **Cray**, the third and final river on this stage and one which will accompany you all the way from suburb to stately home. That 'home' is **Hall Place**, the first of many mansions you'll encounter on the LOOP and a fine place for a picnic. A final bit of sylvan strolling through **Churchfield Woods** leads to your destination at the end of this first stage; **Bexley**, after which the borough is named.

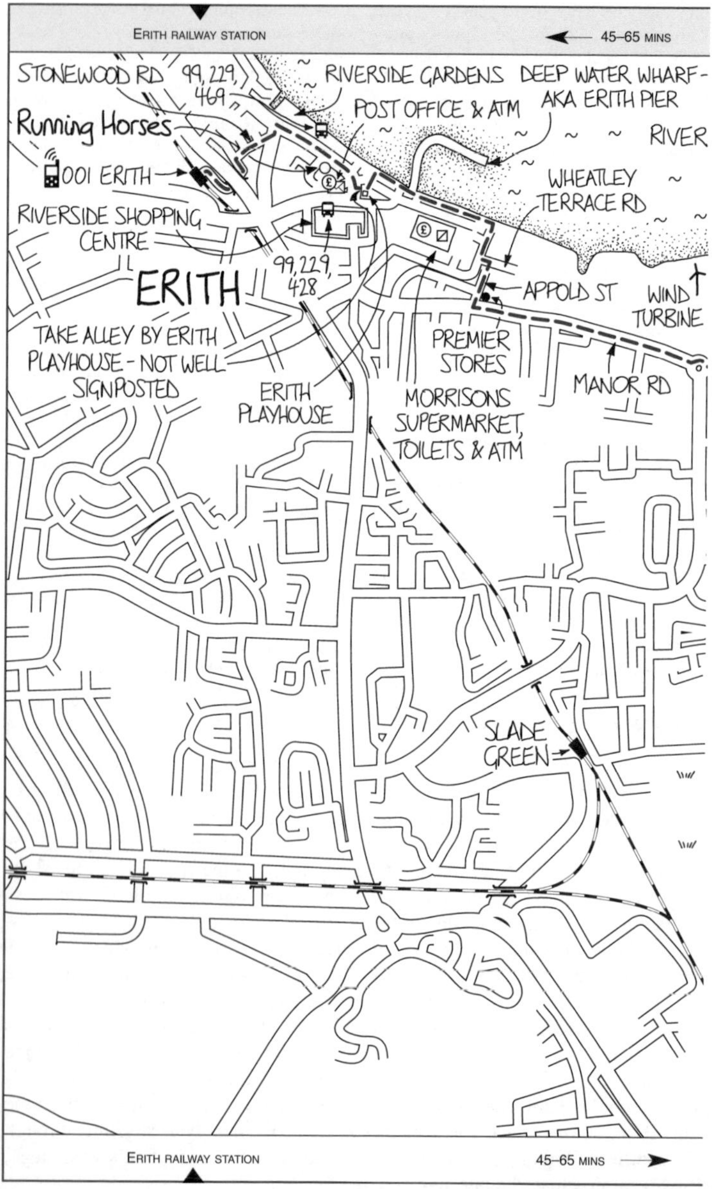
ERITH RAILWAY STATION
45–65 MINS
STONEWOOD RD
99, 229, 469
RIVERSIDE GARDENS
DEEP WATER WHARF - AKA ERITH PIER
POST OFFICE & ATM
Running Horses
RIVER
001 ERITH
WHEATLEY TERRACE RD
RIVERSIDE SHOPPING CENTRE
99, 229, 428
ERITH
APPOLD ST
WIND TURBINE
TAKE ALLEY BY ERITH PLAYHOUSE - NOT WELL SIGNPOSTED
PREMIER STORES
MANOR RD
ERITH PLAYHOUSE
MORRISONS SUPERMARKET, TOILETS & ATM
SLADE GREEN
ERITH RAILWAY STATION
45–65 MINS

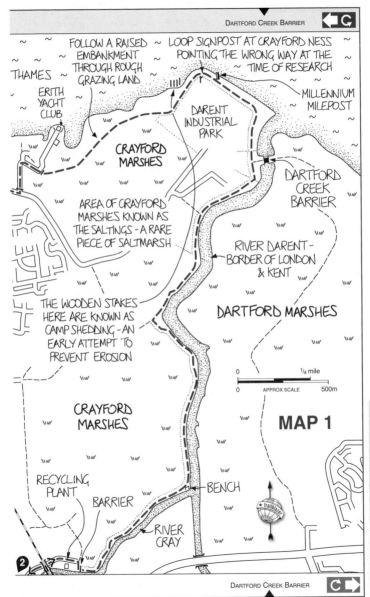

FOLLOW A RAISED EMBANKMENT THROUGH ROUGH GRAZING LAND

LOOP SIGNPOST AT CRAYFORD NESS POINTING THE WRONG WAY AT THE TIME OF RESEARCH

THAMES

ERITH YACHT CLUB

MILLENNIUM MILEPOST

DARENT INDUSTRIAL PARK

CRAYFORD MARSHES

AREA OF CRAYFORD MARSHES KNOWN AS THE SALTINGS - A RARE PIECE OF SALTMARSH

DARTFORD CREEK BARRIER

RIVER DARENT - BORDER OF LONDON & KENT

DARTFORD MARSHES

THE WOODEN STAKES HERE ARE KNOWN AS CAMP SHEDDING - AN EARLY ATTEMPT TO PREVENT EROSION

0   ¼ mile
0   APPROX SCALE   500m

CRAYFORD MARSHES

MAP 1

RECYCLING PLANT

BARRIER

BENCH

RIVER CRAY

trailblazer

2

Crayford Marshes [Map 1, pp66-7]

Even in this protected area (Crayford Marshes has been designated both as a Site of Special Scientific Interest, or SSSI, and as an Area of Metropolitan Importance for Nature Conservation), the hand of man is still very evident, with **Darent Industrial Park**, home to several recycling centres, right at its heart by Crayford Ness. Nevertheless, I'm not alone in thinking that the marshes are a great place for a stroll, with plenty of positives to distract you from the stench and screeching. For one thing, there are the extensive views over the Thames, with the mighty **Queen Elizabeth II Bridge** looming large to the east. Then there's the tranquillity of the marshes themselves, with the pleasant rustle of the wind caressing the reeds mingling with the call of the birds, including herons and hawks, owls and egrets, that have made the marshes their home. And I can't finish my description of the marshes without mentioning the blackberries that grow alongside the path – to my mind, the best I've ever tasted.

Dartford Creek (Tidal Flood) Barrier The major landmark on the marshes stands silent and austere for most of the time though, should floodwaters threaten, two gigantic 160-tonne drop-leaf gates are lowered to prevent the sea inundating the land.

Incidentally, the Darent marks the eastern border of Greater London; the land you can see on the other side of the creek, **Dartford Marshes**, is in Kent. If you're coming from Erith you may have noticed that you've been following an extension of The Thames Path, a National Trail which starts in the Cotswolds and *officially* finishes 184 miles later at the Thames Barrier in Woolwich. The path has been extended for nine miles beyond this to the Darent (though this extension is not officially part of the national trail), and if trekkers had their way, they would be able to cross the barrier and continue their riparian adventure. As yet, however, the barrier is out of bounds and the nearest crossing is the A206, which you encounter at the northern end of the...

Thames Road Wetland [Map 2, pp70-1]

This 6-acre (2.4 hectare) strip of beauty packs quite a punch for such a small site. Not only are there 12 species of *odonata* (ie dragonflies and damselfies) thriving here, but, almost incredibly, the booming call of the bittern has also been heard to resonate around the wetlands. True, the noise of the traffic is never quite out of earshot – but it's a lovely lush little corridor nevertheless.

From Crayford Way, to the west of the Wetlands, **bus** No 428 (Bluewater Shopping Centre to Erith via Dartford & Slade Green; daily 2-4/hr) can take you back to Erith.

CRAYFORD [Map 2, pp70-1]

The Ford over the **River Cray** has, like most places round here, a lengthy history, with artefacts from the Iron Age and the Roman era discovered within its boundaries down the years. Indeed, Roman Watling Street crossed at the ford (the ford, incidentally, lay where the A207 now crosses; see

Map 2). The town has grown significantly from the '27 householders and 2 smallholders' mentioned in the Domesday Book to a population of around 11,500 today.

As with much of this stage, Crayford may not instantly beguile you, but there are compensations in the details: **Waterside**

Gardens, for example, has some neat little references to Crayford's past as a centre for the brick-making, gunwork and aircraft industries, while the paisley-shaped pattern in the paving and the canopy sculptures are a reminder that the town was, for 158 years, the home of David Evans & Co, producing the finest silks for clients such as Liberty's.

Tannery Gardens, across the busy High St, has had a similar makeover. The last building you come to before entering Hall Place Gardens, the Mazda Garage, has a couple of colourful lamp standards. These were rescued from the Princess Theatre, which once stood where Waterside Gardens now is and which was built, back in 1916, by Vickers for their employees.

Services

For refreshments (eat in or takeaway), *Vintage Lindy Lou Tearoom* (☎ 01322-526797, 🖳 www.vintagelindylou.co.uk; **fb**; Thur-Sat 3-6pm, Sun noon-6pm) is handsdown the most charming place in town and occupies the best spot too, right in the heart of Waterside Gardens. Booking is recommended as they get very busy. They hope to open more hours in 2021 (so check their website) but they never open on Monday or Tuesday. Note that dogs aren't allowed in the tearoom.

Across the High St, the *Bear and Ragged Staff* (☎ 01322-522906, 🖳 greene king-pubs.co.uk; 🐾) serves food daily (noon-9pm); or, even more charming,

there's *Penny Farthing* (☎ 07837 021170, 🖳 pennyfarthingcrayford.co.uk; **fb**; Tue-Thur 3-9pm, Fri & Sat noon-10pm, Sun to 3pm) to the north of the gardens; they specialise in real ales and ciders. In 2021 they hope to return to their normal weekday hours (noon-3pm & 5.30-9pm).

For provisions there's a **food store** (Mon-Sat 8am-11pm, Sun 9am-10.30pm) also north of the gardens and a big Aldi **supermarket** (Mon-Sat 8am-10pm, Sun 10am-4pm) a little further on behind Tannery Gardens, while if you want a **post office** (Mon-Fri 9.30am-5.30pm, Sat to 5pm) that's in the Town Hall Square on the way to the station.

Transport [see map pp42-3]

Crayford railway station is about 500 metres from the trail. Simply turn south down the A207, before taking a right down Station Rd, after which it's a second right down Lower Station Rd. Southeastern (see p47) offers plenty of options for getting back to Central London, including **trains** to Charing Cross and Cannon St. Heading the other way, there are services to Gravesend and to Dartford.

For **buses** near the LOOP, the No 428 (Bluewater Shopping Centre to Erith via Dartford & Slade Green; daily 2-4/hr) stops just north of the gardens. The No 492 (Sidcup to Bluewater via Foots Cray, Bexley, Bexleyheath, Barnehurst & Dartford; daily 2/hr) also stops here.

Hall Place Gardens

The Cray runs right through the centre of this large park, with the eponymous house (see box below) after which the park is named on the park's western end.

❏ HALL PLACE

The house (🖳 hallplace.org.uk; house 9am-5pm; £8/7/4/20 for adult/concession/child/family, discount for National Trust and Art Fund members) and its grounds (Apr-Sep 9am-9pm, Oct-Mar 9am-5pm; free) are open to the public.

The highlight of Hall Place is the large topiary known as the **Queen's Beasts**, planted in 1953 to celebrate the coronation. The house itself was built in 1537 and has a lovely flint checkerboard façade, though a large red-brick extension was added just over a hundred years later. There is also a smart, glass-fronted riverfront *café* (daily 9am-5pm) in the grounds.

ROUTE GUIDE AND MAPS

Frustratingly, the high hedge on the garden's eastern side deliberately prevents LOOP walkers from enjoying even a brief glimpse of the house and its grounds, though both are open to the public.

Churchfield Wood

Those who've started their LOOP in Erith will find this wood significant in two ways. Firstly, to gain access to it you have to cross a **stile**, the first you will have encountered along the trail. Secondly, you will also encounter something that resembles **a climb**, only smaller – a rarity thus far on your walk. The wood is

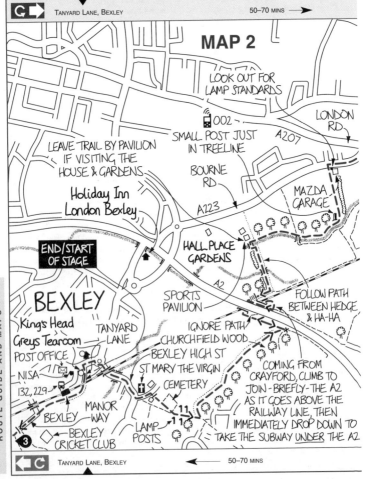

also dominated by something of a rarity, field maple – a good indication that Churchfield, though just a remnant of what was once a much bigger forest, is **ancient woodland**.

BEXLEY [Map 2]

It's often said that London is nothing but a collection of villages all stitched together. Well, there are few places where this is more obvious than at Bexley, often called **Old Bexley** or **Bexley Village** to distinguish itself from the wider borough.

Despite the presence of the non-stop traffic roaring along the High St, Bexley

WATERSIDE GARDENS   100–120 MINS TO DARTFORD CREEK BARRIER (MAP 1) →

SUPERIOR ROUTE GOES THROUGH WATERSIDE GARDENS

NOW FOLLOWING THE **THAMES ROAD WETLAND** – MUCH LUSHER AND MORE OVERGROWN THAN THE CRAYFORD MARSHES

Penny Farthing

CRAYFORD STORE

428

BUS TO ERITH

A206

RIVER CRAY

BARNES CRAY RD

SHORT-CUT BYPASSES PEDESTRIAN CROSSING

TANNERY GARDENS

CRAYFORD WAY

MALDEN LANE

Bear & Ragged Staff

ALDI POST OFFICE

CRAYFORD

492

PATH SQUEEZED BETWEEN BACK GARDENS & RIVER

A207

LOWER STATION RD

0   ¼ mile

0   APPROX SCALE   500m

ROCHESTER WAY

WATERSIDE GARDENS ← 100–120 MINS FROM DARTFORD CREEK BARRIER (MAP 1)

still looks like a village, perhaps because it actually became, like many places along the trail, part of London only in 1965.

There are few sights in town, though the **church of St Mary the Virgin**, the first church you come to heading clockwise on the LOOP, has an unusual octagonal-upon-pyramid spire. The most famous resident of the church's **cemetery** is Henry Oldenburg, one of the original members of the Royal Society. In his role as secretary to the Society, it was his habit to send manuscripts submitted by members to other experts in the field, who could judge them for quality and accuracy before publication. Thus the practice amongst scientists of 'peer review', where one's peers are encouraged to criticise and evaluate one's work, began.

Another renowned resident of Bexley lived next to the church: John Thorpe (1715-92), who earned the blue plaque that now commemorates him by discovering the Roman Lulingstone Villa in Darent Valley.

Services
Facility-wise, there's a **post office** (Mon-Fri 9am-5pm, Sat to 2pm) right on the trail and a Nisa **supermarket** (Mon-Sat 7am-10pm, Sun 8am-9pm) just off it, by the turn-off up to the station, though there are a

couple of **delis** before you reach it with more interesting stock.

There are several **takeaways** and **cafés** including *Grey's Tearoom* (☎ 01322-522826; **fb**; 🐾; daily 9am-4pm), right by the path where it turns off into Tanyard Lane, and quite a few **pubs** including the 14th-century *King's Head* (☎ 01322-553137, 🖥 www.thekingsheadbexley.com), a copper-pan-and-horse-brass affair providing real ales, lunches (Mon-Sat noon-3pm, Sun 11am-4pm, Thur-Sat 5-8pm) and, if you've overdone it, a **bed for the night** (3S/3Tw, most en suite others share facilities) too; **B&B** costs from £50 for two sharing (sgl from £35). Alternatively consider *Holiday Inn London Bexley* (🖥 hilondon bexleyhotel.co.uk).

Transport   [see map pp42-3]
Bexley is well served by Southeastern **trains**, with regular services to London Charing Cross (approx 30 mins) and Cannon Street (approx 37 mins), and east to Dartford, Gravesend & Strood. See p47.

For **buses**, both No 132 (Bexleyheath to North Greenwich via Eltham; daily 2-6/hr) and No 229 (Thamesmead to Sidcup via Erith & Barnehurst; daily 3-5/hr) call at the railway station, as does the 492 Sidcup-Bluewater service.

STAGE 2: BEXLEY TO PETTS WOOD   [MAPS 2-5]

If you didn't find the scenery to your taste on the previous stage (and I'll admit that the large dollops of industrial blight it served up won't be everyone's cup of tea) hopefully this will make up for it.

For pretty much the entire length of this **7¼-mile stage (11.7km; C: 2hrs 40mins to 3½hrs, A/C: 2¾hrs to 3hrs 35mins)** is conducted in, well, countryside, or at least a very good impression of it, with only the briefest of interruptions from civilisation, one at Foots Cray and another to cross the A20 (in Sidcup). That the path manages to remain so 'green' is all the more remarkable given that the trail is cutting through suburbia and one of the most densely populated parts of the country.

Yet, wonderfully, the 'rural' scenery begins almost as soon as you pass through Bexley's tiny **Tanyard Lane** to pass Bexley Cricket Club – founded in 1805 – to join **Old Bexley Conservation Area**. This in turn leads back, via a Water Pumping station, to your old friend the River Cray, which takes you through serene **Foots Cray Meadows**.

From there it's but a few minutes to **Sidcup Place**, after which one can enjoy a lengthy, tranquil sylvan walk in **Scadbury Park & Park Wood** and neighbouring **Petts Wood**; and, without realising it, you find yourself thinking that the bus depots and recycling plants of Erith suddenly seem a very long way away indeed.

Old Bexley Conservation Area [Map 3, pp74-5]

Also known as **Upper College Farm**, this large open meadow is a bit of a haven for nature – quite remarkable, given its proximity to Bexley, which abuts it to the north. Rare plants you may encounter include yellow vetchling, a member of the pea family, and crosswort. Even more remarkable is the fact that this was, until relatively recently, an old landfill site and gravel quarry.

Foots Cray Meadows

This is a lovely place to stroll, with ducks and moorhens gliding beneath the tendrils of weeping willows as you amble along the riverbank. Foots Cray Meadows is a **Local Nature Reserve** and **Site of Metropolitan Importance for Nature Conservation**. The meadows were formed from the grounds of two large but vanished mansions: Footscray Place, which burnt down in 1949, and North Cray Place, which was bombed in 1944 and pulled down in 1961.

At the heart of the meadows is **Five Arches Bridge**, built when the grounds of North Cray Place were landscaped by Lancelot 'Capability' Brown. Usually one of the most photographed features on the LOOP, the current and hopefully temporary addition of security fencing along its length – probably not part of Capability Brown's original design – has undoubtedly made it less photogenic. The bridge stands over a weir. Immediately to the south of the bridge is a small lake, where red-eared terrapins can occasionally be seen sunning themselves on logs or one of the small islands. Though they are non-native species (apparently, terrapins were native to Britain around 8000 years ago, but any you see today were probably bought over in the 1980s during the era of the *Teenage Mutant Hero Turtles*), there *are* several native animals in the park, including kingfishers and greater-crested newts.

A second crossing, **Penny Farthing Bridge**, built at the same time though less grand, links the park to....

Foots Cray

Beyond the southern end of the ponds the LOOP meets up with Rectory Lane by ancient **All Saints Church**. Built in 1330, the church is an amalgamation of different eras, with a Norman font, Tudor arch and a door that dates back to the Civil War.

South of the church, busy Sidcup Hill has stops for several **bus services** including: No 51 (Woolwich to Orpington via Woolwich Arsenal & St Mary Cray; daily 2-6/hr); 233 (Swanley to Eltham via New Eltham & Sidcup; daily 2-3/hr); 321 (to New Cross Gate via Sidcup, New Eltham, Eltham, Blackheath Park & Lewisham; daily 2-5/hr); 492 (Sidcup to Bluewater via Bexley, Crayford & Dartford; daily 2/hr) and R11 (Sidcup to Green Street Green via St Mary Cray & Orpington; daily 2-5/hr).

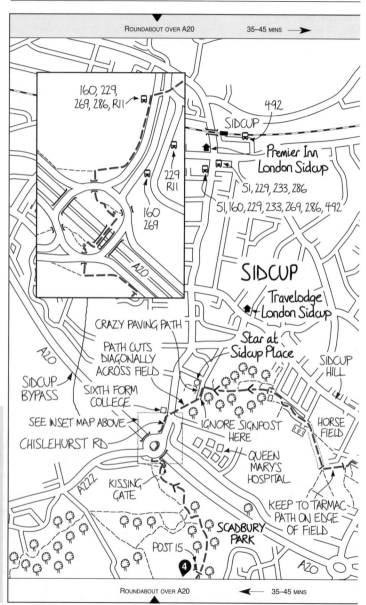

ROUNDABOUT OVER A20   35–45 MINS →

160, 229, 269, 286, R11

492

SIDCUP

Premier Inn London Sidcup

229 R11

51, 229, 233, 286

160 269

51, 160, 229, 233, 269, 286, 492

SIDCUP

Travelodge London Sidcup

A20

Star at Sidcup Place

SIDCUP HILL

CRAZY PAVING PATH

PATH CUTS DIAGONALLY ACROSS FIELD

A20

SIDCUP BYPASS

SIXTH FORM COLLEGE

SEE INSET MAP ABOVE

CHISLEHURST RD

IGNORE SIGNPOST HERE

HORSE FIELD

QUEEN MARY'S HOSPITAL

A222

KISSING GATE

KEEP TO TARMAC PATH ON EDGE OF FIELD

SCADBURY PARK

POST 15

4

A20

ROUNDABOUT OVER A20   ← 35–45 MINS

ROUTE GUIDE AND MAPS

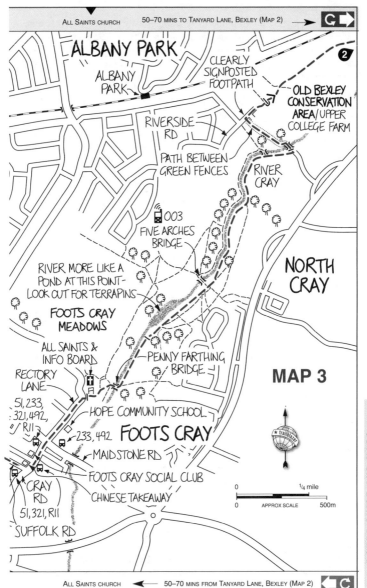

ALBANY PARK

ALBANY PARK

CLEARLY SIGNPOSTED FOOTPATH

OLD BEXLEY CONSERVATION AREA/UPPER COLLEGE FARM

RIVERSIDE RD

PATH BETWEEN GREEN FENCES

RIVER CRAY

003
FIVE ARCHES BRIDGE

NORTH CRAY

RIVER MORE LIKE A POND AT THIS POINT— LOOK OUT FOR TERRAPINS

FOOTS CRAY MEADOWS

ALL SAINTS & INFO BOARD

PENNY FARTHING BRIDGE

MAP 3

RECTORY LANE

51, 233, 321, 492, R11

HOPE COMMUNITY SCHOOL

233, 492

FOOTS CRAY

MAIDSTONE RD

FOOTS CRAY SOCIAL CLUB

CRAY RD

51, 321, R11

CHINESE TAKEAWAY

0   ¼ mile

0   APPROX SCALE   500m

SUFFOLK RD

ROUTE GUIDE AND MAPS

Sidcup Place

You can tell just by looking that there's some history to the pub that today is known as ***The Star at Sidcup Place*** (☎ 020-8308 9870, 🖳 sidcupplacepub sidcup.co.uk; 🐾 bar area; food daily noon-8.30pm). The building was in fact once a manor house and, before that, a fort, built in 1743. The fort was initially designed in a star-shape – hence the name of the pub.

From Chislehurst Rd, to the west of Sidcup Place, **bus** Nos 160, 229, 269, 286 and R11 run up to Sidcup railway station; for details see below.

SIDCUP

Note that, officially at least, you're still in London, though people round here (including the pub) insist they're in Kent. But with London buses driving by and a London telephone code, the evidence would suggest otherwise (though, to be fair, the postcode is a Dartford one, DA, rather than London).

Services

For those wanting accommodation Sidcup offers both a branch of a ***Premier Inn*** (🖳 premierinn.com), near the railway station, and a ***Travelodge*** (🖳 travelodge.co.uk).

There are several **cafés** and **restaurants** on the road down from the station.

Sidcup has a good number of bus services (most of which stop at or near the station) including the: No 51 (Woolwich to Orpington via Woolwich Arsenal & Foots Cray; daily 2-6/hr; 160 (to Catford via Chislehurst, New Eltham & Eltham; daily 3-4/hr); 229 (to Thamesmead via Erith & Bexley; daily 3-5/hr); 269 Bromley North to Bexleyheath via Chislehurst; daily 4-5/hr); 286 (to Greenwich via Eltham & Kidbrooke, daily 3-5/hr); 321 (Foots Cray to New Cross Gate via New Eltham, Eltham, Blackheath Park, Lewisham & New Cross Gate; daily 2-5/hr); 492 (to Bluewater via Foots Cray, Bexley, Bexleyheath, Barnehurst, Crayford & Dartford; daily 2/hr) and R11 (to Green Street Green via Foots Cray & Orpington; daily 2-5/hr).

Rail services are provided by Southeastern; see p47 for more details and map pp42-3.

Scadbury Park & Park Wood   [Map 3, pp74-5; Map 4]

For almost the next three miles you stick to the trees through lovely Scadbury Park, formerly the grounds of an ancient manor. For nearly all the time you follow the **Friends of Scadbury Park Acorn Nature Trail**. The path is waymarked by numbered wooden posts; you will walk the section between post number 15 (Map 3; the first number you encounter if coming from Sidcup Place) to 5 (Map 4; near the A208). In doing so you will also cross the border between the Borough of Bexley and the Borough of Bromley.

Remains of Scadbury Manor At the heart of the woods are the remains of the house itself (signposted **Moated Manor** rather than Scadbury). The ruins are just a few metres off the trail and no effort to reach, which is just as well as there's little there today save for a few old walls and foundations plus, of course, the moat. The complex is fenced off, presumably so people don't go swimming, though the colour of the water in the moat will be deterrent enough for most visitors.

By the way, if you started your LOOP in Erith it may have come to your attention that you have now passed through the grounds of no fewer than *five* mansions, manor houses and country estates, or at least the ruins of them

REMAINS OF MOATED
SCADBURY MANOR
POST 14
POST 13
POST 11
POST 10
POST 8
POST 9
SIGNPOST TO
MOATED MANOR
& POST 12
St Paul's
Cray Rd
PARK
WOOD
004
MASSIVE
OAK TREE
SCADBURY PARK
& PARK WOOD
POST 5
ST PAUL'S
CRAY
PETTS
WOOD
WILLETT MEMORIAL
NATIONAL TRUST SIGN
EDLMANN MEMORIAL

MAP 4

St Paul's Cray Rd ← 40–50 MINS FROM ROUNDABOUT OVER A20 (MAP 3)

❏ SCADBURY MOATED MANOR

The original house that stood on this site was built sometime in the 12th century, though that was destroyed in 1738 and the pillars of bricks you can see are largely of a more recent vintage, built by one of the last owners of the mansion, Hugh Marsham-Townshend, early in the 20th century. He constructed his own version of a Tudor manor house on top of the original foundations, though the over-reliance on concrete as a building material for his Tudor house suggests that authenticity was never a major consideration; that, too, was largely destroyed before the century was over.

The building is now a scheduled 'ancient monument' and, unsurprisingly, on English Heritage's 'At Risk' register. Looking at the place today, it's tempting to conclude that that ship has already sailed, and whatever 'risks' it was under have probably already happened.

(namely Hall Place, North Cray Place, Footscray Place, Sidcup Place and Scadbury Manor) – and that's in just 14 miles or walking. So no matter how pretty you may think the LOOP is now, just imagine how beautiful it must have been a couple of hundred years ago when these houses were in their heyday. (Though, of course, in all probability, a couple of hundred years ago the likes of you and me wouldn't have been allowed anywhere near these estates unless we were part of the staff.)

Petts Wood

These woods are named after a local family of shipbuilders who bought the forest to supply timber – particularly oak – for their business in the 16th century, producing ships for more than 200 years from their shipyards in Woolwich and Deptford. The woods themselves are very pleasant to amble through, and there are a couple of man-made features that are worth diverting from the trail for:

Willett Memorial It may seem slightly odd to come across a memorial to the great-great-grandfather of Coldplay's frontman, but William Willett, while never as famous as his distant descendant, can nevertheless be said to have had a greater effect on the lives of Britons than the musical outpourings of Mr Chris Martin. For Willett was one of the prime campaigners behind the introduction of **British Summer Time**.

The story goes that while out riding in the woods early one bright sunny morning, he noticed that few others were savouring the sunshine with him, but instead the shutters on most houses were still closed. This gave him the simple idea of resetting the clocks, laying out his argument in a pamphlet in 1907 entitled *The Waste of Daylight*. Willett's proposal was to move British time forward by a total of 80 minutes over successive Sundays in April. With powerful backing in parliament, including a young Winston Churchill, 'Daylight Saving', as it became known, was finally introduced in 1916, though neither in the form that Willett suggested (as you'll know, the clocks go forward only once, not on successive Sundays as Willett proposed, and only by an hour rather than eighty minutes) – nor precisely for the reason he gave either (the act was introduced in 1916 mainly to help the country save coal during wartime).

Other countries had already introduced daylight saving too, including Britain's wartime foes the Germans, so Willett can hardly claim to have been the inventor of daylight saving. Nevertheless, it is arguable that, without his efforts, daylight saving may never have been introduced in this country. Sadly, Willett never got to see his concept being adopted, having died the year before following a bout of influenza.

The memorial itself is in the form of a **sundial**, and lies a 3-minute walk away from the path: just follow the faint but distinctive trail to the east of the National Trust 'Petts Wood' sign. (Incidentally, in addition to this memorial

---

❏ **IMPORTANT NOTE – WALKING TIMES**

All times in this book refer only to the time spent walking. You will need to add 20-30% to allow for rests, photography, checking the map, drinking water etc.

there's also a pub in Petts Wood village near the station called The Daylight Inn that was named in tribute to his work; an honour that, as far as I can recall, has never been bestowed on any member of Coldplay.)

Edlmann memorial The second memorial in Petts Wood lies even closer to the path than William Willett's, and is dedicated to the man who saved the woods from disappearing – or, at least, a significant chunk of them.

When Petts Wood came up for sale in 1927, the locals, worried that it would all be bought by developers and turned into a housing estate, clubbed together and purchased 88 acres (35.6 hectares) of woodland, which they then promptly gave to the National Trust for safekeeping. Unfortunately, that still left 47 acres (19 hectares) on the wood's western edge, which the residents simply didn't have the cash to buy. Step forward **Colonel Francis Edlmann**, who bought this section to add it to his neighbouring estate at Hawkwood.

When Edlmann died in 1950 the whole of Hawkwood came up for sale, but was promptly bought up and, once again, given to the **National Trust**. The monolithic Edlmann Memorial, hewn from Cornish granite, was unveiled in gratitude in 1958.

PETTS WOOD [Map 5, p81]

Though the name of the town comes from the Pett family, who leased the woods in the 16th century to source the timber for their prosperous shipbuilding business, the suburb of Petts Wood is a 20th-century invention, built by developers to provide a residential estate in a rural setting close to London. The railway station, less than half a mile (800m) from the path, was the first building erected, in 1928, and the rest of the town followed from there.

With such a brief history, it's not surprising that the town has, perhaps, less to boast about than its neighbours. That said, it was here that the last branch of the Woolworths chain shut for good, after the chain was forced into bankruptcy in 2009 following the financial crisis. The enterprising manager, realising that this honour had fallen to his store, collected the remains of their Pick 'n' Mix sweet section – always the most celebrated section of any Woolworths store – put the sweets in a bag, and sold them at auction for £14,500.

The town's illustrious forbears are celebrated in the names of the pubs. On one side of the station you have the **Daylight Inn**, while on the other side of the tracks, on the link path, is **Sovereign of the Seas**, named in honour of one of the ships built by the Pett firm.

Services

The town is actually divided by the train line. The border is more than just geographical, as you'll notice if you cross the railway bridge to the eastern side of the line. This is where you'll find the best facilities including a Sainsbury's **supermarket** (daily 7am-11pm) with **ATM**, and there's a **post office** (Mon-Sat 9am-8pm) down the road.

Two decent **cafés**, *Cow & Bean* (☎ 01689-826845; Mon-Thur 7am-5pm, Fri to 10pm, Sat 8am-10pm, Sun 8am-4pm) and a branch of *Costa* (Mon-Fri 6am-6pm, Sat 6.30am-6pm, Sun 7.30am-5.30pm), are both on this eastern side of the tracks too. I also think *Daylight Inn* (☎ 01689-877402, 🖥 thedaylightinn.co.uk; **fb**; food daily noon-9pm) is the better of the pubs.

Back on the western side of the line, opposite the turn-off to the station is a Boots the **chemist** (Mon-Fri 9am-7pm, Sat to 6pm) and a **supermarket**, a branch of Morrisons (Mon-Sat 7am-10pm, Sun 10am-4pm).

You'll also find **Chinese, Indian, Thai** and several **Mediterranean** restaurants scattered on both sides of the line but particularly so on the western side. *Sovereign of the Seas* (🖥 jdwetherspoon .com; daily 9am-11pm) serves pizza.

There are branches of *Travelodge* (🖳 travelodge.co.uk) in Bromley and *Premier Inn* (🖳 premierinn.com) near Bromley South station and also in Orpington; both Bromley and Orpington can be reached by train from Petts Wood (see below).

Transport   [see map pp42-3]

Regarding transport, Petts Wood is in Zone 5 and is very well connected to Central London, with Southeastern services to Cannon St, Charing Cross (via London Bridge) and Victoria. In the other direction there are trains to Orpington and two to

Sevenoaks, from where you can catch trains down to Tunbridge Wells and Hastings. Petts Wood is also a stop on Thameslink's Luton to Orpington service. See p47 for details of these **rail** services.

Bus-wise, the R3 (Orpington to Locksbottom, nr Farnborough; daily 2-3/hr) and 273 (for Lewisham via St Mary Cray & Lee; daily 2-3/hr) call at Station Sq on the eastern side of the station. The No 208 (Lewisham to Orpington via Bromley South; daily 4-5/hr) calls at Queensway on the western side of the station.

STAGE 3: PETTS WOOD TO CONEY HALL (FOR HAYES STATION)
[MAPS 5-7]

If you started your walk in Erith and are completing the stages in order, it is on this **8-mile stage (12.9km; C & A/C 2hrs 50mins to 3hrs 20mins)** that, for the first time, you'll be confronted (and possibly affronted) by several climbs. True, none of them are particularly long, though a couple can be fairly described as 'steep'. Add to this the fact that there's a heavy dollop of woodland and perhaps you'll understand why I think that, for the first time on the trail, the LOOP starts to feel like a 'proper' hike rather than just an amble through the suburbs. Indeed, wonderfully, sometimes you can peer between the trees and not see anything but fields and greenery stretching all the way to the horizon.

The reason this third stage is so green and (by comparison with the previous stages) hilly, is largely due to the fact that you are for much of it wandering in the foothills of the North Downs (the National Trail, the North Downs Way, is at some points only around six miles to the south of here). The downs are renowned for their large stretches of woodland so it's no surprise that you pass a fair few trees here too, particularly at **Crofton Wood** and **Darrick and Newstead Woods Nature Reserve**.

But this is the LOOP and, as you've learnt by now, that also means a fair bit of meandering through the grounds of old country estates, including an encounter with one, **Holwood House**, that is, refreshingly, still in private hands. You also pass through **Farnborough**, to my mind the most 'villagey' of the villages on the entire trail.

When it comes to **facilities**, you can find most things in **Farnborough** including café, pub, post office, takeaway etc – as well as buses. **High Elms Country Park** also has a highly regarded café. Further along the trail, **Keston** has a post office, a pub and a bus service.

Jubilee Country Park   [Map 5]

The Queen has celebrated quite a few jubilees during her time on the throne, of course, and this particular park is named in honour of her silver jubilee, way back in 1977, when the land was bought by Bromley Council, having previously been the site of a golf course and allotments, as well as a further source of wood for shipbuilders. Given its varied history it's no surprise that most of the trees here are fairly young, though in August the park puts on a great display with bright

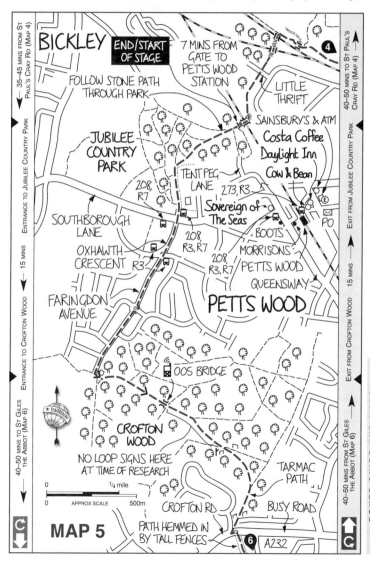

blue chicory flowers dotted everywhere; great to look at, though less wonderful if you've got a dog (you'll be pulling the seeds out for weeks). Your trail sticks to the southern edge of the park.

For **buses** the No 208 (Lewisham to Orpington via Bromley South & Petts Wood; daily 4-5/hr, R3 (Orpington to Locksbottom, nr Farnborough, via Petts Wood; daily 2-3/hr) and R7 (Chislehurst to Chelsfield via Bickley, Petts Wood & Orpington; daily 1-2/hr) call on Southborough Lane and Oxhawth Crescent.

Crofton and Darrick Woods   [Map 5, p81; Map 6, pp84-5]

This dappled tangle of holly, hawthorn, birch and oak lying at the southern end of Faringdon Avenue is **Crofton Wood**. It was saved from the developers in the 1970s by a concerned group of nature-loving locals, so where there could have been a series of suburban semis you'll now see a Site of Special Scientific Interest.

The woods are actually made up of two smaller patches of woodland, **Sparrow and Roundabout Woods**. Unfortunately, the provision of signposts hereabouts is not great but if you stick to the main path and keep to the same direction (south-east) you have a fair chance of emerging at the top of Ormonde Ave, from where a thread of alleyways and roads leads you to the next con-glomeration of coppice, **Darrick Wood**, part of **Darrick & Newstead Woods Local Nature Reserve**. The name is believed to have come from the words 'dark oak' though there are plenty of other species here including field maple, alder, cherry, hazel and birch – but it's the springtime bluebell display for which the woods are most renowned.

Tubbenden Meadow

After what seems like an eternity under the gloomy canopy of Crofton and Darrick Woods, it comes as something of a relief to emerge blinking into the sunlight at Tubbenden Meadow. This wildflower slope is a haven for some of the smaller members of the animal kingdom, with pollinators and pipistrelles aplenty. The meadow is criss-crossed by various paths shaved into the grass, with the LOOP running north–south diagonally across the field.

FARNBOROUGH   [Map 6, pp84-5]

Less renowned than its namesake in Hampshire, the venue for a famous airshow, this village in Greater London (though orig-inally part of Kent) nevertheless has some history. Its name comes from *Fearn-biorginga*, meaning 'village among the ferns on the hill', and is first mentioned in official records in AD862. The village was a major stop for travellers heading between London and Hastings, and the modern A21 still thunders near it today, though merciful-ly to the north of the old High St.

There is also a handful of cutesy, ancient cottages and a lovely church, **St Giles the Abbot**, which is largely 19th cen-tury in origin (William Morris designed the stained-glass windows), but which has a 12th-century nave and a 14th-century font.

Services

If you started your walk in Erith this is prob-ably the first place you come to that feels like a 'proper' village, with all the accou-trements that implies: a little flower-filled square at its heart, an old **pub**, *Change of Horses* (☎ 01689-852949; fb; 🐾 bar only; food Wed-Sun noon-2pm, Thur-Sun 5-7.30pm), and plenty of other amenities all clustered hereabouts, including a **post office** (Mon-Wed & Fri 9am-5.30pm, Thur & Sat to 1pm), general food store (Mon-Sat 9am-7pm, Sun 10am-4pm), **pharmacy** (Mon-Wed & Fri 9am-1pm & 2-6pm, Thur & Sat to 1pm).

There are a few small **restaurants** and **takeaways** including a kebab house, a chippy and *The Café @ Farnborough Village* (☎ 01689-851578, 🖥 cafefv.com; fb; Tue-Fri 8am-3pm, Sat 9am-3pm, Sun 9am-noon). When things are more normal they may open daily and anyhow their opening hours aren't certain so check their Facebook page. The menu includes vegan and gluten-free options and, weather permitting, there is outdoor seating where dogs are welcome. Finally there is a seasonal **farm shop** (summer Fri & Sat 9am-2pm).

Transport   **[see map pp42-3]**
There is no railway station in Farnborough but **bus** No 358 (Crystal Palace to Orpington; daily 2-4/hr) calls there; stops en route include Beckenham Road tram stop (see Tramlink box on p49), Bromley South and Shortlands railway stations (for train service details see Southeastern p47).

High Elms Country Park

Just south of Farnborough is the rather grand High Elms Country Park, named after the 19th-century mansion that – before it was razed to the ground by fire in 1967 – used to sit in its centre.

The focus for most people is the **Visitor Centre** (Sat & Sun 11am-4pm, also Mon, Wed & Fri during school summer holidays) and the neighbouring *Green Roof Café* (☎ 01689-855439, 🖥 thegreenroofcafe.co.uk; summer Mon-Fri 10am-5pm, Sat & Sun from 9.30am, winter to 4pm) – as well as the **toilets** that sit in what was once the estates' stable block and coach-house.

By the entrance to the stable block is an **Eton fives court** (fives is a game similar to squash, though you use your hand rather than a racquet). The LOOP passes these as it follows, briefly, the path of the mansion's former drive, past sequoia and sculpture.

Though nothing is left of the mansion itself, tiles and bricks have been set in the ground that trace the outline of some of its main rooms; the LOOP actually takes you right though the site of the old **kitchen**. The history of the estate dates back to the Norman Conquest, though the house itself dated from the 19th century; luminaries such as Charles Darwin, who lived nearby, would have stayed here as guests of the estate's owners, the Lubbock family, who had made their fortune in banking.

High Elms Golf Club Much of the southern part of the High Elms estate was sold off and converted into a golf club in the 1920s; the LOOP takes you through both the club car park and, after crossing High Elms Rd and through the restored **Clocktower Community Orchard**, through part of the course itself. (The **clocktower** after which the orchard is named, by the way, is clearly visible by the road, mounted on top of what was once the estate's farm stables.) The path through the golf course does a good job of screening walkers from the sight of golfers and their pastel fashions; and, I presume, golfers are just as glad not to have to see walkers either.

LOVIBONDS AVENUE

CROFTON AVENUE

CROFTON ❺

PATH SIGNED TO FARNBOROUGH — DON'T TAKE IT

LA TOURNE GARDENS

SIGNPOST OFTEN HIDDEN BUT IS CORRECT PATH

DARRICK WOOD

PLAYING FIELD

TENNIS COURTS

LOCKSBOTTOM

TUBBENDEN MEADOW

BOTTOM CORNER OF MEADOW

GLADSTONE RD

A21

POST OFFICE

Change of Horses

358

FARNBOROUGH

1 2 3 · 4

5 6

CHURCH RD

1 KEBAB HOUSE
2 FISH BAR
3 PHARMACY
4 THE CAFÉ @ FARNBOROUGH VILLAGE
5 GROCERY STORE
6 INDIAN RESTAURANT

SEASONAL VILLAGE FARM SHOP

ST GILES THE ABBOT

Green Roof Café
VISITOR CENTRE & TOILETS

HIGH ELMS COUNTRY PARK

SHIRE LANE

WATCH OUT - NO PAVEMENT

KEEP TO TARMAC

CROSS FLAT LAWN - FORMERLY THE MANSION'S KITCHEN

BE CAREFUL - NO PAVEMENT & SHARP BENDS

NORTH END LANE

BOGEY LANE

HIGH ELMS RD

CAR PARK

CLUBHOUSE

HIGH ELMS GOLF COURSE

FARTHING ST

ALTERNATIVE PATH IN FIELD IF MAIN PATH IS MUDDY

OVERGROWN ORCHARD

CLOCKTOWER

Bogey Lane

With chalky ground underfoot, plump rolling hills and delightful rural scenery, if you needed any further proof that you are now meandering close to the North Downs, this pretty amble along ancient Bogey lane will provide you with it. The lane can turn into a quagmire if it's not high summer, so if you find it too muddy the landowner has given permission for walkers to stroll alongside the hedge in the field to the south. Presumably the road is called Bogey Lane because, if you hit the golf ball this far off course, a bogey is probably the best score you could hope for.

Shire Lane & Holwood House

Another kindly landowner has allowed the construction of a path that runs parallel to busy Shire Lane, thereby saving walkers from having to take their life in their hands along this pavement-less highway.

Along the way, through a gap in the trees to the north, you can see the oh-so-grand **Holwood House**, built in 1826 by Decimus Burton. It stands on the site of a previous, smaller country house that was once owned by Britain's youngest ever prime minister, William Pitt the Younger, who was just 24 when he became the most senior politician in the country.

❏ WILLIAM WILBERFORCE AND THE END OF THE SLAVE TRADE

William Wilberforce was born in Kingston-upon-Hull (better known as Hull) in Yorkshire in 1759. The only child of a wealthy merchant, upon his father's death in 1780 William was forced to move down south to live with his uncle and aunt in Wimbledon. Their devout Christianity had a profound and enduring effect on Wilberforce, and can be seen as the main influence on his subsequent career.

The friendship between William Wilberforce and William Pitt can be dated back to their time together at St John's College, Cambridge, where they were both undergraduates. Wilberforce, the more garrulous and, at that time, dissolute of the pair, used to visit the House of Commons to watch the debates together with the studious Pitt, who had already set his heart on a career in politics. But it was Wilberforce who first became an MP, winning the seat of his hometown of Kingston-upon-Hull in 1780, at the age of just 22 and while still at university. Pitt stood as a candidate for the University of Cambridge in the same general election, but lost.

The fact that Wilberforce spent a gargantuan £8000 on his election campaign, having inherited a great deal of money on the death of his grandfather, went a long way to ensuring young Wilberforce's victory in the election. This financial independence his inheritance had provided for him also enabled him to sit as an independent MP in parliament, and he frequently garnered plaudits for his speeches, and in particular his authoritative speaking style, which belied his rather puny frame.

It was a reawakening of his Christian faith, however, which had rather lapsed during his college years but was reignited during a tour of Europe in 1784, that gave Wilberforce's political career both purpose and passion. From being something of a *dilettante*, Wilberforce became a zealous advocate on a number of pressing social issues – most famously, of course, slavery. By 1783 the slave trade was, together with tobacco, constituting about 80% of Britain's foreign income. But the appalling living conditions of the slaves had led many to question the morality of such a trade.

The current, Grade I property was last on the market in 2014 for £12 million, and is now owned by Barnardos-boy-made-good, Mr Peter Waddell, who made his fortune from car dealerships.

At the western end of the path, as the LOOP jags north, you'll find **Jack Frost Pet and Country Store** (Mon-Sat 8.30am-5.30pm, Sun 10am-4pm), where you can pick up an ice-cream.

For something more substantial, just to the south across Shire Lane sits **Holwood Farm Shop** (☎ 01689-638381, 🖥 holwoodfarm.co.uk) and its *café* (Tue-Fri 9am-4pm, Sat to 4.30pm, Sun 10am-3.30pm; 🐾 lobby area only). Be careful how you cross the junction here.

The No 146 **bus** (Bromley North to Downe via Bromley South, Hayes & Keston; daily 1/hr) stops near Holwood Farm Shop.

The Wilberforce Oak

One of William Pitt's closest friends, and a frequent guest at Holwood, was the slave reformer William Wilberforce (see box below).

The story goes that while out walking together, one day in early summer, 1787, the pair chatted about the slave trade, then the UK's most lucrative industry. What was said between them is described in a diary entry written by

On 13 March 1787 a dinner, attended by leading abolitionists, such as the artist Sir Joshua Reynolds and the diarist James Boswell, had the specific purpose of persuading Wilberforce to bring the case for abolition to parliament. Wilberforce, though sympathetic to their cause, thought himself 'unequal to the task'. But by the end of the dinner, he had agreed to bring the subject to parliament, 'provided that no person more proper could be found'.

Further pressure on Wilberforce was applied by his old friend Pitt, in the famous meeting underneath an old oak tree at Pitt's home, Holwood House (see p86). There the two of them, together with fellow abolitionist (and future prime minister) William Grenville, discussed the campaign for the end of slavery, with Pitt asking his friend directly:

'Wilberforce, why don't you give notice of a motion on the subject of the Slave Trade? You have already taken great pains to collect evidence, and are therefore fully entitled to the credit which doing so will ensure you. Do not lose time, or the ground will be occupied by another.'

It was to prove a lengthy fight, but the Slave Trade Act was eventually passed in 1807, a year after the death of William Pitt. Wilberforce apparently broke down in tears on the news. But his work was not yet finished: though the bill put an end to the slave trade in Britain, it did not put an end to slavery itself, a campaign to which Wilberforce dedicated the next two decades of his life.

With his health deteriorating, Wilberforce was eventually forced to resign from parliament. He moved to Highwood Hill, now called Mote End Farm (see p160), where he died in July 1834. The following month, the House of Lords passed the Slavery Abolition Act, which abolished slavery in most of the British Empire.

ROUTE GUIDE AND MAPS

Wilberforce, and now carved into the ornate stone bench that sits behind the fence in the grounds of Holwood:

'At length, I well remember after a conversation with Mr Pitt in the open air in the root of an old tree at Holwood, just above the steep descent into the vale of Keston, I resolved to give notice on a fit occasion in the House of Commons my intention to bring forward the abolition of the slave trade.'

The tree under which this discussion was supposed to have taken place became known as the **Wilberforce Oak**, in honour of the monumental conversation that took place that May. Incidentally, if you're wondering which oak it is that we're talking about, well it's not the massive (but dead) tree just down the hill.

In fact, the oak tree under which they stood no longer stands, though you can make out its slowly decaying remains in the ground; the remains form a circle that surrounds a recently planted replacement. The nearby information board with photo gives an idea of how it once looked.

Keston Common, Ponds and Caesar's Well

It was William Pitt who ordered that the Westerham Road, which you cross on your hike, be moved further away from his home at Holwood House. The road now marks the eastern border of **Keston Common**, which boasts not only an **Iron Age earthwork** (which the LOOP passes by, just south of the car park) but also a series of fishing lakes known as the **Keston Ponds**, originally constructed in the early 19th century to provide water for Holwood House.

The brick-encircled spring that feeds the ponds is known as **Caesar's Well**. Of the several stories that surround the origins of the name, the most common is one where the Roman emperor and his army camped near here, and were led by ravens to this spring after they had run dangerously short of water. The fact that the Romans never got this close to London under Caesar's command would suggest that there's little truth behind the tale, though the river, of which this is the source, is called the **Ravensbourne**. It flows north from here to empty into the Thames somewhere east of Deptford.

KESTON   **[Map 6, pp84-5]**

If it wasn't for the unending traffic roaring along the roads, your experience of Keston on the LOOP would probably be entirely positive. The place itself is not unattractive and the LOOP takes you past the village green and obligatory pub, *The Greyhound* (☎ 01689-856338, 🖥 greyhoundkeston.co .uk; 🐾; food Mon-Sat noon-8pm, Sun to 6pm).

The Fox Inn, which lies right on the trail, closed in 2020 but perhaps by the time you are here someone will have reopened it.

Nearby is the **local store and post office** (Mon-Fri 9am-5.30pm, Sat to 12.30pm).

Both the No 146 (Bromley North to Downe via Bromley South & Hayes; daily 1/hr) and 246 (Bromley North to Westerham via Hayes & Coney Hall; daily 1-2/hr) **bus** services leave from outside The Fox.

West Wickham Common [Map 7, pp90-1]

Just east of Hayes at the end/start of this stage is West Wickham Common, home to another **Iron Age earthwork**, though it's hard to make out the Iron Age stuff from the remains of a medieval field system, Elizabethan military camp and artificial rabbit warren that are also said to lie here. More impressive than the ditches are the massive **old oak trees**, some over 600 years old, that stand, pollarded, broken but unbowed, by the side of the trail.

CONEY HALL [MAP 7, pp90-1]

With Hayes station (see below) just over a kilometre from the trail, this is not the most convenient place for those looking to start or end their day's walk here. But there's no need to venture far to visit a Londis (daily 6am-10.30pm) **supermarket**, which lies just a few metres from the path on Kingsway, with a Co-op (daily 7am-10pm), with an **ATM,** a little further along on the corner.

There are several **takeaways** and **restaurants** along the A232/Croydon Rd, including Indian, Thai, and a chippy, as well as a **café**, *Coney's* (☎ 020-3719 2656; Mon-Sat 7am-4pm, Sun from 8am).

If you want a **post office** (Mon-Thur 6am-9pm, Fri & Sat to 10pm, Sun 7am-9pm), however, you'll have to head to Hayes station.

Transport [see map pp42-3]

Bus-wise, the No 119 (Bromley North to South Croydon via Bromley South, Hayes, West Wickham, Shirley & East Croydon; daily 2-4/hr), 138 (to Bromley North via Hayes & Bromley South; daily 1-3/hr), 246 (Bromley North to Westerham via Hayes & Keston; daily 1-2/hr) and 314 (New Addington to Eltham via Hayes, Bromley South, New Eltham & Eltham; daily 2-5/hr) all call in Coney Hall.

Getting to Hayes station from the LOOP

The walk to Hayes station is the longest of any of the 'official links' on the LOOP (**1.1km**), and one of the more complicated, too. From the end of the stage turn back onto the A232/Croydon Rd, turning left onto a tarmac footpath adjacent to Nash College. This leads, eventually, to Warren Wood Close, where you turn left, continuing onto the pedestrian-only path at its end. The road at the end of that path is Warren Rd, that in turn leads to Station Hill (the first turning on the left). A shimmy left then, 100m later, right leads to the station, as well as the main parade of shops in Hayes.

Hayes **railway station** is at the end of Southeastern's Hayes line (see p47 and map pp42-3) to/from both London Charing Cross and Cannon Street (approx 40 mins). **Bus** service Nos 119, 138, 246, & 314 call at Hayes station (see above for details).

STAGE 4: CONEY HALL TO HAMSEY GREEN [MAPS 7-10]

As with the previous stage, there's plenty of wonderful woodland wandering – interspersed with some pleasant parkland pootling – on this **8¾-mile hike (14.1km; C & A/C 3hrs 20mins to 4hrs)**. Indeed, it is, once again, quite striking how the LOOP manages to stick to the countryside as much as possible, stitching together various meadows, fields, woods and parks, even though suburbs often encroach on every side, as the briefest of glances at the route on Google Earth will show.

ROUTE GUIDE AND MAPS

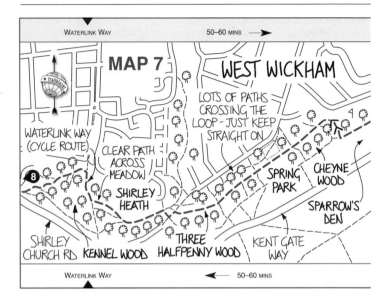

WATERLINK WAY 50–60 MINS ——→

MAP 7 WEST WICKHAM

LOTS OF PATHS
CROSSING THE
LOOP - JUST KEEP
STRAIGHT ON

WATERLINK WAY
(CYCLE ROUTE) CLEAR PATH
ACROSS
MEADOW

8 SHIRLEY
HEATH

SPRING
PARK

CHEYNE
WOOD

SPARROW'S
DEN

SHIRLEY
CHURCH RD KENNEL WOOD THREE
HALFPENNY WOOD KENT GATE
WAY

WATERLINK WAY ←—— 50–60 MINS

A woodland ramble is always a pleasant way to spend a day, of course, but there's a lot more to this stage than that, including, perhaps, the **best viewpoint on the southern half of the LOOP** – one that allows you to look over the whole of London and beyond.

If the stage does have an unofficial subtitle, it would be something like **'Borders and boundaries'**. Not only do you pass from the borough of Bromley to the borough of Croydon in this section – and thus cross the old border between Kent and Surrey – but, towards the end of the stage, you also step outside of London to join Tandridge Border Path, following the edge of Surrey's Tandridge district. And not forgetting, of course, that right at the start of this stage you cross the **Greenwich Meridian** – the imaginary boundary between the planet's Western and Eastern hemispheres.

This fourth stage is one of the longer hikes on the LOOP, and there are a few hills here too, so it's best done as a 'stand-alone' hike rather than trying to combine it with a stage that precedes or follows it. Indeed, for some, the walking may prove to be *too* strenuous, particularly as there **aren't many places to stop for refreshments** *en route*. If this is you, note that there are several places where you can escape the trail using **public transport**, either by tram at Coombe Lane station (see p94), or taking the bus from the suburbs of Shirley and Selsdon.

Coney Hall Park   [Map 7]
Yet another slab of public parkland carved out from an old country estate, Coney Hall Park is largely given over to sports pitches, though by the tarmac

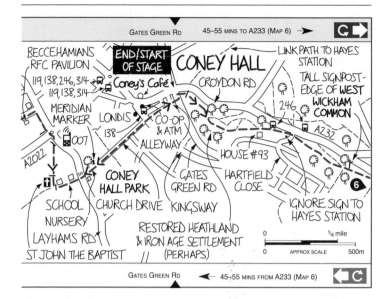

path that takes you from one side of the park to the other you'll find a curious, squat green monument, like a giant's pepper pot. This is actually the **Meridian marker**, marking the point of Longitude 0°, where the Greenwich meridian bisects the park, the country and, by extension, the planet itself. As such, it's a good place to check that your GPS is accurate, if nothing else.

St John the Baptist church

The LOOP takes you through the graveyard of this 15th century church, which sits atop a hill above Coney Hill Park. Next to it is Wickham Court Preparatory School, the main building of which was constructed in the latter half of the 15th century for an ancestor of Anne Boleyn. The school itself, however, was only established in the 1990s.

Sparrow's Den

The large slab of playing fields known as Sparrow's Den is dominated by **Old Beccehamian Rugby Club**, founded by former pupils of Beckenham School (since renamed Langley Park Boys School). The trail runs between the clubhouse and a mini golf-course. The old Roman road, Watling Street, makes another appearance on the trail here – or would do, if any of it was actually visible – as it crosses the pitches.

Spring Park and Shirley Heath

The slope to the west of the mini-golf course is crowned by an extensive stretch of woodland, **Spring Park**, that has survived until now largely due to the fact that the poor soil on which it grows is not really suitable for growing anything

> ❑ **ANCIENT ORDER OF FROTH BLOWERS**
>
> An information board in Spring Park's woodlands describes the Ancient Order of Froth Blowers, which, despite its name, was actually established only in the 1920s. For five shillings, anyone could join the order, and would receive a pair of silver enamelled cufflinks which, according to the society's membership booklet, allowed them to blow froth off any member's beer and *'occasionally off non-members' beer provided they are not looking or are of a peaceful disposition'*. Behind this Pythonesque silliness was a serious purpose, with money raised from membership fees and through fines (imposed for such transgressions as not wearing the cufflinks) being given to charity.
>
> The founder, Bert Temple, established the order as a source of funds for the children's charities set up by surgeon Sir Alfred Fripp, after he had performed life-saving stomach surgery to save Temple's life. The West Wickham Home of Recovery for Children with Heart Disease, which lies nearby, was funded largely by donations from the Froth Blowers.

else. The woods themselves, containing some lovely old stands of oak, is divided into several smaller woods, including **Cheyne Wood** and **Threehalfpenny Wood**. Sadly, behind the charming name of the latter is a grisly tale. A body was discovered in the woods in 1805 and, though badly decomposed, was soon identified as being that of the local parish clerk, a Robert Rutter, who had actually disappeared over two years previously. Mr Rutter was known to be carrying three halfpennies with him when he disappeared, and sure enough three coins of that denomination were found in the corpse's pocket and greatly contributed to the positive identification.

The LOOP crosses several springs – hence the name of the park – as well as the former border of Surrey and Kent (before the boroughs of Bromley, once of Kent, and Croydon, which was previously part of Surrey, were both absorbed into Greater London in the 1960s). At the westernmost point of the park the trails emerges at **Shirley Heath**, a welcome patch of open country amongst the deep, dark woods.

Kennel Wood

So-named because a local resident trained foxhounds for the local hunt in this area, the path through Kennel Wood woods joins, briefly, a cycle route called **Waterlink Way**. You'll need to follow the LOOP signs and the map closely through here to make sure you know when to follow the cycle route, and when to leave it. Fail to do so, and if you were to keep to Waterlink Way to its northern terminus you would arrive at the *Cutty Sark* in Greenwich; while if you followed it south, you would find that the Waterlink Way is actually part of a bigger cycle route, given the rather mundane designation of NCN21, that will eventually take you all the way to the south coast and Eastbourne.

SHIRLEY   [Map 8]

The LOOP sticks to the streets through the suburb of Shirley and this is the best place to break up the stage. There's a Londis **store** (Mon-Sat 7am-9pm, Sun 8am-9pm) on Sandpits Rd. The Sandrock pub opposite has been closed for a while now but a couple of hundred metres down the road is *The Surprise Inn* (☎ 020-8656 5588,

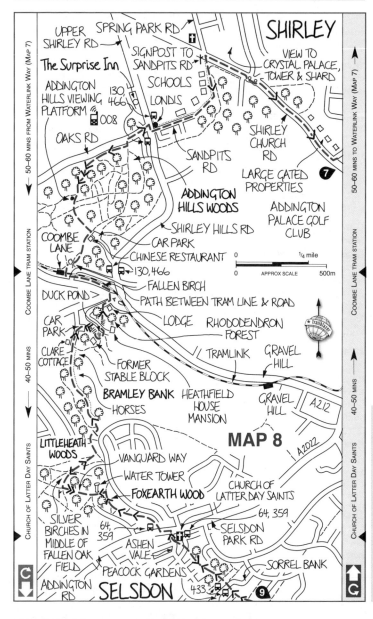

🖥 surpriseinnshirley.co.uk; 🐾; food Mon noon-3pm, Tue-Thur noon-3pm & 5-8pm, Fri & Sat noon-8pm, Sun to 6pm).

Transport   **[see map pp42-3]**
Outside the Londis (on Upper Shirley Rd) is a **bus** stop where you can catch the No

130 (New Addington to Thornton Heath; daily 2-5/hr) and 466 (Addington Village to Caterham-on-the-Hill via East Croydon, South Croydon, Purley & Coulsdon Common; daily 2-6/hr). Both services also stop at Coombe Lane tram stop (see below).

Addington Hills and Woods
This is actually the largest surviving piece of heathland left in London and is also known as **Shirley Hills**. The highlight of the hills is the large **viewing platform** in its centre, from where one can see the City of London; Canary Wharf; if it's a very clear day, even the distinctive arch over Wembley Stadium and, to the north-west, Windsor Castle, over 26 miles away, can be seen! The platform was actually built in the 1960s to celebrate 1000 years of Croydon – the first written record of the place dating from AD960.

Coombe Lane
North-east of the tram platform is a car park and, rather incongruously, a *Chinese restaurant*, both of which the LOOP passes in front of on its way to/from Coombe Lane station.

At its Coombe Lane is a stop on Croydon's celebrated **Tramlink** service (daily 6-8/hr; see box on p49 for details). For **bus** services both the No 130 (New Addington to Thornton Heath via Shirley; daily 2-5/hr) and 466 (Addington Village to Caterham-on-the-Hill via Shirley, East Croydon, South Croydon, Purley & Coulsdon Common; daily 2-6/hr) stop near the tram station.

Heathfield Estate
The path once more plunges into dense undergrowth at Heathfield, though this time it's **rhododendrons** that provide the shade. The 18th-century house, together with the accompanying **stables** and a circular **duck pond**, are at the bottom of the descent. Don't be frightened to look around the grounds and admire the giant trees – They are open to the public even though the house isn't.

The **house** was restored in the 1920s by Raymond Riesco, after whom the road running between the estate and Bramley Bank is named. Riesco was a keen collector of Chinese ceramics, which were sold, together with the house and grounds, to Croydon Council on his death. It turns out to have been a smart piece of business: just 17 pieces from this ceramic collection raised over £8 million for the council when put up for auction.

Bramley Bank, Littleheath Woods, Fallen Oak Field & Foxearth Wood
Once again the LOOP does a great job of stringing together the green gems that decorate the suburbs, and nowhere is this better illustrated on this stage than here. **Bramley Bank** is another part of the Heathfield Estate, though now run by London Wildlife Trust.

At its southern end it links almost seamlessly with **Littleheath Woods**, which quickly opens out into **Fallen Oak Field**. You need to follow the map

---

VANGUARD WAY

It is in Foxearth Wood that the LOOP joins the Vanguard Way (💻 vanguardway.org
.uk). From the name you'd be mistaken for thinking that this was, once upon a time,
some important military thoroughfare, but the truth is much more prosaic: the name
actually comes from a group of walkers who, on one of their early outings, were
forced to sit in the guard's van of a crowded train on their way back home. Vanguards
Rambling Club originally devised the 66-mile/107km Vanguard Way to take
Londoners out of the city to the South Downs at Berwick, near Eastbourne, though
the path has since been extended and now goes all the way to Newhaven on the coast
(from where, if you're so inclined, you can catch a ferry to Dieppe in France and continue your rambling from there).

---

closely here, for the LOOP ignores the more obvious path in favour of one that
heads to a stand of five birches, with the signpost hidden in the shade of the
trees. The ancient woodland immediately to the south is **Foxearth Wood**. It is
in Foxearth Wood that the LOOP joins the Vanguard Way (see box above).

Selsdon
The LOOP and Vanguard Way share the same route between Foxearth Wood
and **Elm Farm**, ducking through the narrow alleyways and across the quiet suburban lanes of Selsdon.

There are **bus** stops near the trail if you decide this stage is just too long,
with the No 64 (New Addington to Thornton Heath, South Croydon, East
Croydon & West Croydon; daily 2-7/hr) & 359 (Addington Village to Purley via
Gravel Hill & Sanderstead; daily 2/hr) crossing the trail at Selsdon Park Rd; and
bus No 433 (Addington Village to East Croydon via South Croydon; daily 4-
5/hr) travelling down both Sorrel Bank and Peacock Gardens.

Selsdon Wood   [Map 9, p96]
The trail eventually emerges at Selsdon Wood, another **nature reserve**, where
you should stick to the main path and ignore all trails heading left and right. If
you're walking in spring you're in for a treat with white wood anemones carpeting the floor, followed soon after by bluebells. There are over a hundred different bird species that call the woods their home, too, and this was also one of
the places where I had an unexpected encounter with some local deer.

Tandridge Border Path
The gate at the northern end of **Baker Boy Lane** marks the point where the
LOOP both leaves London *and* joins Tandridge Border Path, a circular path that
does just as its name suggests, following the border of this East Surrey district.
The wooded lane itself is pretty enough, though can be muddy in the winter
months.

Vanguard Way leaves the LOOP at the southern end of Baker Boy Lane,
though the LOOP and Tandridge Border Path continue together to Hamsey
Green, passing on its way the cluster of farmhouses known as **Farleigh
Common** and, in the valley below, the woods of **Mossyhill Shaw**.

ROUTE GUIDE AND MAPS

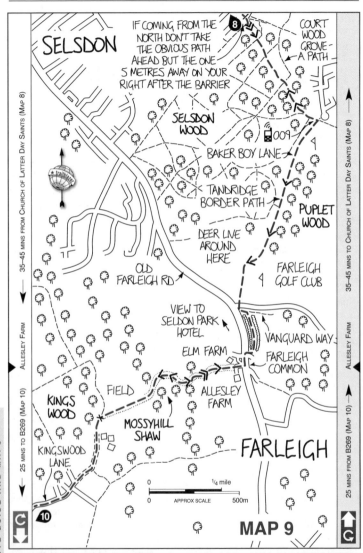

IF COMING FROM THE
NORTH DON'T TAKE
THE OBVIOUS PATH
AHEAD BUT THE ONE
5 METRES AWAY ON YOUR
RIGHT AFTER THE BARRIER

SELSDON

COURT
WOOD
GROVE-
A PATH

SELSDON
WOOD

009

BAKER BOY LANE

TANDRIDGE
BORDER PATH

PUPLET
WOOD

DEER LIVE
AROUND
HERE

FARLEIGH
GOLF CLUB

OLD
FARLEIGH RD

VIEW TO
SELDON PARK
HOTEL

VANGUARD WAY

ELM FARM

FARLEIGH
COMMON

FIELD

ALLESLEY
FARM

KINGS
WOOD

MOSSYHILL
SHAW

FARLEIGH

KINGSWOOD
LANE

0   1/4 mile

0   500m
APPROX SCALE

MAP 9

35-45 MINS FROM CHURCH OF LATTER DAY SAINTS (MAP 8)

ALLESLEY FARM

25 MINS TO B269 (MAP 10)

35-45 MINS TO CHURCH OF LATTER DAY SAINTS (MAP 8)

ALLESLEY FARM

25 MINS FROM B269 (MAP 10)

ROUTE GUIDE AND MAPS

❏ **IMPORTANT NOTE – WALKING TIMES**
All times in this book refer only to the time spent walking. You will need to add
20-30% to allow for rests, photography, checking the map, drinking water etc.

HAMSEY GREEN [Map 10]

Stretched along the busy B269 Limpsfield Rd, Hamsey Green sits on the plateau of the North Downs.

This place is actually divided north/south between Greater London and Surrey; the northbound bus stop by the LOOP, for example, is in the London borough of Croydon, while the southbound one is in Surrey. That said, with its heavy traffic, constant building works and cosmopolitan population you'd have to say it feels more like a London suburb than a Surrey village.

It's not the prettiest place on the LOOP but it does have a **pond** dating back to Neolithic times, very near the trail.

Services

There are several convenient facilities, including a Co-op **supermarket** (Mon-Sat 7am-10pm, Sun 8am-10pm) with its own **ATM** and **post office** (Mon-Fri 9am-5.30pm, Sat to 12.30pm), and a few **takeaways** nearby. What it doesn't have is a pub, thanks to an abstentionist Lord of the Manor in the 1800s who imposed conditions on future land sales that barred pubs and brewers from purchasing them.

Transport [see map pp42-3]

There's no train or tube stop in Hamsey Green but **bus** No 403 daily 3-5/hr) travels along the main road, on its way between Sanderstead and West Croydon (to the north) and Warlingham (southwards).

If you have an aversion to buses a 40-minute walk from Hamsey Green, much of it on Stage 5 of the LOOP, will take you to the twin railway stations of Whyteleafe and Upper Warlingham (see p98).

STAGE 5: HAMSEY GREEN TO COULSDON SOUTH [MAPS 10-11]

This fifth stage maybe the shortest you've encountered so far, but it packs a fair bit into its **6½ miles (10.5km; C: 2hrs 10mins to 2½hrs, A/C: 2¼hrs to 2hrs 35mins)**.

From the lovely **Sanderstead to Whyteleafe Countryside Area** at the start, via **Kenley** and **Coulsdon Commons**, there is some lovely park- and heath-land along the way. But it's **Happy Valley** that really steals the show, and is undoubtedly one of the highlights of the entire LOOP, a delightful patchwork of woodland and wildflower meadow that rarely fails to live up to its name. Nor do the thrills stop there, with the stage finishing with a gentle stroll atop lovely **Farthing Downs**, offering good views all round and lovely, springy downland turf under your feet.

As a final surprise, the stage even has the good grace to drop you right outside the front entrance of **Coulsdon South station**, so your onward journey should be as convenient as possible too. Once in Coulsdon it is not far to walk to Coulsdon Town station if that is more convenient.

Though you shouldn't need to break up this relatively short stage, there is the option of ending your hike early by taking a detour to neighbouring Whyteleafe or Upper Warlingham **railway stations**, and there's a **decent pub** on Coulsdon Common, at about the halfway point.

Sanderstead to Whyteleafe Countryside Area   [Map 10, p97]

The course of the LOOP seems rather irrational as it takes a large northerly detour through this Area, particularly as Tandridge Border Path is far more direct. No matter, for any time spent in this wide-open space of grassland is time well spent. The area park is rather clumsily named, it's true, though the names of the fields you pass – Dipsley Field and Skylark Field to name but two – are perhaps more charming and evocative. On its western side and adjacent to the railway line is **Riddlesdown Common**, home to the rare chalkhill blue butterfly (see p60); the path you take through it is actually part of an old Roman road.

WHYTELEAFE & UPPER
WARLINGHAM   [off Map 10, p97]

There's a Tesco Express **supermarket** (daily 6am-11pm) on Godstone Rd (A22). For accommodation consider *Travelodge Caterham Whyteleafe* (🖳 travelodge.co .uk) which is south of Whyteleafe station but on the No 407 and 434 bus routes.

Bus No 407 (Sutton to Caterham Valley via Carshalton, West Croydon & Purley; daily 3-6/hr) crosses the LOOP at the point where the link path to Whyteleafe station begins.

At the other end of New Barn Lane (on Valley Rd), the No 434 (daily 2/hr) travels

between Coulsdon Town and Whyteleafe and calls at/near both their railway stations.

Whyteleafe and Upper Warlingham **railway** stations are actually on different lines, with Upper Warlingham (see p47) on Southern's Victoria to East Grinstead/ Uckfield line, while Whyteleafe is on their London Bridge to Caterham line (see p48); see also map pp42-3.

These twin railway stations are just three minutes apart, separated by a roundabout, with both lying around 10-15 minutes from the LOOP.

Kenley Common & Aerodrome [Map 11, pp100-1]

Yet another patch of green, **Kenley Common** is owned by the City of London, who took this common (and several others, as we've already encountered) over in 1878 to try to arrest the disappearance of open spaces in Greater London. The star of the show is the pyramidal orchid which is said to thrive around here on the chalky soil of the Downs.

Adjacent to the common's southern side (and reachable via a gate) is **Kenley Aerodrome**, the last of London's Battle of Britain stations to survive in its original World War II state. There is an **RAF monument** here.

Betts Mead Recreation Ground

There's not much to say about this small piece of open grassland except that the path through it takes an unexpected turn at about the halfway point; follow the instructions closely on Map 11, pp100-1, as the signage is not good here.

Norman Fisher Observatory

Smack bang in the middle of some horse paddocks is a squat little dome-shaped, white-painted building, with an even smaller domed construction next to it. This is actually Norman Fisher Observatory, built in the 1970s and belonging to **Croydon Astronomical Society** (🖳 croydonastro.org.uk). Its location, amongst the horses and away from the houses, was presumably deliberately chosen to minimise light pollution. The society runs open evenings at the observatory on any Saturday when it's clear and/or for the observation of special astronomical phenomena (eg when there's a meteor shower). There's no need to book, and there is a kitchen and wi-fi on-site, but there are no toilets.

Rydon's Wood & Coulsdon Common

Rydon's Wood, a tract of secondary woodland, is nothing remarkable but it does serve as a nice enough *hors d'oeuvre* to this stage's main event...Happy Valley.

Another City of London-owned common, **Coulsdon Common** is the home of 18th-century *The Fox* (☎ 01883-340737, 🖳 www.vintageinn.co.uk; 🐕; food Mon-Fri noon-8.30pm, Sat & Sun from 10am), a rather charming dog-friendly inn, with an extensive menu, tucked away on the common's western corner. There's a **bus** stop on the common where both the No 404 (Coulsdon Town to Caterham-on-the-Hill via Coulsdon South; daily 2/hr) and 466 (Addington Village to Caterham-on-the-Hill via Shirley, Sandilands, East Croydon, South Croydon & Coulsdon; daily 2-6/hr) call.

Happy Valley

The highlight of this stage, and indeed the whole of the southern half of the LOOP, is this wonderful slice of chalky downland. It's almost impossible to pass the bench at the top of the steep-sided valley without pausing to drink in the scenery and serenity of this lovely little pocket of the North Downs. Forming a **Site of Special Scientific Interest (SSSI)** with neighbouring Farthing Down, the valley covers some 67 hectares (166 acres) and is famed for its wildflower meadows and collection of orchids, such as the relatively scarce **bee orchid** and the very rare **man orchid**. *(cont'd on p102)*

ROUTE GUIDE AND MAPS

COULSDON SOUTH railway station   60–70 MINS ⟶

12
404
COULSDON
SOUTH   END/START
OF STAGE

NARROW ALLEY
BETWEEN
HOUSES

REDDOWN RD

B276   MAP 11

CAN SEE CANARY
WHARF FROM HERE

OFFICIAL PATH RUNS ALONG
DITCHES LANE BUT MUCH
BETTER TO FOLLOW GRASSY
PATH TO WEST OF ROAD

COPSE &
SIGNPOST   JUST FOLLOW MAIN TRACK
THROUGH WOODS

TOPOSCOPE

FARTHING
DOWNS

0   ¼ mile
0   APPROX SCALE   500m

ONE OF THE MOST BEAUTIFUL PARTS
OF THE WHOLE LOOP – THE LOVELY
MEADOWS OF HAPPY VALLEY

CIRCLE OF SEATS
& INFO BOARDS

011
DOUBLE BENCH –
GREAT PLACE TO
REST & ENJOY
THE SCENERY

CAR
PARK
TOILETS

BARRIER

HAPPY VALLEY

NETHERNE-
ON-THE-HILL   DEVILSDEN
WOODS   KEEP BY TREES   TO CHALDON
CHURCH

COULSDON SOUTH railway station   ◀ 55–65 MINS

ROUTE GUIDE AND MAPS

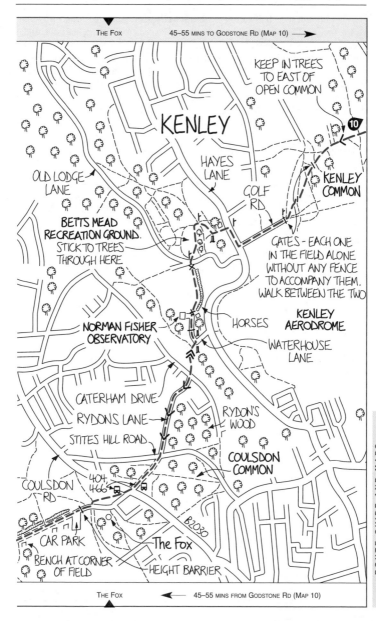

THE FOX   45–55 MINS TO GODSTONE RD (MAP 10) →

KEEP IN TREES
TO EAST OF
OPEN COMMON

KENLEY

10

HAYES
LANE

GOLF
RD

KENLEY
COMMON

OLD LODGE
LANE

BETTS MEAD
RECREATION GROUND.
STICK TO TREES
THROUGH HERE

GATES - EACH ONE
IN THE FIELD ALONE
WITHOUT ANY FENCE
TO ACCOMPANY THEM.
WALK BETWEEN THE TWO

KENLEY
AERODROME

HORSES

NORMAN FISHER
OBSERVATORY

WATERHOUSE
LANE

CATERHAM DRIVE

RYDONS LANE

RYDON'S
WOOD

STITES HILL ROAD

COULSDON
COMMON

COULSDON
RD

404,
466

The Fox

B2030

CAR PARK

BENCH AT CORNER
OF FIELD

HEIGHT BARRIER

THE FOX   ← 45–55 MINS FROM GODSTONE RD (MAP 10)

ROUTE GUIDE AND MAPS

In addition, over half of the UK's **butterfly** species can be found fluttering on the breeze. That there are so many butterfly species is in large part due to the sheer number and variety of wildflowers that thrive in the meadows carpeting the valley floor, which in turn is in large part due to the presence of **yellow rattle**. This relatively rare plant is unusual in that it is semi-parasitic; that is to say, as the roots of the yellow rattle develop they seek out the roots of other plants growing nearby, particularly grasses, drawing water and nutrients away from them. In doing so, they suppress the growth of grasses by as much as 60%, thereby allowing the wildflowers to flourish in the sun. The plant is called yellow rattle, by the way, because at the end of their life the seeds rattle inside the brown calyxes (containing the sepals), making a distinctive sound as the wind stirs them.

Devilsden Woods

These Woodland Trust-owned woods provide a sylvan bridge between the twin glories of Happy Valley and Farthing Downs. The ancient yews that are dotted around the wood used to mark the boundaries between farms. The LOOP cuts straight through the centre of Devilsden, following a local nature trail.

Farthing Downs

The official LOOP path follows the road along the spine of Farthing Downs, the most extensive area of semi-natural downland left in Greater London. A much better option, however, is to walk on the soft springy turf to the west of the road, watching out for any (usually docile) cattle that graze the Downs. There are great views looking north towards the City of London, with a **toposcope** along the way helping walkers to interpret what they see.

The Downs not only form (with Happy Valley) an **SSSI**, but in its own right is also a **Scheduled Ancient Monument**, with evidence of human occupation going back over 6000 years. After the Neolithic and Bronze Age people cleared the downs of trees, Iron Age man took advantage by farming the land; an Iron age field system, including the banks and ditches made by the Iron Age farmer's plough, can still be made out at the northern end of the downs. (The Iron Age, incidentally, lasted from around 700BC to the arrival of the Romans in AD43.) Much later and slightly further north, the Anglo-Saxons of the 7th century dug 16 barrows, divided between two cemeteries, on the other side of the path. The circular mounds of these excavated graves are still visible today. With the poor chalky soil exhausted by the early farmers, the land was only really good for grazing, a practice that continues to this day.

COULSDON SOUTH
[Map 12, pp104-5]

Coulsdon is an ancient settlement, appearing as *Colesdone* in the Domesday Book, though with evidence of human habitation going back to the Neolithic period.

The 'old town', however, is actually some way off the trail (you see it as you're walking across Farthing Downs); the section that you do see, **Coulsdon South**, formally known as **Smitham Bottom**, is much newer, with the focus of Coulsdon having shifted thanks to the arrival of the railway and not one, but two railway stations.

The whole aspect of the parish has been completely transformed during the last twenty years by building. It was a little while ago entirely rural with a few new houses scattered along the line of the rail-way and up the valley towards Caterham, whence another deep depression in the chalk runs down to Smitham Bottom. Now there are continuous rows of villas and cottages and shops from Croydon to south of Coulsdon station.

Victorian History of the Counties of England, 1912

The stage ends at the door of one of these railway stations – Coulsdon South – with the shops around 10 minutes away, close to the course of Stage 6.

Supermarkets here include an Aldi (Mon-Sat 8am-10pm, Sun 10am-4pm) and, across the road, a Tesco (daily 6am-11pm) and a Waitrose (Mon-Fri 7.30am-9pm, Sat to 8pm, Sun 10am-4pm), further down the road. Just before it is a Boots the **chemist** (Mon-Fri 8.30am-6.30pm, Sat 9am-5.30pm, Sun 10am-4pm) and a couple of **cafés** including *Cyco* (☎ 020-8660 2259, 💻 cycocafe.com; 🐾; Tue-Fri 8am-5pm,

Sat & Sun 9am-4pm) and several **take-aways** too.

East Croydon provides many accommodation options with branches of Premier Inn, Travelodge, Holiday Inn and Jury's Inn (see p27) all a short journey by train (see below) from Coulsdon and then within a 5- to 15-minute walk of East Croydon station.

Transport [see map pp42-3]
Coulsdon has two railway stations: Coulsdon South (Map 11) is a stop on Southern's **train** services to London Victoria, Redhill & Horsham as well as Thameslink's Horsham to Peterborough service; Coulsdon Town (off Map 12) is on Southern's London Bridge to Tattenham Corner line. See pp47-8 for details.

Bus services include the: No 404 (to Caterham-on-the-Hill; daily 2/hr); 405 (Redhill to Croydon; daily 2-4/hr); and 463 (to Pollards Hill via Woodmansterne; daily 2-4/hr).

STAGE 6: COULSDON SOUTH TO BANSTEAD DOWNS
[MAPS 11-13]

Though much of the first part of this short **4¾ mile stage (7.6km; C & A/C 1hr 50mins to 2hrs)** is dominated by a lengthy stretch of perambulating along pavements, much of the last part is conducted amongst the fairways and foliage of **Banstead Downs Golf Course**. But it is the farm that you march across during the middle part of this stage that will probably linger in your memory the longest, especially if you're walking this stage in summer. This is **Mayfield Lavender Farm**, a place quite unlike any other in the UK, at least in the summer months when people flock here in their finest summer frocks to have their photo taken amongst the neat rows of organically grown lavender.

While the lavender fields, and the crowds they attract, are undoubtedly an unusual phenomenon, I found the neighbouring **Oaks Park** to be the most pleasant part, not least because its **café** is pretty much the only place on this stage where you can get a bite to eat.

Note that if you're looking to escape the trail before the end of the stage, the **bus services** from Grove Lane/Clock House Village near the stage's start provide the only option. However, assuming that you have the necessary time and energy, **I advise that not only do you complete this stage in one go, but you consider combining it with the next one too**. The total distance of the two stages is only just over 8 miles (13km), which is a sensible length for a day's stroll. It also means you don't have to finish your day in the middle of Banstead Downs Golf Course, which is where this stage rather arbitrarily ends, though from there you only need to hike a further 500m to Banstead railway station for a connection to London.

The A237 through Coulsdon   [Map 12]

Running west of the station the trail follows the busy A237. This used to be the main road south out of London to Brighton; you will pass an old milepost near the station stating that it's 14 miles to Westminster Bridge and 37½ miles to Brighton. The main road now thunders above you on the viaduct.

Further north along the A237 you'll come to a new development of apartments on what used to be the site of Cane Hill Psychiatric Hospital. Michael Caine's brother and Charlie Chaplin's mother were both treated here, as was, most famously of all, David Bowie's half-brother, Terry Burns. The hospital

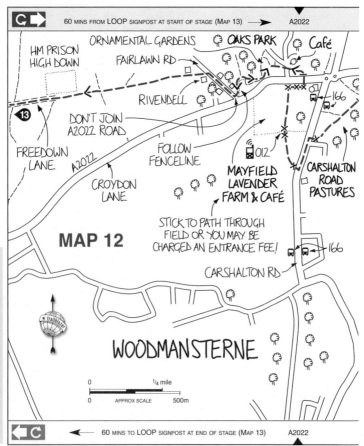

features, in cartoon form, on the cover of the US version of Bowie's album *The Man Who Sold The World*.

CLOCK HOUSE VILLAGE [Map 12]

At the end of the lengthy climb out of Coulsdon is Clock House village, named after a local farm (long since demolished), though more commonly and appropriately known as The Mount.

There's a **convenience store** (Mon-Sat 6.30am-8pm, Sun 8-6pm) across the road from the trail, a **post office** (Mon-Fri 9am-5pm, Sat to noon), round the corner, and a pub, *Jack & Jill* (☎ 07939 291860; **fb**; 🐾; bar 2-10pm), right on the trail. They hope to be serving food again (bar food; daily 2-8pm) in 2021 and may also open a café.

Bus No 463 (daily 2-4/hr) travels along Grove Lane (and then turns off onto The Mount) on its way to Pollards Hill from Coulsdon South. It also stops near Woodmansterne railway station (see p48).

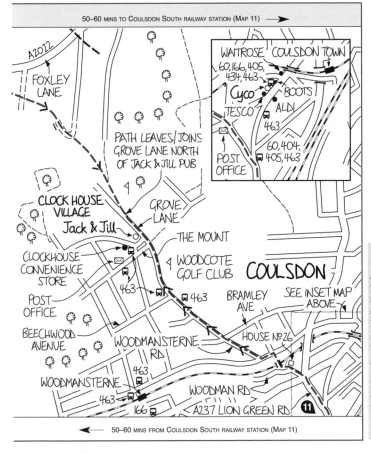

50–60 MINS TO COULSDON SOUTH railway station (MAP 11) →

← 50–60 MINS FROM COULSDON SOUTH railway station (MAP 11)

ROUTE GUIDE AND MAPS

Carshalton Road Pastures

Sitting on the most northerly ridge of the North Downs, this small bumpy patch of seemingly untamed grassland is home to 100 species of wildflower, shrub and tree.

Despite appearances, the Pastures are actually carefully managed, in order to allow rare species of flora and fauna to thrive here, including the small blue and brown hairstreak **butterflies** – just two of 18 butterfly species that make their home here – and animals such as **slow worms** and the occasional visiting **roe deer**.

Mayfield Lavender Farm

It comes as something of a surprise, having crossed mile after mile of lonely field and woodland, suddenly to stumble upon the crowds at the organic lavender fields of **Mayfield Farm** (⌨ www.mayfieldlavender.com). But during the summer months (June-Aug daily 9am-6pm) when the lavender is in bloom, and particularly at the weekend, these fields are full of crowds of men and (mostly) women, the latter in their finest flowing summer dresses, flouncing around the rows of lavender taking photos for their Instagram accounts. It's really quite jaw-dropping. Thankfully, whereas they will have had to pay the £4 entrance fee, walkers, providing they stick to the obvious large track across the field, are not obliged to pay anything, though there is an outdoor *café* **and gift shop** (daily 9am-5pm) on the site which may persuade you to part with your pennies.

Between Mayfield and Oaks Park, you can catch the No 166 **bus** (West Croydon to Banstead via Purley & Coulsdon; daily 2-5/hr – Mon-Sat 1-2/hr continues to/starts in Epsom). The Oaks Park stop (on Carshalton Rd) is for the lavender farm.

Oaks Park

If you're tackling the LOOP clockwise, you're probably thinking that it's been a while since you strolled through a municipal park that used to be part of a large country estate. Well the wait is over, for The Oaks was one of the great 18th-century country houses in this part of Surrey, and attractive Oaks Park has been carved out of its land.

The park is an engaging mix of formal gardens, woodland, natural chalk meadows (not on the trail) and informal parkland. There's also a man-made **grotto** dating from the late 19th century, and a *café* (daily 10am-5pm) and **toilets**, all just a few steps from the path. The park is famous for its flocks – or 'charms' to use the correct collective noun – of goldfinches, which are attracted to Oaks Park by the wildflowers that have been able to flourish since the park lost 13,000 trees in the great storm of 1987.

The estate was once in the hands of the sports-loving politician Edward Smith-Stanley, the 12th Earl of Derby, and it was here on the estate that two of the world's most prestigious horse races, the Oaks (named after his house) and the Derby (named after himself), both run at nearby Epsom racecourse, were devised.

The house was pulled down in the 1950s due to its dangerous condition, but several of the outbuildings remain including the stable block, which has now been repurposed as artists' studios.

Fairlawn Road and Freedown Lane
The unsealed road to the west of Oaks Park is Fairlawn Rd, home to several large houses. The road marks the border between London and Surrey. Branching north of it into Surrey is the bridleway Freedown Lane. Its name is quite ironic given that it takes you past the concrete walls of **HM Prison High Down**, built on the site of a former asylum.

Banstead Downs   [Map 13, p109]
While many a walker may be sighing at the sight of yet another golf course blighting the countryside, at least it can be argued that the one here is in an appropriate location. For Banstead Downs has long had sporting associations. Indeed, there was once a horse-track that led all the way from Banstead Downs to Epsom Downs, home of the Derby; and the **railway line** that you cross via a bridge is the Epsom Downs line, built to traffic spectators to the race course. The royal train even ran along here for many years on Derby Day (the Queen has in fact missed only a couple of Derby races since first attending in 1946).

Besides, the golf course, which is bisected by the busy multi-lane A217, is obliged to manage Banstead Downs for both sport *and* conservation, and the Downs have been designated an **SSSI**. They also play host to the most curious finish of any stage on the LOOP, with the walk coming to an abrupt end by a signpost hidden in the middle of a small copse of trees between fairways. The signpost points to the link path down to the station, but, as outlined on p103 in the introduction to this 6th stage, I advise you to continue onto Stage 7 if you can.

BANSTEAD   [Map 13, p109]
The Anglo-Saxons are believed to have been the first to settle in the area now called Banstead and it gets a mention in the Domesday Book (as *Benestede*).

Much later, the town earned a reputation for its clean air (presumably because of its proximity to the North Downs) and doctors regularly recommended a visit to Banstead to their patients. I, of course, recommend you do the exact opposite and bypass Banstead to continue along the trail, especially as the shops and facilities of the village are a fair distance beyond the station, which is in turn 500 metres off the LOOP.

Services
As for those facilities, most of the cafés etc are east of the A217 in central Banstead. But there are a few shops around Banstead station in the residential district of **Contiguous Nork** – a name that makes me very happy. Here, on Nork Way, you'll find a Co-op **supermarket** (daily 6am-11pm). A shuffle further down the road will also reveal Madison's **Pharmacy** (Mon-Fri 9am-1pm & 2-6pm, Sat 9am-1pm only) and the smallest WH Smith I've ever seen, with a **post office** (Mon-Sat 6.30am-6.30pm, Sun 7am-1pm) inside.

Transport
Banstead is a stop on Southern's London Victoria to Epsom Downs **railway** line (see p48).

The No 166 **bus** to West Croydon calls at Oaks Park, Woodmansterne & Coulsdon Town (daily 2-5/hr); some services (Mon-Sat 1-2/hr) continue to/start in Epsom.

STAGE 7: BANSTEAD DOWNS TO EWELL (BOURNE HALL PARK)
[MAPS 13-15]

This is the equal shortest stage, along with Stage 10, on the whole trail at just **3½ miles (5.6km; C: 1¼hrs to 1hr 35mins, A/C: 1hr 20mins to 1hr 40mins)**. It begins by taking you past the desirable residences of Cuddington Way and ends by taking you through the grounds of what was designed to be the most 'des res' ever built, Henry VIII's **Nonsuch Palace**.

It's a steady downhill stroll for much of the stage (though obviously uphill for those walking anti-clockwise), and though there are **no eateries** on the way, and the only place to catch a **bus** is on the A232, most people will find Stage 7 to be a straightforward, stress-free saunter.

Through Banstead's suburbs   [Map 13; Map 14, p111]
Though bookended by greenery, for much of this stage you'll be walking through the London Borough of Sutton, and the Surrey districts of Epsom and Ewell. These suburbs were laid out between the wars, though many of the houses, particularly on affluent Cuddington Way, are much later.

The only landmark on this stretch is **St Paul's**, the church on the corner of the Northey Avenue and Nonsuch Walk. The church is actually the third built on this site in the last 100 years, the rebuilds required to house the increasing number of churchgoers; this Evangelical church is clearly managing to buck the trend of declining congregations that's afflicted the Church of England over the past century.

The No 470 **bus** (Colliers Wood to Epsom; Mon-Sat 2/hr) travels along the A232, with stops at the south-eastern corner of Nonsuch Park, opposite the top of Bramley Rd, and also at Ewell East railway station (see Southern p48 for rail service information and map pp42-3).

Warren Farm & Nonsuch Park   [Map 14, p111]
Though unexceptional when compared to many parks on the LOOP, if you've come from Banstead it's quite a relief finally to reach the open meadow of **Warren Farm**. Managed by the Woodland Trust, this former hay farm is a mix of open grassland and broadleaved woodland and is, of course, a favourite with local dog-walkers and joggers. Dogs should be kept on a lead, by the way, due to the presence of ground-nesting birds such as the skylark.

Separated from Warren Farm by two concrete tracks – all that remains of a proposed arterial road that was, thankfully, never completed – is the much larger **Nonsuch Park**.

This is the last surviving remnant of Little Nonsuch Park, a deer park established by Henry VIII in 1538 as part of his vanity project, Nonsuch Palace – so named because Henry, so he hoped, thought that there could be 'none such place like it' in the whole of Europe. No expense was spared in building the palace, and an entire village, Cuddington, was flattened to make room for it. Unfortunately, the house was not finished by the time of Henry's death in 1547, though that which was completed was apparently everything Henry had hoped

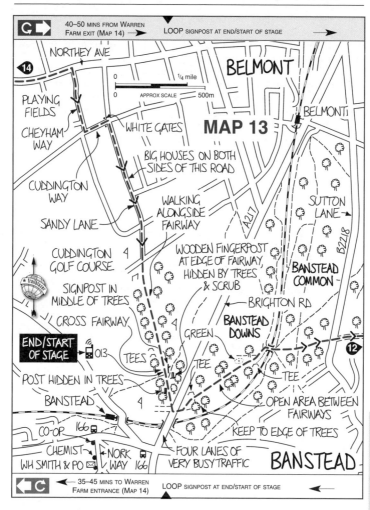

it would be. The writer Paul Hentzner, writing 50 years after Henry's death in his book *Travels in England during the reign of Queen Elizabeth*, described it thus:

The palace itself is so encompassed with parks full of deer, delicious gardens, groves ornamented with trellis-work, cabinets of verdure, and walks so embrowned by trees, that it seems to be a place pitched upon by Pleasure herself, to dwell in along with Health.

ROUTE GUIDE AND MAPS

Unfortunately, the whole building was pulled down in the late 1600s so the building materials could be sold off to pay the gambling debts of the then owner, Barbara, Countess of Castlemaine. She was one of the many mistresses of Charles II, who is said to have fathered five of her six children.

The LOOP follows the unfinished arterial road, now called The Avenue, which loops north to where Henry's palace once stood, with the footprint of the building marked by small obelisks. (The signposts pointing to the Mansion House, by the way, are referring to a later, 18th-century construction.) The LOOP, however, diverts off The Avenue away from the palace to one of the few visible ruins from Henry's time, the **Banqueting House**, though there's little to see save a very overgrown retaining wall behind a fence. The cellars and fireplace are still intact, apparently, but have been filled in.

EWELL   [Map 14; Map 15, p113]

Ewell's history is a long one. The town was first mentioned in the 11th-century Domesday Book, though the most ancient part of Ewell today is the Grade I listed 13th-century **tower** which the LOOP passes by. This is all that remains of Ewell's original St Mary's Church – a replacement church was built nearby in the 19th century. Opposite the tower is 19th-century **Ewell Castle**, now a private school where hell-raising actor Oliver Reed was a pupil. This castle was also the venue of the first meeting between the artist John Everett Millais and his wife-to-be Effie Gray. They eventually married nine years later, a lengthy delay to their nuptials caused because they had to wait for Effie's marriage to critic (and Millais fan) John Ruskin to be annulled due to non-consummation – a story that has inspired countless books and movies.

The LOOP also visits **Bourne Hall Park** (Map 15; 🖳 bournehall.org) home to a *coffee shop* (Tue-Sat 10am-4pm), and a **museum** (Mon-Sat 9am-5pm) charting the borough's history. Both of these can be found in the futuristic circular building at the back of the park. There is also a 19th-century **water wheel** in the manicured grounds, and a couple of large duckponds. The stage ends in the park, by a LOOP signpost pointing the link path off to Ewell West station.

The path actually diverts away from the centre of Ewell, which lies just a couple of minutes off the trail to the south.

Services

There are facilities enough to warrant a diversion, including a Co-op **supermarket** (daily 7am-11pm), with a decent café, *All Things Nice* (☎ 020-3754 3873, 🖳 allthings nice-ewell.com; 🍴; Mon-Fri 8.30am-4.30pm, Sat from 9.30am) above it and a lively pub, *The Famous Green Man* (☎ 020-8393 9719, 🖳 famousgreenman.com; 🍴; food Mon-Thur 11.30am-2.30pm, Fri-Sun to 5.30pm), opposite. If you need the **post office** (Map 15; Mon-Sat 7am-7pm, Sun to 2pm) you'll find one on the trail just before Bourne Hall Park.

There are branches of both *Premier Inn* and *Travelodge* (see p27) near Epsom station, a bus or train journey away.

Transport   [see map pp42-3]

Ewell East railway station (Map 14) is a stop on Southern's **train** services between London Victoria and Epsom. From **Ewell West** (Map 15) SouthWestern Railway operates trains to Waterloo and, in the other direction, to Dorking and Guildford (see p48).

For **buses**, the No 293 (Epsom to Morden via North Cheam; daily 2-3/hr) and 406 (Epsom to Kingston-upon-Thames via Tolworth; daily 2-3/hr) stop at the southern end of Bourne Park. The No 467 (Epsom to Hook via Chessington; Mon-Sat 1/hr) calls near Ewell West railway station and the 470 (Colliers Wood to Epsom via Sutton & Cheam; Mon-Sat 2/hr) stops at Nonsuch Park and Ewell East railway station.

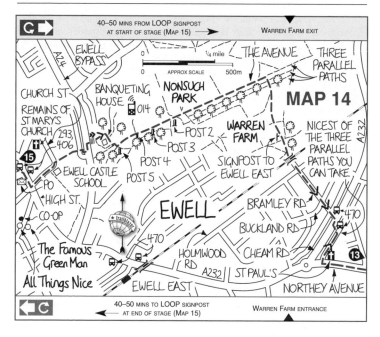

40–50 MINS FROM LOOP SIGNPOST AT START OF STAGE (MAP 15) →   WARREN FARM EXIT

EWELL BYPASS

A24

CHURCH ST

REMAINS OF ST MARY'S CHURCH 293

406

BANQUETING HOUSE 014

NONSUCH PARK

THE AVENUE

THREE PARALLEL PATHS

MAP 14

POST 2

WARREN FARM

NICEST OF THE THREE PARALLEL PATHS YOU CAN TAKE

A232

POST 3

POST 4

EWELL CASTLE SCHOOL

POST 5

SIGNPOST TO EWELL EAST

15

PO

HIGH ST.

CO-OP

EWELL

trailblazer

470

BRAMLEY RD

BUCKLAND RD

470

The Famous Green Man

All Things Nice

HOLMWOOD RD

A232

EWELL EAST

CHEAM RD

ST PAUL'S

13

NORTHEY AVENUE

¼ mile

0 APPROX SCALE 500m

40–50 MINS TO LOOP SIGNPOST ← AT END OF STAGE (MAP 15)   WARREN FARM ENTRANCE

STAGE 8: EWELL (BOURNE HALL PARK) TO KINGSTON BRIDGE
[MAPS 15-17]

This **7¼-mile stage (11.7km; C: 2½hrs to 3hrs 5mins, A/C: 2hrs 25mins to 2hrs 55mins)** is all about the **Hogsmill**, a stream/river that you follow (save for three notable diversions) from its source at the start of the stage in Ewell, all the way to its confluence with the Thames at Kingston at the stage's end.

While you may not have heard of the river before now – or, rather, the stream, for the Hogsmill doesn't officially become a river until it's joined by Green Lanes Stream, about half a mile (800m) into the stage – you may well be familiar with the art that it has inspired.

Sir John Everett Millais' ***Ophelia***, on display at Tate Britain, is one such work. Ophelia (from *Hamlet*) is depicted in the picture singing as she drowns in a river. Shakespeare set his play in Denmark, of course, but Millais used the Hogsmill (see Map 16) as the model for his backdrop, painting *en plain air* to better capture the essence of nature, before heading inside to paint Ophelia herself. (As a model he used Elizabeth Siddall, who, aged just 19, agreed to immerse herself in a bath for long periods to enable Millais to complete his work. Perhaps unsurprisingly, Siddall ended up with a severe cold and Millais was forced by her father to pay the doctor's bills.)

In the same year Millais's close friend and fellow founder of the Pre-Raphaelites, William Holman Hunt, painted several landscapes around Ewell and the Hogsmill, most famously his masterpiece *The Hireling Shepherd*, in which a young shepherd boy tries to show a beautiful young maiden a death's-head hawkmoth that he's caught, while neglecting his sheep that are seen in the background wandering into a wheat field. A few years later, Hunt was back by the Hogsmill, this time using the overgrown and disused door of an old barn that was attached to one of the Hogsmill's gunpowder mills as the main 'prop' for his work *The Light of the World*. In the picture Jesus is shown knocking at a door, an image that illustrates this verse in Revelations: *'Behold, I stand at the door and knock; if any man hear My voice, and open the door, I will come in to him, and will sup with him, and he with Me.'*

To judge by the **wooden sculptures** of the local fauna that line the Hogsmill, the waterway is still clearly a source of inspiration for artists to this day, and a walk along it makes for a pleasant afternoon. Indeed, the only negative aspects of this 8th stage are the places where you are forced to divert away from the Hogsmill: firstly at Grafton Rd, a tedious schlep; and secondly, along the Kingston bypass, which is positively unpleasant; and thirdly, through the suburbs of Surbiton, which is untaxing but unenthralling.

These last two places are also where you can catch a **bus** away from the trail, in addition to **railway stations** at Malden Manor and Berrylands. There's also a **pub** and **supermarket** at Berrylands, though few other places to get food on this stage. That's not a problem, however, for the wealth of dining options by the Thames in Kingston indubitably makes up for this shortfall.

Hogsmill Riverside Open Space   [Map 15]

Hogsmill Riverside Open Space is part of Hogsmill Local Nature Reserve. The LOOP jumps from one side to the other fairly regularly in Ewell. One such crossing is at **Upper Mill**, a traditional 18th-century weatherboard mill that still has several original features and is the last surviving of several mills that used to be here (and which were mentioned in the Domesday Book). The mill was last used for its original purpose in the 1950s, and in the 1970s it was owned by actor Oliver Reed.

The LOOP crosses the water again after taking the wooden walkway through the **tunnel** under the London to Dorking railway line. The signage thereafter was not the best at the time of research, but as long as you stick to the river you shouldn't go too far wrong. It's a pleasant, easy stroll, with plenty of places to stop for a picnic or lie in the grass while watching out for kingfishers, which are supposed to live and fish by the Hogsmill.

Packhorse Bridge Further north, the LOOP passes Packhorse Bridge, a reminder of when a **gunpowder mill complex** used to operate just north of here on the river's western bank, with the gunpowder then being transported by mule to storage facilities nearby. Today you can turn east at the bridge to reach **Ewell Court House** (🖳 ewellcourthouse.org), a Grade-II listed building constructed by the mill owners that is now used as a venue for weddings.

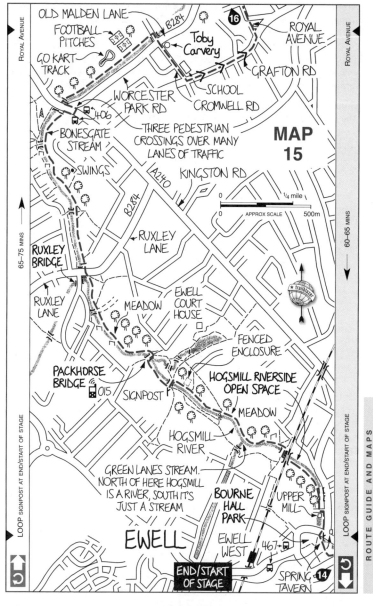

ROYAL AVENUE

OLD MALDEN LANE

FOOTBALL PITCHES

GO KART TRACK

B284

Toby Carvery

16

ROYAL AVENUE

GRAFTON RD

WORCESTER PARK RD

SCHOOL

CROMWELL RD

406

BONESGATE STREAM

THREE PEDESTRIAN CROSSINGS OVER MANY LANES OF TRAFFIC

MAP 15

SWINGS

A240

KINGSTON RD

0   1/4 mile

0   500m
APPROX SCALE

B284

RUXLEY LANE

RUXLEY BRIDGE

★ trailblazer

RUXLEY LANE

MEADOW

EWELL COURT HOUSE

PACKHORSE BRIDGE   015

SIGNPOST

FENCED ENCLOSURE

HOGSMILL RIVERSIDE OPEN SPACE

MEADOW

HOGSMILL RIVER

GREEN LANES STREAM. NORTH OF HERE HOGSMILL IS A RIVER, SOUTH IT'S JUST A STREAM

BOURNE HALL PARK

UPPER MILL

EWELL

EWELL WEST

467

SPRING TAVERN

14

END/START OF STAGE

65–75 MINS

60–65 MINS

LOOP SIGNPOST AT END/START OF STAGE

LOOP SIGNPOST AT END/START OF STAGE

ROYAL AVENUE

ROYAL AVENUE

Ruxley Bridge   North of here the LOOP ignores the lane crossing Ruxley Bridge – once better known as the **Ruxley Splash** as cars used to have to ford the Hogsmill while pedestrians could take a bridge.

Soon the Hogsmill is joined by its major tributary, the **Bonesgate**. Here the Thamesdown Link (a path connecting the North Downs Way at Westhumble with the Thames Path at Kingston-upon-Thames) meets the LOOP and a little further north of here the Hogsmill marks the border between London and Surrey.

Diversion from the Hogsmill   [Map 15, p113; Map 16]
The intended route along the Hogsmill has never materialised so sadly you still have to deviate off it for a fairly long, tedious and often steep schlepp along Grafton Rd. Compensations are few but there is a *Toby Carvery* (☎ 020-8337 5221, 🖥 tobycarvery.co.uk; 🐾 bar area only; food Mon-Fri 11.30am-8pm, Sat & Sun 8am-8.30pm) at the start of the diversion if you're desperate for a roast dinner.

On the descent (Map 16) back down to the river you pass the **Church of St John the Baptist**, Old Malden. Not only is this church mentioned in the Domesday Book but the name Malden comes from the Saxon *Mael-dun*, meaning Cross on a Hill, and there are a few remains of an earlier Saxon church on the site, and in the fabric of the present building.

The LOOP makes use of a steep track running down from the church to the Hogsmill; note that this can get very muddy in the winter.

> ### Link to Malden Manor station   [Map 16]
> It's a straightforward stroll to Malden Manor, from where SouthWestern Railway operates **trains** (London Waterloo to Chessington South; see p48 and map pp42-3). If you feel slightly discombobulated on reaching the station, it could be because you have reached the dizzying heights of Zone 4 – one of the very few places on the LOOP where you get this close to central London!
>
> The K1 (New Malden to Kingston-upon-Thames via Surbiton; Mon-Fri 6-8/hr, Sat 3-6/hr, Sun 2-4/hr) **bus** stops near the station.

Malden Way/Kingston Bypass
Your serene progress along the Hogsmill is interrupted once more, this time by the roaring A3 Kingston bypass. You can complain about the horrors of the modern industrial world as you trudge along the pavement to the subway, but in fact the congestion through Kingston had always been an issue, and this road was first proposed way back in 1912, and built in 1927.

There are **bus** stops, one on either side of the subway, for the K1 (see above) and the 265 (Tolworth to Putney Bridge via Barnes; daily 4-6/hr).

BERRYLANDS (SURBITON)
                    [Map 16; Map 17, pp118-19]
The Hogsmill now snakes its way through Surbiton. If you're heading towards Kingston-upon-Thames, you'll feel the houses start to close in on either side as you make your way along the course of the river, until, eventually, you have to quit the banks altogether to climb on a short detour to the Duke of Buckingham pub (closed at the time of writing), in the district of **Berrylands**.

The Berrylands (🖥 theberrylands.co .uk; 🐾; daily noon-10pm) serves food and welcomes dogs!

Beyond Berrylands station but still on the LOOP, where Lower Marsh Lane meets Villers Rd, there's a Co-op **supermarket** (daily 7am-10pm).

Transport   **[see map pp42-3]**
The LOOP passes very close to Berrylands **railway** station, which is a stop on

SouthWestern Railway's London Waterloo to Hampton Court service (see p48).

Bus K2 (Hook to Norbiton via Tolworth, Surbiton & Kingston-upon-Thames; daily 3-6/hr) travels along Surbiton Hill Park.

Through Kingston-upon-Thames

The trail does its best to follow the Hogsmill through Kingston, and in doing so passes through several landmarks, including the **county courts** and the impressive circular **Guildhall**. You can also take a very short detour to visit the **Coronation Stone**, also known rather pompously as the **Chair of Majesty**. Depending on which source you read, this is either the very stone on which at least six Saxon kings were crowned (see below), or it's nothing more than a bit of masonry rescued from the ruins of a 12th-century church, which a 19th-century mayor, in his wisdom, decided was the very stone on which kings were anointed, and announced it as such to much fanfare. What isn't in dispute is that before the mayor had unveiled the stone, it had previously seen service helping riders mount their horses in the marketplace.

Back on the trail you'll cross the medieval **Clattern Bridge** (medieval name *clateryngbrugge*), the oldest in Kingston and so-called because of the noise horses' hooves make when crossing it.

KINGSTON-UPON-THAMES
[Map 17, pp118-19]

Depending on how you measure these things, Kingston is perhaps the most 'historic' of all the places on the LOOP: it may or may not be the oldest, but there's no denying that Kingston's past is more intriguing, and more colourful, than anywhere else you'll encounter on your round-London circuit. It was first mentioned in a historical record dating back to AD838 ('*Cyninges tun*'), as the venue of a meeting between Ceolnoth, Archbishop of Canterbury, and Egbert, then ruler of the Kingdom of Wessex. The negotiations that day eventually led to the unification of the entire country of England under the kings of Wessex (under Ceolnoth's grandson, Alfred), and thereafter around five further Saxon kings were crowned here.

The importance of Kingston was not lost on the invading Normans over a century later, when William the Conqueror himself claimed the town (now known as '*Chingestune*') for his own *demesne* (ie a piece of land attached to a manor and retained by the owner for their own use). The place has long been very prosperous, not least because of its bridge, versions of which have been hereabouts since the 12th century, and possibly even earlier, and for a while it was the pre-eminent crossing of the Thames west of London.

The construction of **Hampton Court**, just across the river gave the town a further economic filip as well as further connections with royalty. Small wonder then, that when in 1927 the Mayor of Kingston petitioned George V for the right to use the title 'Royal Borough', the king agreed, saying that it had been described as a 'royal borough since time immemorial'. (By allowing the mayor's request, Kingston joined an exclusive club of royal boroughs, with only Kensington & Chelsea, Windsor & Maidenhead, and Greenwich the other members.) The town was allowed to keep its royal status even after its absorption into London in 1965, though this act created something of an anomaly: Kingston is the county town of Surrey, even though it's no longer part of the county.

Services

The waterfront promenade, which the LOOP takes, is lined with *cafés, bars and restaurants* – you won't go hungry, or be short of options, in Kingston. Close to the station is a Tesco **supermarket** (daily 6am-11pm). There's a **post office** (Mon-Fri 8.30am-7pm, Sat 9am-5pm, Sun 10am-5pm) on Eden St, a few minutes from the trail and a Boots the **chemist** (Mon-Sat 8am-6.30pm, Sun 11am-5pm) in Eden Shopping Centre. There is no shortage of outdoor/trekking shops either, including Ultimate Outdoors on Thames St (daily 10am-6pm) and a Cotswold Outdoor (Mon-Fri 10am-5.30pm, Sat 9.30am-5.30pm, Sun 11am-5pm) on Clarence St.

There are branches of both *Premier Inn* (London Kingston-upon-Thames hotel; ⌨ premierinn.com) and *Travelodge* (Kingston-upon-Thames Central; ⌨ travelodge.co.uk) near the station.

Transport [see map pp42-3]

The **railway station** is around seven minutes from the LOOP (500 metres). SouthWestern Railway operates services to/from here (see p48).

There are bus stops all over town but most services call at the **bus station** which is about 50m to the east of the railway station, on Cromwell Rd (part of the one-way system).

There are buses to many parts of London and beyond including the: No 71 (to Chessington via Hook; daily 4-6/hr); 111 (to Heathrow Airport via Hampton, Hounslow, Hounslow East & Cranford; 4/hr); 213 (to Sutton via New Malden; daily 2-3/hr); 216 (to Staines via Hampton Wick, Hampton Court, Hampton, Sunbury & Ashford; daily 2-3/hr); 281 (Tolworth to Hounslow via Kingston-upon-Thames, Hampton Wick, Fulwell & Twickenham; daily 5-7/hr); 285 (to Heathrow Airport via Hampton Wick, Hampton Hill, Feltham, Great South West Rd & Hatton Cross; daily 2-3/hr); 406 (to Epsom via Tolworth, West Ewell & Ewell; daily 2-3/hr); 411 (to West Molesey via Hampton Wick & Hampton Court; daily 2-4/hr); 481 (to Isleworth via Hampton Wick, Teddington, Fulwell & Whitton; daily 1-2/hr); and K1 (to New Malden via Surbiton & Malden Manor; Mon-Fri 6-8/hr, Sat 3-6/hr, Sun 2-4/hr).

The X26 (West Croydon to Heathrow Central via Worcester Park, New Malden & Hatton Cross; daily 2/hr) buses heading towards Hatton Cross stop on Clarence St near the station and those heading towards West Croydon stop on Cromwell Rd; both are part of the A307 but the one-way system divides the road.

Both the No 85 (to Putney; daily 2-6/hr) and the 371 (to Richmond; daily 4/hr) stop on Kingston Hall Rd.

STAGE 9: KINGSTON BRIDGE TO THE A30 (FOR HATTON CROSS STATION) [MAPS 17-21]

This **9½-mile stage (15.3km; C & A/C 3¼hrs to 4hrs)** is rather a monumental one. Not only do you **cross the mighty Thames** for your first and only time on the LOOP, but you also traverse the only royal park on the trail – and the best park, in this author's opinion at least, on the whole route. That park is **Bushy Park**, once the happy hunting ground of Henry VIII, and still filled with deer to this day.

The next park on the trail, which hugs the **Crane River**, can't quite match up to Bushy in terms of scale or interest, but nevertheless many people are very pleasantly surprised by this waterway, and in particular how it's become the home of some rarely seen members of the animal kingdom. Indeed, the only real complaint that people have about it is that the LOOP doesn't follow it for longer.

Nor do the charms of this stage end there, for there's another large swathe of greenery, in the form of **Hounslow Heath**, towards the walk's end – and who knew Hounslow could be so tranquil, and so serene?

Unfortunately, you do have to work for these rewards. For one thing, this is one of the longest stages on the LOOP (though, to be fair, there are several **bus** services and a **railway station** within easy walking distance of the trail, as well as a lovely **café** in Bushy Park's Woodland Gardens). What's more, between

MAP 17

each of the above attractions there are some lengthy stretches of roadside rambling to be tackled. The stage also finishes at what most walkers would agree is the worst end to any stage on the entire trail, the A30; indeed, it's one of the worst parts of the LOOP full stop.

But let's ignore those drawbacks for now, because I promise you that, at the end of this stage, it will be the bucks of Bushy Park, or the kingfishers of the Crane, that will be your abiding memories.

Crossing Kingston Bridge

There's been a bridge across the Thames at Kingston for at least the last 800 years, and very possibly a lot longer – perhaps as far back as Anglo-Saxon times. The current bridge, however, was opened only in 1828. Until 1965, crossing the

END/START OF STAGE

ULTIMATE OUTDOORS

KINGSTON-UPON-THAMES

CROMWELL RD BUS STATION   NORBITON
71,85,111,213,216,281,285,406,411,481,K1,X26

KINGSTON

TESCO

Travelodge London Kingston-upon-Thames

COTSWOLD OUTDOOR

Travelodge Kingston-upon-Thames Central

IRON GATE

CLATTERN BRIDGE

Premier Inn London Kingston-upon-Thames

EDEN SHOPPING CENTRE - POST OFFICE & BOOTS

PATH OFF ROAD THROUGH COUNTY COURTS

CORONATION STONE

BLUE BRIDGE

GREEN BRIDGE

SWAN WALK

SCHOOL

PEDESTRIAN CROSSING

ZEBRA CROSSING

HOGSMILL RIVER

IGNORE SIGNPOST

3 BRIDGE PATH   K1

ALLEY

K1

LOWER MARSH LANE

SEWAGE WORKS

VILLIERS RD

DUKE OF BUCKINGHAM

CO-OP

SURBITON CEMETERY

16

0   ¼ mile

0   APPROX SCALE   500m

bridge meant leaving Surrey for Middlesex, before the latter county was abolished in 1965, having already seen most of its territory absorbed into Greater London. (Today, Middlesex exists as little more than a cricket team whose home is also the home of the sport, Lords.)

Hampton Wick

On the western side of the river is Hampton Wick, and it is here that the LOOP says farewell to the Thames Path, at the end of their 400 metres together.

White Hart Hotel Hampton Wick (🖥 whitehearthoteluk.co.uk; food daily noon-9pm), which dates back to the 1600s, is just over the bridge on the western side and a 5-minute walk from Hampton Wick station. It offers both accommodation and food and dogs are welcome.

The No 481 (to Isleworth to via Teddington, Fulwell & Whitton; daily 1-2/hr) **bus** stops on Church Grove, and on Hampton Court Rd for services to Kingston. Hampton Wick **railway station** is a stop on some of SouthWestern Railway's services (see p48; map pp42-3). Other bus services visiting Hampton Wick include the 111, 216, 285, 406 and 411 (see p206).

Bushy Park

At 445 hectares (1100 acres), Bushy Park is the second largest royal park, behind only Richmond Park. It's a magnificent place. First-time visitors are often struck by how wild the park appears, with copses of mature trees surrounded by swathes of rough open land, filled with tall grass and bracken, through which the Longford River gently meanders. Unsurprisingly, the park is a real haven for birdlife; on my visit I spotted woodpecker, kingfisher, a little owl and many species of waterfowl.

But without doubt the most memorable feature of Bushy Park are the **deer**. This is as it should be, for the park started out as a hunting ground for Henry VIII, who in the 1530s was spending most of his time at neighbouring Hampton Court Palace, having been gifted it by his Lord Chancellor, Thomas Wolsley, in 1529. (It should be noted that this 'gift' was not quite as it seems; Wolsley had fallen from favour in Henry's court after he'd failed to secure the king's divorce from Catherine of Aragon, and thus gave the estate to the king knowing full well that, if he didn't, he would probably have it taken from him anyway.)

There are both **fallow and red deer** roaming in the park, around 320 in total, but don't be fooled by their seemingly laconic natures; they can attack if annoyed, particularly rutting stags (the rutting season usually takes place in Oct-Nov), mothers protecting their young (usually May-July) and during the mating season (Sep-Oct). The park recommends that you keep 50m away from them and, while this might be difficult at times, given how numerous they are and the fact they've learnt to approach people for food, it's certainly wise not to approach them too closely.

The LOOP plots a course through the park that visits several of Bushy's best-known features, including:

The Longford River Henry may have been the first, but he certainly wasn't the only king to reside at Hampton Court, with each resident embellishing Bushy Park to his or her taste. In 1639 Charles I created an artificial river to improve the supply of water to the palace by diverting water from the River Colne (a river that you'll be encountering on Stage 11; see p135). The 19km hand-dug waterway was named the Longford River, though unofficially it was nicknamed the **King's Hosepipe**. Over the years the river has been embellished with various ponds along its route, attracting many species of waterfowl to the park.

❏ **IMPORTANT NOTE – WALKING TIMES**

All times in this book refer only to the time spent walking. You will need to add 20-30% to allow for rests, photography, checking the map, drinking water etc.

Chestnut Avenue & the Diana Fountain Despite the 'wild' appearance of much of the park, Bushy does have its formal side too, and nowhere more so than the parallel rows of trees leading up to the Diana Fountain that you can just see glinting in the sunlight to the south. This is **Chestnut Avenue**, first laid out by Charles I. The name is actually rather misleading, for the dominant species, on the outer rows at least, is lime rather than chestnut. Indeed, it was two parallel rows of lime trees that King Charles originally had planted in 1622. The Avenue was then redesigned by Christopher Wren in the early 1700s.

The **Diana Fountain** lies a quarter of a mile (400m) off the LOOP but is worth a detour. Supposedly a depiction of Diana, the Goddess of Hunting, some commentators think it could actually be a depiction of Arethusa, a nymph and daughter of Nereus; the carvings of four water nymphs and the repeated sea-shell motif that surround the statue would suggest they have a point. As with Chestnut Avenue, the statue was made on the orders of Charles I, and stood in the privy garden of Hampton Court, though it was moved to the southern end of Chestnut Avenue at the behest of Christopher Wren as part of his improvements to the park.

Several **buses** travel along Hampton Court Rd: No 111 (Heathrow Airport to Kingston-upon-Thames via Cranford, Hounslow East, Hounslow, Hampton & Hampton Wick; daily 4/hr); 216 (Kingston-upon-Thames to Staines via Hampton Wick, Hampton, Sunbury & Ashford; daily 2-3/hr); and 411 (Kingston-upon-Thames to West Molesey via Hampton Wick; daily 2-4/hr) and all stop near the palace.

Woodland Gardens (Map 18, p122) Do note that **dogs are not allowed in the fenced-off** Woodland Gardens – the only part of the LOOP that is off-limits to them. If you're hiking with your hound you'll have to follow the detour shown at the bottom of Map 18. It's a shame, as the gardens are yet another of Bushy's unexpected treats, a carefully curated woodland walk along **Keeper's River** past pond, lodge, plantation and glade. The gardens are actually divided into two sections. The first, **Pheasantry Plantation**, is home to *Pheasantry Café* (🖥 royalparks.org.uk/parks/bushy-park; daily Apr-late Oct 9am-6pm, late Oct-Mar to 4pm) with accompanying visitor centre and toilets.

The second section, reached by crossing the park's pedestrian highway, **Ash Walk**, is the scruffier **Waterhouse Plantation**, which has been, quite deliberately, less strictly managed in order to benefit the wildlife.

Hampton Hill
Bus No 285 (Heathrow Airport to Kingston-upon-Thames via Hatton Cross, Great South West Rd, Feltham, Teddington & Hampton Wick; daily 2-3/hr) stops on Hampton Rd.

Fulwell   [Map 19, p123]
The LOOP passes reasonably close to **Fulwell railway station**, a stop on SouthWestern Railway's London Waterloo to Shepperton service (see p48; map pp42-3). On Wellington Rd, near the station, there are bus stops serving the R70 to Hanworth and, across the road, to Richmond.

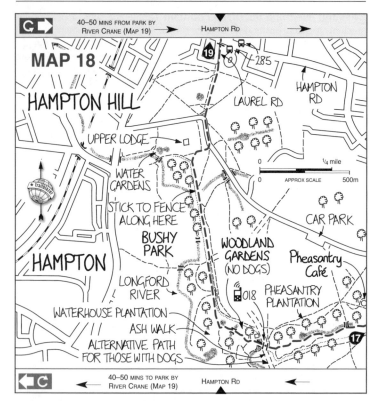

On Twickenham Rd **bus services** include: 290 (Twickenham to Staines via Strawberry Hill, Hanworth, Sunbury & Ashford; daily 2-4/hr) and 490 (Richmond to Heathrow Airport via Feltham & Hatton Cross; daily 2-6/hr). While on Hospital Bridge Rd services include: 110 (Hounslow to Isleworth via Twickenham; daily 3/hr) and 481 (Isleworth to Kingston-upon-Thames via Whitton, Fulwell, Teddington & Hampton Wick; daily 1-2/hr).

The LOOP passes near a branch of *Premier Inn* (London Twickenham East; 🖳 premierinn.com).

River Crane

While nothing can reach the heights of Bushy Park in this author's opinion, the River Crane does at least provide a soft landing for those who've just come from there. The Crane flows for only 8½miles (13.6km) before it empties into the Thames at Isleworth, and the LOOP follows it for much of its course (though, as is typical on the LOOP, there are several diversions away from its banks), both to the end of this stage and the start of the next one. Nobody is sure where its name comes from, though the possibility that it's named after the elegant, long-legged, long-necked birds can't be ruled out (though they haven't bred here since the Middle Ages).

If you're heading clockwise on the LOOP, you'll first encounter the Crane at **Hospital Bridge**, so-called, according to the information board nearby, because a hospital was situated nearby that was attached to the army encampment that mustered there under the orders of James II, when everything hereabouts was just heath. It's worth nipping back under the bridge away from the LOOP, by the way, to see the **bench with a kingfisher** carved on it, the work of artist Paul Sivell. He's also responsible for the **dragonfly bench** that you see a bit further on that *is* on the LOOP.

Though **Crane Park** (as this wild area surrounding the river is called) never feels that rural – the sound of traffic and glimpses of back-garden fences

ensure you always know you're in an urban environment – it's still home to an impressive register of wildlife, including kingfishers, dragonflies and the endangered water vole.

Shot Tower   [Map 20]
This marks the point where the LOOP joins/leaves the Crane. Perhaps the best aspect of this 25m-high tower is that, because of the surrounding tree cover, you don't actually see it until you're almost at its base. The tower is all that remains of **Hounslow Powder Mills**, which operated for over 150 years from 1766 to the 1920s, though the tower dates 'only' from 1828. Surprisingly, nobody is 100% sure what it was used for. Originally it was thought it was used in the manufacture of lead shot, the molten lead being poured from the top of the tower into a pool of cooling water below. Some, however, think it served merely as a watchtower, enabling workers to look out for fires at the plant. Whatever its original purpose, today it serves as a **visitor centre** though its opening times are limited (Sun 1.30-4pm).

The **third of Sivell's benches** (see p123), this time with an oak leaf carved on the back-rest, sits near the tower.

Hanworth Road, Heathfield
It's long and dull, but in order to get between the Crane and Hounslow Heath you have to march along this arrow-straight road although there is a **chemist**, a branch of Boots, and a **post office** should you require. And if walking really doesn't appeal you could hop on **bus** No 111 (Heathrow Airport to Kingston-upon-Thames via Cranford, Hounslow, Hanworth, Hampton Court & Hampton Wick; daily 4/hr) for a couple of stops as it travels along Hanworth Rd.

Hounslow Heath
Once upon a time pretty much the whole of Hounslow and beyond looked like this 82-hectare (200-acre) swathe of grass, bramble, hawthorn and gorse – an area of 1619 hectares (4000 acres) that's now reduced to something just a 20th of that size. But we should be thankful that this swathe of serenity is here at all given how developed so much of Hounslow is today.

Hounslow Heath boasts an interesting past. Used by the Tudors for falconry and hunting, James II established a military encampment on the heath as a show of might, intimidating Londoners in order to promote his idea of absolute monarchy, where the king has total (and, as a result, often tyrannical) power. You have already crossed Hospital Bridge (see p123) which was attached to the camp; this gives you some idea how far the heath once stretched. It later became notorious as a place where highwaymen could carry out their nefarious activities; the heath was crossed by a couple of major roads, and there was plenty of 'wilderness' where the bandits could hide out.

It was this reputation for lawlessness that eventually encouraged the authorities to develop the land. The first airport to offer international commercial flights in the capital, **London Terminal Aerodrome**, was built on the heath in the 1920s, taking advantage of the flat terrain. The first flight to Australia,

which left the UK on 12 November 1919 and arrived just under a month later, took off from here.

As for the rump of the heath that remains you need to follow the instructions on Map 20 carefully as, on its eastern side at least, there are few signposts.

At its western end it crosses a **golf course**. If, like me, you consider golf courses in general a waste of good countryside, in this instance we should be placated by the fact that a) you only get the briefest of glimpses of it as you push on through the undergrowth, and b) the site was formerly landfill, so at least it's an improvement on that.

Brazil Mill Woods
The trail rejoins the **Crane** to pass through this narrow ribbon of woodland, with the trail threading its way between river bank and back-garden fence. These woods were once the site of a mill that extracted red pigment from Brazil trees to use as dye during the 18th century, hence the name. You can still make out the **millrace** (the channel that carries the water that drives the wheel) and the **sluices** (the gates that control the flow of water) by the path.

Staines Road, Feltham
Separating Brazil Mill from Donkey Wood, and temporarily interrupting your progression along the Crane, the LOOP crosses Staines Rd by a **24hr petrol station** with a Spar **store** where you can get snacks and hot drinks. There's a **Tesco** (daily 6am-midnight) with an **ATM** three minutes down the road, as well as a *café* and *takeaways*. Staines Rd, incidentally, follows the course of the Roman road from London to Chichester; the cul-de-sac opposite the petrol station is Roman Close.

Donkey Wood
Rejoining the Crane, you'll find evidence of another **mill**, producing gunpowder. The **earth banks** you encounter in the woods are also part of the same mill complex. You'll also cross the **Duke of Northumberland's River**, an artificial waterway dug to connect the Crane with the River Colne, another tributary of the Thames. But it is the lengthy duckboards (boardwalks) that are the highlight of this stage, taking you across ground that is often saturated.

A30/The Great South-West Road   [Map 21]
The stage eventually finishes, ingloriously at the Great South-West Road, the A30 (together with the Piccadilly underground line, which also pokes its head above ground here). From here either follow the signposts and head west to Hatton/Hatton Cross; or head in the opposite direction to take a shorter detour, using pedestrian crossings to get across the A30, so as to continue onto the next stage. Don't expect the walking to be pleasant, whichever way you choose.

HATTON   [Map 21]
The least pleasant link walk (**half a mile/ 800m**) of them all leads to Hatton/Hatton Cross – which some may consider scant reward for their efforts. Beloved by highwaymen thanks to its proximity to the wild and lawless Hounslow Heath (see p124), Hatton is today a land of large industrial units and wide, busy roads.

There are pockets of interest, including the hamlet's oldest pub, *The Green Man* (☎ 020-8890 2681, 🖥 greeneking-pubs.co .uk; 🐕 on lead; food daily noon-9pm, but

they may also open from 10am), which has a hiding hole behind the fireplace designed, so it is said, deliberately for the benefit of outlaws. The fact that a nearby road is called Dick Turpin Way is not, I suggest, a coincidence.

These days, of course, it's rather overshadowed by Heathrow Airport which dominates everything around here. There's little for the trekker, even by the station, and I suggest that, if you can, you run Stages 9 and 10 together and forego Hatton

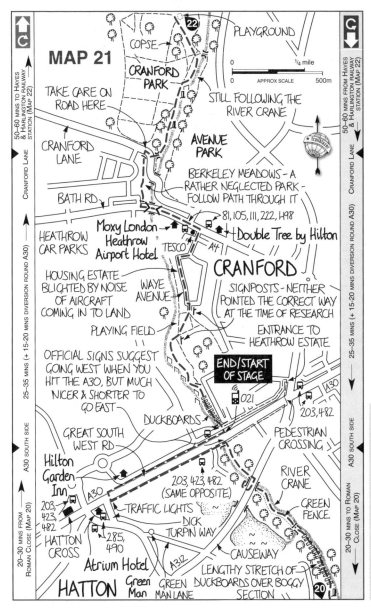

MAP 21

Cross's charms. However, due to the proximity of Heathrow Airport, there are plenty of hotels. *Atrium Hotel Heathrow* (🖥 atriumhotelheathrow.co.uk) is between the Green Man and Hatton Cross station and rooms include studio apartments with a kitchenette. Also nearby is *Hilton Garden Inn Hatton Cross* (🖥 hilton.com).

Transport   **[see map pp42-3]**
But if you do need to leave or join the LOOP here, you'll find that Hatton Cross is on the **Piccadilly underground line**, with westbound trains heading to Heathrow Airport and eastbound trains heading to Central London.

Bus services which stop at the tube station and run along the A30 (Great South-West Rd) include the: No 203 (Staines to Hounslow via Ashford, Bedfont, Cranford & Hounslow West; daily 2-3/hr); 423 (Heathrow Airport to Hounslow via Hounslow West; daily 2-3/hr) & 482 (Southall to Heathrow Airport via Hounslow West & Cranford; daily 2-3/hr).

STAGE 10: (HATTON CROSS STATION FOR) THE A30 TO HAYES & HARLINGTON   [MAPS 21-22]

This is the equal shortest stage on the LOOP, a **3½-mile (5.6km)** skip, though in order to get to its start you do have a **half-mile (800m)** detour round the A30 to negotiate too. There's no reason why you can't complete this stage in just **C & A/C 1¼hrs to 1hr 35mins (plus 15-20 mins** at the start of the stage to negotiate the A30).

This is actually something of a relief, for just as Heathrow Airport dominates the landscape around here, so it dominates this stage too. The screaming of jet engines is a constant presence, and it's fair to say that poor old Cranford has been roared into cowering submission by the airlines that skim its rooftops. This is also the stage when you have to cross the A4 Bath Rd (Great West Rd) and then pass under the M4. But there are compensations: **Cranford Country Park** is tidy and serene (at least in those moments between the planes landing and taking off); the **church** and **stables** at the park's northern end are interesting; and by the end you'll be basking in the relative tranquillity of the **Grand Union Canal**, a canal you'll be walking alongside, on and off, for the next couple of stages. Besides, it's always a good feeling to tick off another stage – especially when minimal effort was required to do so.

If Cranford and its environs are all too much there are **cafés** there to escape the noise, as well as **buses** both on Cranford's main road and towards the end of the stage on North Hyde Rd.

CRANFORD   [Map 21, p127]
No other place on the LOOP has been so blighted by modern development as Cranford, which sits under the flight path of Heathrow's northern runway. This was probably a pleasant place once, with the Crane flowing gently through its centre. Today there is no ford but a bridge, which used to mark the crossing into Middlesex (the Middlesex crest is still carved into the stone) and today marks the boundary between the boroughs of Hounslow and Hillingdon, the latter being London's second largest borough, though perhaps one of its least well known.

Services
There is a Tesco **supermarket** (daily 6am-11pm) on the LOOP and a *café* or two too – though most walkers will presumably prefer their cappuccino without a side-order

of screaming turbine, and will thus shuffle on to the next pit stop.

Cranford's proximity to Heathrow means it also has plenty of accommodation options such as *Moxy London Heathrow* (🖥 marriott.com) and *DoubleTree by Hilton Hotel London Heathrow Airport* (🖥 hilton.com) – dogs are welcome at both.

Transport   [see map pp42-3]
Buses running along the A4 Bath Rd include the: No 81 (Slough to Hounslow via Harmondsworth; daily 4-5/hr); No 105 (Heathrow Airport to Greenford via Southall; daily 4-5/hr); 111 (Heathrow Airport to Kingston-upon-Thames via Hounslow East, Hounslow, Whitton, Hanworth, Hampton, Hampton Court & Hampton Wick; daily 4/hr); 222 (Uxbridge to Hounslow via West Drayton & West Hounslow; daily 5-6/hr) and H98 (Hounslow to Hayes End via Hounslow West & Great West Road, Hayes, and Hayes & Harlington station; daily 4-6/hr).

Cranford Park

Whatever direction you're coming from, it's a relief to enter Cranford Park. It's a bit of a surprise too, to find such a large and peaceful place thriving amongst the housing estates. Even the roar of the planes overhead doesn't seem so intrusive here as you stroll along the Crane via paths cut into the long grass, with meadows stretching away to the west. At the northern end of the park is a **visitor centre** with **toilets**.

St Dunstan's Church and Cranford House stables   [Map 22, p131]

At Cranford Park's northern end is **St Dunstan's Church**, with a 16th-century **tower** housing a 14th-century bell. The church is perhaps best known today as the place where the ashes of troubled comedy genius Tony Hancock are buried, thanks largely to the efforts of fellow satirist Willie Rushton, who brought them back home from Australia following Hancock's suicide in 1968.

The most substantial **remains of Cranford House**, the centre of the estate from which the park was carved, are the **stables** next to the church. The circle of benches in front of the stables are a decent place for a picnic, with the stables themselves doing a reasonable job of screening you from the noise of the M4, just a few paces away under the stable arch. The park continues to the north of the M4, though this strip is officially called **Dog Kennel Covert** for this is where the manor's dog kennels once stood.

Bus No 195 (Brentford to Hillingdon Heath via Hanwell, Southall, Cranford, Hayes & North Hillingdon; daily 5/hr) travels along North Hyde Rd, at the northern end of Dog Kennel Covert.

Between Cranford Park and the Grand Union Canal

If you're coming from Cranford you have to tackle a particularly unpleasant piece of pavement strolling, past a rubbish-strewn pedestrianised area leading down to a subway under the A312 (which you don't take). It is with no small amount of relief that you eventually turn off the highway and unwind down the switchback ramps to reach the towpath of the Grand Union Canal. The distance from here to the northern end of this stage by the turn-off to Hayes & Harlington station is just half a straightforward mile (800m) away. Before tackling that, however, head south for a few metres from the ramp and you'll come to **Bulls Bridge Junction** – where the Grand Union meets the Regent's Canal (see box p130).

ROUTE GUIDE AND MAPS

❏ THE GRAND UNION CANAL

The Grand Union runs for 137 miles between Brentford, on the Thames in London, and the heart of Birmingham. Contrary to popular belief, it's more than just a single canal, but is in fact an amalgamation of 10 separate waterways, and has many 'arms' branching off to places such as Leicester, Aylesbury, Slough and Northampton.

The canal was actually born out of a sense of panic. With railways having taken the place of much of the canal system at the end of the 19th century, and with roads emerging as a threat too, the owners of several smaller canals decided that the only way to survive was to amalgamate. The largest of these canals was **Grand Junction**, which had been operating in 1805, between Birmingham and London. In 1894 the owners of Grand Junction bought the canals which together make up the 41-mile Leicester Line, then in 1929 they were joined by **Regent's Canal**, an 8½-mile long canal through North London from west (Paddington) to east (Limehouse Basin). The resulting network of waterways was called the Grand Union Canal, the word 'union' emphasising the fact that this is more than just a single branch. By the way, the point where the LOOP meets the Grand Union is within a few metres of the junction between the Regent's and Grand Junction canals; see p129.

Though little freight is carried by the canal today, the waterway is still popular with tourists and holidaymakers – as well, of course, as walkers.

HAYES & HARLINGTON　　　[Map 22]

Hayes' most famous resident, George Orwell, who worked as a schoolmaster in Hayes in the early 1930s, described the town as '...*one of the most godforsaken places I have ever struck. The population seems to be entirely made up of clerks who frequent tin-roofed chapels on Sundays and for the rest bolt themselves within doors*.'

LOOP walkers, however, will probably wonder to themselves that if Orwell could be so excoriating about Hayes, whatever would he have made of Cranford?

Services

Because Hayes, for all its noise and litter, isn't so bad, and LOOPers will probably appreciate the fact that everything they might need in Hayes is pretty conveniently close to the trail, including a Tesco **supermarket** (daily 6am-11pm), with **ATM,** right outside the station, which itself is only a couple of hundred metres from the LOOP.

There's also the *Village Café* (☎ 020-8573 5413; Mon-Fri 8am-7pm, Sat & Sun 8am-7pm) away from the road on your right as you're walking from the towpath to the station.

Before that, just at the top of the slope above the towpath, is *The Old Crown* (☎ 020-8813 5553, 🖳 oldcrown-hayes.craft unionpubs.com; 🐕; daily 11am-10pm).

About 200m north there's a Superdrug **chemist** (Mon-Sat 9am-6pm, Sun 11am-5pm), and next door to that a **post office** (Mon-Sat 9am-5pm).

Staycity Aparthotels London Heathrow (🖳 staycity.com/london) is near the Tesco.

Transport　　　[see map pp42-3]

Hayes & Harlington is a stop on GWR's London Paddington to Didcot Parkway **train** service (see p47) and is also on TfL Rail's London Paddington to Heathrow

---

SYMBOLS USED IN TEXT

🐕 Dogs allowed; see pp34-5 for more information
fb signifies places that have a Facebook page (for latest opening hours)
C = walking clockwise　A/C = walking anti-clockwise

BRIDGE 198 & GOOD BIT OF 'STREET ART' THOUGH NOTE CAREFUL 'NON-ATTRIBUTION' TO BANKSY

HAYES

PRINTING HOUSE LANE

LITTER & FLYTIPPING BY CANAL IS A BIG PROBLEM, PARTICULARLY HERE

GRAND UNION CANAL

BRIDGE 199

DAWLEY RD

END/START OF STAGE

WESTERN VIEW

HELTER-SKELTER RAMPS BETWEEN CANAL AND BUSY ROAD

022

1 SUPERDRUG
2 HAYES POST OFFICE
3 THE OLD CROWN
4 THE VILLAGE CAFÉ
5 TESCO & ATM
6 STAYCITY APARTHOTELS LONDON HEATHROW

90, 140, 195, 350, E6, H98, U4, U5

HAYES & HARLINGTON

GRAND UNION CANAL

THE PARKWAY

195

WALK ALONG NOISY PAVEMENT FOR A FEW HUNDRED METRES

0   ¼ mile
0   APPROX SCALE   500m

LITTER-STREWN PATHWAYS IGNORE SUBWAY

NORTH HYDE RD

BULL'S BRIDGE JN, 50M

MAP 22

STABLES – NICE PLACE FOR A PICNIC WITH LOTS OF BENCHES

DOG KENNEL COVERT

J3

M4

HARLINGTON   GO THROUGH ARCH   21   ST DUNSTAN'S

Airport line and when the full Elizabeth Line opens you will be able to travel from here across London to Harold Wood (which is on the LOOP!). Services will be operated by TfL Rail; for more details see p48.

There is no shortage of **buses** departing from Hayes & Harlington station, either, including: No 90 (to Feltham via Hatton Cross; daily 3-5/hr); 140 (to Harrow & Wealdstone via Northolt & South Harrow; daily 4-7/hr); 195 (Brentford to Hillingdon Heath via Hanwell, Southall, Cranford & North Hillingdon; daily 5/hr); 350 (to Heathrow Terminal 5 via Stockley Park, West Drayton & Yiewsley; daily 3/hr); E6 (Greenford to Cranford; daily 4-5/hr); H98 (Hounslow to Hayes End via Hounslow West, Cranford & Hayes; daily 4-6/hr); U4 (to Uxbridge; daily 4-6/hr); and the U5 (to Uxbridge via West Drayton; daily 4-5/hr).

STAGE 11: HAYES & HARLINGTON TO UXBRIDGE [MAPS 22-25]

The **Grand Union Canal** dominates this **7¼-mile stage (11.7km; C & A/C 2¾hrs to 3hrs 20mins)**, which will be music to many walkers' ears. It's an interesting and very historical waterway, after all, with plenty to see along the way. It's also very flat, of course, which makes for some easy strolling and a chance to really eat up the miles. And, like many canals, it's quite photogenic, particularly on a sunny day when the greenery overhangs the canal and the joyful livery of the boats is reflected in the water. This is also true of the **River Colne**, another waterway that the path hugs for much of this stage; you join it at picturesque **Little Britain**, a lake that does indeed bear a passing, cursory resemblance to the shape of this island if you view it from above while squinting. (Take a look at it on Google Earth and you'll see what I mean.)

Another advantage of following the Grand Union is that the **railway stations** that bookend this stage, as well as West Drayton station at about halfway, are all conveniently close to the canal, indeed often just a bridge away, so there's no lengthy hiking involved to make your escape from the LOOP. And while there aren't many facilities actually on the canal or the Colne, civilisation is only moments away for much of the time, with cafés, shops and further transport options aplenty.

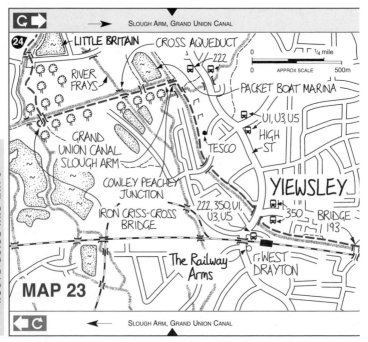

The Grand Union Canal west of Hayes & Harlington

The canal continues its gently drifting course west of Hayes and Harlington. It's a pleasurable, effort-free stroll along the towpath, though the fly-tipping that is rampant around here is dismaying.

Note there's a piece of **graffiti on Bridge 198**. The authorities have covered the work in clear perspex to protect it from the elements (and, more likely, other, less-talented artists who will doubtless want to scrawl over it with their 'tags'). They have, however, been careful *not* to attribute the work to celebrated artist Banksy, even though, if it's not by the man himself, it's clearly by someone from the Banksy 'school'; it even has a rat, a recurring motif in Banksy's work. There's no doubting the skill of the artist, but if I had to guess, I'd say it wasn't by the master himself: the piece lacks the trademark originality and social commentary for which he's renowned. Still, I'm no expert in these matters and if it *was* by him, of course, it would be worth a fortune – though that could lead to some unscrupulous soul trying to remove it from the wall, with presumably terrible consequences for Bridge 198.

Stockley Park [Map 23]

If you're wracking your brains trying to think why you've heard the name Stockley Park mentioned repeatedly over the past year or so, the answer is

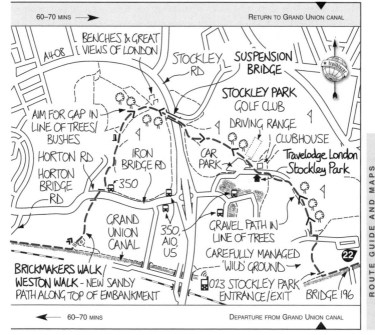

probably because the English Premier League have their **VAR Hub** here. Every time there's a controversial incident in a Premier League game, the video footage of that incident is sent to a panel of three men (a Video Assistant Referee, or VAR, an assistant, or AVAR, and a Replay Operator) to scrutinise and come to a definitive decision. The system has been controversial ever since its introduction for the start of the 2019-2020 season.

For walkers, however, this new business park is more memorable for the **single-column suspension bridge** that conveys both walkers and golfers across from one half of the golf course to the other; and the **viewpoint**, complete with benches, that lies to the west of the bridge, from which you can see over great swathes of central London and beyond.

Should you wish to rest your head here the LOOP passes near *Travelodge London Stockley Park* (💻 travelodge.co.uk). The No 350 (Hayes to Heathrow via West Drayton & Yiewsley; daily 3/hr), A10 (Uxbridge to Heathrow Airport; daily 2-3/hr) and also the U5 (Hayes & Harlington to Uxbridge via West Drayton & Yiewsley; daily 4-5/hr) **bus** services stop on Bennetsfield Rd/ Longwalk Rd near the hotel and also on Iron Bridge Rd.

At the southern end of Stockley Park the LOOP crosses Horton Rd by a **bus** stop (Horton Close) served by the No 350.

Weston Walk
This is a new part of the LOOP. The path takes you along a raised embankment termed **Brickmakers Walk** (though signposted Weston Walk), that celebrates the main industry in Stockley at the beginning of the 19th century, an industry that existed thanks in large part to the clay soil underfoot that was actually called 'brick earth'. Work in the brickmakers' was typically long and hard, with both adults and children as young as seven working up to twelve hours a day, six days a week.

At the western end of the Walk the LOOP rejoins the Grand Union Canal.

Link to West Drayton station
A simple crossing of the canal over Bridge 193 (aka Colham Bridge) brings you to West Drayton **railway station** and its accompanying **bus** station.

You'll find a **pub**, *The Railway Arms* – and also a Boots and various convenience stores, along the adjacent West Drayton High St, with further options opposite down Yiewsley High St.

West Drayton is a stop on TfL's London Paddington to Reading service (see p48; map pp42-3). In addition to the trains several **bus** services call in at the station, including the: No 222 (Uxbridge to Hounslow; daily 5-6/hr); 350 (Hayes to Heathrow via Stockley Park & Yiewsley; daily 3/hr); U1 (to Ruislip via Uxbridge, Ickenham & West Ruislip; daily 2-3/hr); U3 (Uxbridge to Heathrow via Harmondsworth; daily 3-5/hr), and U5 (Hayes to Uxbridge via Hayes & Harlington; daily 4-5/hr).

Yiewsley
Back on the trail, heading from the link you'll find a giant Tesco **superstore** (Mon-Sat 7am-11pm, Sun 11am-5pm) by the canal.

The No 222, 350, U1, U3 & U5 **bus** services (see above) stop in Yiewsley.

The Slough Arm (Grand Union Canal)

At busy **Cowley Peachey Junction**, by **Packet Boat Marina**, the LOOP deviates away from the main canal to take the Slough Arm of the Grand Union, one of the last canals to be dug, as late as 1885, even though the railway had now superseded the canal system in Britain.

The LOOP stays on this Arm for a mere half a mile (800m), though it's enough to take in a cast-iron **aqueduct**, a **pillbox** left over from WWII, and a fine example of a **coal-tax post**. These posts were dotted on the perimeter of 19th-century London, around 12-18 miles from the centre of the city, to mark the boundary of outer London in the 1860s. Beyond this point, taxes on coal had to be paid to the Corporation of London. There were approximately 280 of these posts erected, of which three-quarters remain in situ.

Little Britain   [Map 23, pp132-3; Map 24, p136]

Named after the shape of the lake rather than the comedy series (and if you asked a child to draw the outline of Britain it might indeed resemble the shape of the lake), Little Britain is a **former gravel pit** and a pleasant place for an amble, once you've learnt to block out the noise from the nearby M25. Indeed, on a still day, with the willows reflecting in the lake's glassy surface, it can be rather charming, if often rather busy with day-tripping families. The LOOP actually doesn't spend too much time on the lakeshore, preferring instead to follow the course of the River Colne.

The Colne River   [Map 24, p136; Map 25, p137]

The LOOP stays in **Colne Valley Regional Park** for several miles, between the shores of Little Britain and the outskirts of Harefield, sticking largely to the river's west bank south of Iver Lane, but to its eastern banks after that. Note that when construction of the HS2 line commences there may be some temporary disruption of the LOOP route through Colne Valley Regional Park.

The Colne, incidentally, forms part of the border between Greater London and Buckinghamshire (though at one time this would have been Middlesex, before that county was effectively abolished).

At a business park the river and trail part ways for the LOOP to rejoin the Grand Union Canal on the outskirts of Uxbridge.

UXBRIDGE   [Maps 24-5, pp136-7]

Yet another place on the LOOP that was absorbed into Greater London in 1965, Uxbridge is a logical place to end a stage, with plenty of facilities and good transport connections back to the centre of London.

The name Uxbridge comes from **Wixan's Bridge**, which crossed the Colne near the Swan & Bottle pub (see p138). (The Wixan, incidentally, was a Saxon tribe that settled in the area around the 7th century.) That pub is not the only inn with a historical connection, for the Crown & Treaty (then just called the Crown Inn),

which you pass by on the link path from the LOOP to the station, was the venue for negotiations between Charles I and the parliamentarians. Uxbridge had been chosen for that meeting as it stood between the Parliamentary stronghold of London and the royalist stronghold at Oxford.

By the way, **Kate Fassnidge**, who has a community centre and municipal park named after her in Uxbridge, as well as a giant mural painted in her honour – all visible from the link path – was a local landowner who gave land and properties to the borough.   *(cont'd on p138)*

(cont'd on p138)

ROUTE GUIDE AND MAPS

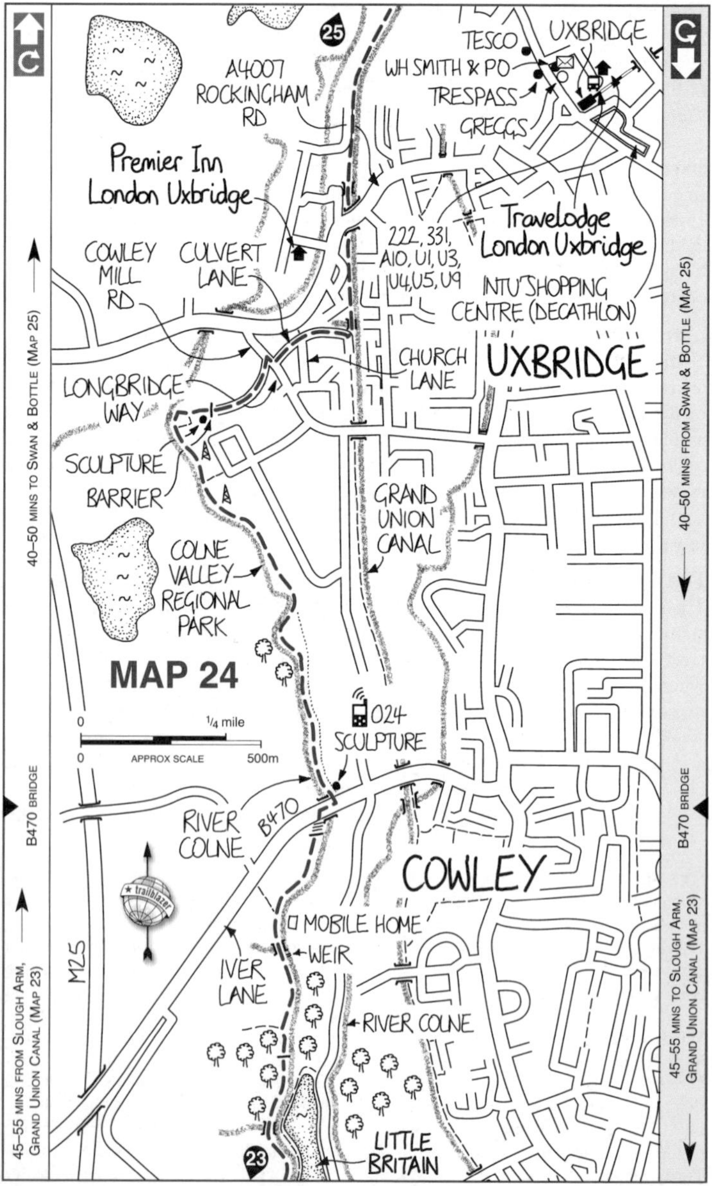
MAP 24
A4007
ROCKINGHAM
RD
Premier Inn
London Uxbridge
TESCO
WH SMITH & PO
TRESPASS
GREGGS
UXBRIDGE
222, 331,
A10, U1, U3,
U4, U5, U9
Travelodge
London Uxbridge
INTU SHOPPING
CENTRE (DECATHLON)
COWLEY
MILL
RD
CULVERT
LANE
CHURCH
LANE
UXBRIDGE
LONGBRIDGE
WAY
SCULPTURE
BARRIER
GRAND
UNION
CANAL
COLNE
VALLEY
REGIONAL
PARK
024
SCULPTURE
0
1/4 mile
0
APPROX SCALE
500m
RIVER
COLNE
B470
COWLEY
MOBILE HOME
WEIR
IVER
LANE
RIVER COLNE
M25
LITTLE
BRITAIN
trailblazer
25
23
40–50 MINS TO SWAN & BOTTLE (MAP 25)
40–50 MINS FROM SWAN & BOTTLE (MAP 25)
B470 BRIDGE
B470 BRIDGE
45–55 MINS FROM SLOUGH ARM, GRAND UNION CANAL (MAP 23)
45–55 MINS TO SLOUGH ARM, GRAND UNION CANAL (MAP 23)

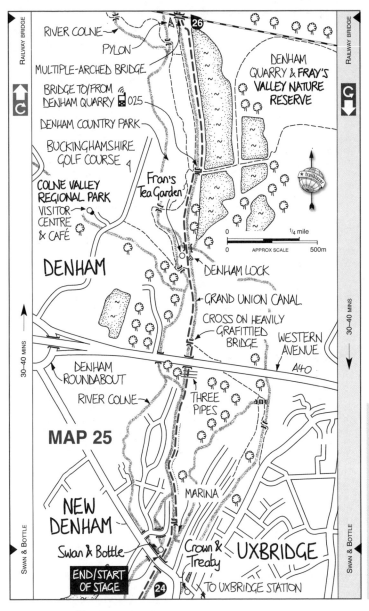

RAILWAY BRIDGE

RAILWAY BRIDGE

RIVER COLNE

PYLON

MULTIPLE-ARCHED BRIDGE

BRIDGE TO/FROM
DENHAM QUARRY

025

DENHAM COUNTRY PARK

BUCKINGHAMSHIRE
GOLF COURSE

COLNE VALLEY
REGIONAL PARK

VISITOR
CENTRE
& CAFÉ

DENHAM

Fran's
Tea Garden

A

26

DENHAM
QUARRY & FRAY'S
VALLEY NATURE
RESERVE

trailblazer

0   ¼ mile

0   500m
APPROX SCALE

DENHAM LOCK

GRAND UNION CANAL

CROSS ON HEAVILY
GRAFITTIED
BRIDGE

WESTERN
AVENUE

A40

30-40 MINS

30-40 MINS

DENHAM
ROUNDABOUT

RIVER COLNE

MAP 25

NEW
DENHAM

Swan & Bottle

END/START
OF STAGE

24

THREE
PIPES

MARINA

Crown &
Treaty

UXBRIDGE

TO UXBRIDGE STATION

SWAN & BOTTLE

SWAN & BOTTLE

ROUTE GUIDE AND MAPS

UXBRIDGE   (cont'd from p135)
Services

You'll pass by most things you need on your way between the LOOP and the station, including a Boots the **chemist** (Mon-Sat 9am-6pm, Sun 10.30am-5.30pm), a **post office** in WH Smith (Mon-Sat 9am-5.30pm, Sun 11am-3pm), and a Tesco **supermarket** (Mon-Sat 7am-10pm, Sun noon-6pm).

There are a couple of **outdoor/ trekking shops** too, including Trespass (Mon-Fri 10am-6pm, Sat 9am-6pm, Sun 11am-5pm), in Pavilions Shopping Centre, and a Decathlon (Mon-Sat 9.30am-6pm, Sun 10.30am-5pm), in Intu Shopping Centre just beyond the station.

There's a good pub right at the end of the stage where you leave the canal to reach Uxbridge station. *The Swan & Bottle* (Map 25; ☎ 01895-234047, 🖳 chefandbrewer .com; 🐾 on lead) is a large place with some outdoor seating and serves food daily 11.30am-9pm.

For accommodation *Premier Inn London Uxbridge* (🖳 premierinn.com) is on the River Colne near the A4007 (south-west of the tube station) and *Travelodge London Uxbridge* (🖳 travelodge.co.uk) is near the tube station.

Transport   [see map pp42-3]

Uxbridge is the western terminus of branches of both the **Metropolitan Line** and the **Piccadilly Line**, so you don't have to wait long for a train to central London.

Bus services stopping at or near the station include: No 222 (to Hounslow via Yiewsley, West Drayton, Cranford & West Hounslow; daily 5-6/hr); 331 (to Ruislip via Denham, South Harefield, Harefield, Batchworth Heath & Northwood; daily 2-3/hr); A10 (to Heathrow Airport via Hillingdon; daily 2-3/hr); UI (West Drayton to Ruislip via Ickenham & West Ruislip; daily 2-3/hr); U3 (to Heathrow Airport via West Drayton & Harmondsworth; daily 3-5/hr); U4 (to Hayes via Hayes & Harlington; daily 4-6/hr); U5 (to Hayes & Harlington via Yiewsley, West Drayton & Stockley Park; daily 4-5/hr) and U9 (to Harefield via Ickenham; Mon-Sat 3/hr, Sun 1/hr).

❑ UXBRIDGE ENGLISH DICTIONARY

If you look up Uxbridge on Wikipedia, you'll find that the town is rightly renowned as the administrative headquarters of the London Borough of Hillingdon. It is also a town of some historical import, with Charles I and the Parliamentarians negotiating here during the Civil War (see p135). All of which is worth celebrating, of course. But if there's one thing that Uxbridge is best known for, at least amongst listeners of Radio 4, it is *Uxbridge English Dictionary*. This spoof dictionary features as a round in the long-running comedy panel show, *I'm Sorry I Haven't a Clue*, where contestants have to think up 'alternative' definitions to words.

Here are a few of my favourites:

Accomplish: a drunken sidekick
Befuddle: a tight group of cattle
Croquette: a tiny little crocodile
Dictaphone: someone you really don't like calling
Economist: cheap fog
Falsetto: fake ice-cream
Ghoulish: Hungarian stew that comes back to haunt you
Hobnob: cooking accident
Intercontinental: someone who has wet themselves all over the world
Juniper: Did you bite that woman?

STAGE 12: UXBRIDGE TO WEST HAREFIELD   [MAPS 25-27]

On this **5-mile stage (8km; C & A/C 1½hrs to 1hr 50mins)** the LOOP continues to hug the Grand Union Canal, never straying too far from it until the last
few hundred metres. It's an untaxing, if largely unenthralling trudge, though the
canal certainly feels more rural now than it did on the previous stage, which is
a blessing. Highlights are few – though I'm a fan of Fran's Tea Garden, one of
several **cafés** on this stage; but, by the same token, there's not much to moan
about on this section either.

South Harefield is the most convenient place to escape by **bus** if you need
to, but the stage is relatively short and relatively straightforward, so, many will
want to combine it with Stage 13, especially as the public transport connections
at the end of this stage, Harefield West, are very limited. If you have the requi-
site time and energy, I think it's a good idea too.

Denham Lock & Country Park
About half a mile (800m) north of Uxbridge the Colne flows into and feeds the
Grand Union canal. Nearby, a path separates off the towpath to head west to
Denham Country Park and, 10 minutes away, **Colne Valley Park Visitor
Centre** (🖳 colnevalleypark.org.uk; Apr-Oct Mon-Fri 9.30am-4pm, Sat, Sun &
school hols to 5pm; Nov-Mar daily 10.30am-3.30pm), which has a natural his-
tory exhibition, its own *café* (daily 11am-3pm) and toilets.

If you are only interested in the last two items, it's probably best you stick
to the LOOP for at **Denham Lock** there's the idyllic *Fran's Tea Garden* (☎
01895-271070; fb; 🐾 on lead; summer Wed-Sun 10.30am-5.30pm, winter
Wed-Sun 11am-4pm). It's a lovely looking place with a delightful garden in
which to sit and fill your face with their homemade cakes.

Denham Quarry and Frays Valley Nature Reserve
The LOOP takes a brief diversion away from the towpath to visit this nature
reserve, which lies just a few metres to the east of the canal. The reserve is made
up of **four large lakes**, former gravel pits that now house an abundance of
wildlife, with waterfowl including grebe, shoveler, tufted duck and pochard,
while cormorants roost in the trees above. The lake also has sailing and fishing
clubs, though swimming is not allowed and dogs should be kept on leads.

South Harefield   [Map 26, p140]
North of Harefield Marina the LOOP leaves the canal towpath once more to
reach Moorhall Rd in South Harefield. On the road is Widewater Place where
there's a **café**, *Thought 4 Food* (☎ 07980 714458, 🖳 www.thought4food.co
.uk/widewater-cafe; Mon-Fri 8am-3pm), and **toilets**.

The LOOP returns to the canal via the bridge, with the large pub garden of
The Bear on the Barge (☎ 01895-831407, 🖳 www.thebearonthebarge.com; 🐾
bar area; food daily 11am-9pm) backing onto the towpath.

The No 331 **bus** (Ruislip to Uxbridge via Northwood, Batchworth Heath &
Denham; daily 2-3/hr) stops near the front door of The Bear.

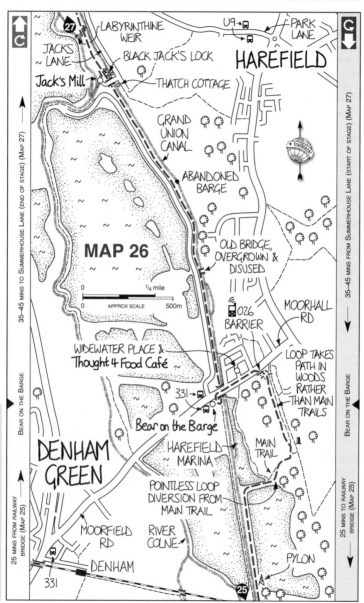

Black Jack's Lock

You can still see the 17th-century part-timber-framed **mill house**, now a listed building, by this lock, with the Colne River once again also making an appearance. The place is now a **café**, *Jack's Mill* (☎ 01895-822205, 🖳 jacksmillpantry .co.uk; Mon-Fri 9.30am-4.30pm, Sat & Sun 9.30am-6pm; 🐾). It also used to offer B&B and was one of the more charming accommodation options along the LOOP, with views over either the canal or neighbouring Troy Lake. However, at the time of writing the accommodation was only let as a whole property.

West Harefield   [Map 27, pp142-3]

By **Coppermill Bridge** is the dog-friendly *Coy Carp* (☎ 01895-821471, 🖳 vintageinn.co.uk; 🐾; food daily noon-8.30pm) a pub that was formerly known as the Fisheries, and which actually pre-dates the canal. Regardless of whether you visit the pub, the bridge is still an important landmark on the LOOP, for it's here that the path says a fond farewell to the Grand Union Canal (or, of course, an even fonder 'hello' if you're walking the trail in the opposite direction!). Five minutes and a steep climb later, you're also saying goodbye/hello to this stage, the walk ending at the junction of Coppermill Lane and Summerhouse Lane.

Annoyingly, it's one of those stages where the **transport** connections are, to say the least, rather tenuous, but you can continue up Park Lane for 200m to a turning circle, where the U9 **bus** (Uxbridge to Harefield via Ickenham; Mon-Sat 3/hr, Sun 1/hr) stops. More options are a further kilometre away in Harefield village.

STAGE 13: WEST HAREFIELD TO MOOR PARK   [MAPS 27-28]

The most memorable part of this **4¾-mile hike (7.6km; C: 1hr 40mins to 2hrs 5mins, A/C: 1hr 35mins to 2hrs)** about the unhurried hills of Hertfordshire is that, in places at least, it really feels like you're in the English countryside, and the capital feels a long, long way away. True, there is still some lengthy road walking to do, mainly through the very salubrious suburbs of **Moor Park**. But there are also parts where you're surrounded by hawthorn hedgerows, not houses, and it's horses and not humans that will be watching your progress for much of the stage. There are some lovely sylvan stretches along the trail too, including venerable **Park Wood** and the restored **Bishop's Wood**, a previously neglected brush of trees that's now home to the rare purple emperor butterfly.

In addition to this natural splendour there are also a couple of **pubs** worthy of your attention; and if you really have to leave the stage before the end you can do so by catching a **bus** from Batchworth Heath.

Summerhouse Lane

If you're starting your stage at Summerhouse Lane, your first job is to climb out of Colne Valley, which you've been enjoying since Little Britain. It's a steep climb which may cause you to curse those on Colne Valley Trail, who have the much easier task of continuing north. Hillingdon Trail, however, will be your companion for a little while longer as both trails follow Summerhouse Lane as it bends up the hill.

Park Wood

Overlooking Colne Valley at the top of the climb is Park Wood, a surprisingly ancient coppiced wood flanked by horse fields and, later on, **allotments**. Indeed, the official website describes it as 'possibly the most varied piece of woodland in Middlesex', and while of course they may be biased – and the county of Middlesex doesn't really exist anymore – there's no doubting it's a charming place, particularly in spring when the bluebells are flourishing. The wood is actually located behind the famous **Harefield Hospital**, the largest specialist heart and lung centre in the UK.

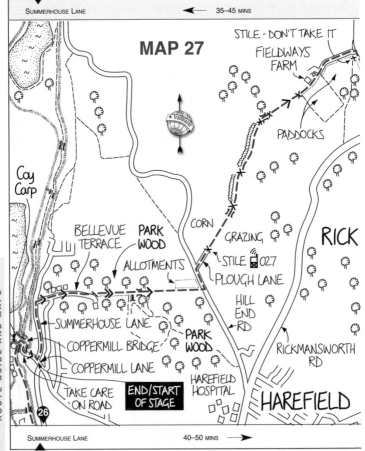

SUMMERHOUSE LANE   ←   35–45 MINS

MAP 27

STILE - DON'T TAKE IT

FIELDWAYS FARM

PADDOCKS

Coy Carp

BELLEVUE TERRACE   **PARK WOOD**

CORN

GRAZING   **RICK**

ALLOTMENTS

STILE 027

PLOUGH LANE

HILL END RD

SUMMERHOUSE LANE

COPPERMILL BRIDGE   **PARK WOOD**

RICKMANSWORTH RD

COPPERMILL LANE

HAREFIELD HOSPITAL

TAKE CARE ON ROAD

END/START OF STAGE

HAREFIELD

26

SUMMERHOUSE LANE   40–50 MINS →

ROUTE GUIDE AND MAPS

Fieldways Farm, Rickmansworth

Between Plough Lane and the Rose & Crown pub (see p144) the path traces a 'proper' countryside route through fields, past hedgerows and over stiles, with both cattle and corn thriving in the neighbouring fields. The fields belong to Cripps House Farm, off the trail to the west. The farm that *is* on the route, Fieldways Farm, is actually in Hertfordshire; the border between the county and London runs along the substantial hedge, that you cross through via a stile, immediately south of the farmhouse. The farm itself is surrounded by **paddocks**, but these are no normal horses. This is the home of Steve Dent Stunts,

ROSE & CROWN   ← 35–45 MINS   A404

KEEP TO FENCE OUTSIDE PADDOCK

GAP IN TREES HERE

LONDON RD

Ye Olde Greene Manne

HAREFIELD RD

THE NINE OF HERTS GOLF CLUB

FIELD

A404

WHITE POST

BATCHWORTH HEATH

BISHOP'S WOOD

LONE HAWTHORN - THE PATH INTO/OUT OF WOODS EMERGES OPPOSITE HERE

WOODCOCK HILL

Rose & Crown

28

MANSWORTH

WHITE HILL

331

RICKMANSWORTH RD

MUDDY SECTION WITH POSTS BOTH SIDES

0   1/4 mile
0   APPROX SCALE   500m

ROSE & CROWN   35–45 MINS →   A404

suppliers of horses, carriages and period horse tack to the film and television industry. The farm has over 80 'celebrity' horses, and their collective CV is an impressive one, with roles in everything from *Gladiator*, *Casino Royale* (the modern Daniel Craig version) and *The League of Gentlemen*. Just like their human counterparts, these four-legged thespians can be a bit sniffy about mere mortals getting too close, so the path plots a deliberate course around – and not through – the paddocks.

Rose & Crown pub, Rickmansworth
The LOOP crosses right through the car park of this quiet and humble 17th-century country *pub* (☎ 01923-773826, 🖳 roseandcrownrickmansworth.co.uk; 🐾 bar area; food Mon-Fri noon-4pm & 5-9pm, Sat noon-8pm & 5-9.30pm, Sun noon-7pm) with a pleasant beer garden. It probably appears too early in your day's walk for you to be considering a pint – but if you can find an excuse to stop there are certainly worse places to pause for an hour. Or more.

Bishop's Wood
You would never think, looking at Bishop's Wood today, that just half a dozen years ago these woods were in a rather parlous state. The problems really started in World War II, when the woods were understandably neglected – Britain, at the time had more pressing concerns. Fast-forward to the 1960s and well-meaning managers planted quick-growing conifers in order to restore the 'look' of the woods and make them appear healthy and vigorous. Unfortunately, this had the unwanted outcome of leaving the floor of these woods with little light, which impacted significantly on their biodiversity. As a final insult, it even lost its status as an SSSI.

Thankfully, in these enlightened times efforts are being made to remove the conifers and replace them with more native species and these woods are proving that they don't need much encouragement to thrive again. Already it's become home to such rarities as the **wild service tree**, *Sorbus torminalis*, and rarely seen native butterflies such as the white admiral, silver-washed fritillary and even the purple emperor. which is so rarely seen due to its preference for the treetops. Your best chance of seeing one is mid morning, when they may descend to the ground to feed on salt from animal dung.

Batchworth Heath
The heath is dominated by a pub that may date from the late 16th or early 17th centuries. Always known as the Green Man, though now, alas, adjusted to *Ye Olde Greene Manne* (☎ 01923-826433, 🖳 vintageinn.co.uk; 🐾; food daily noon-8.30pm), it's dog-friendly and quite attractive, despite its location by the busy A404. Beyond the pub is a grand entrance leading to the **Moor Park Mansion**, now a golf course.

Opposite is the **Prince of Wales** pub, now closed, a handsome flint-walled building that's in good shape, especially when one considers that half of it was blown up by a flying bomb during WWII. Back across the A404 again there's a second **coal-tax post** (see p135), indicating that, once again, you're close to the boundary of Greater London.

Buses leave from opposite Ye Old Green Manne: the most reliable service is the No 331 (Ruislip to Uxbridge via Northwood, Harefield, South Harefield & Denham; daily 2-3/hr).

Northwood

It will be hard for people of a certain vintage – let's say 50 years old or more – to resist the temptation to take a detour off the LOOP for a few metres to the corner of Ebury Close and Kewferry Rd. The house on the corner at No 55 was the location for the '70s classic sitcom *The Good Life*, starring Richard Briers and the always-mesmerising (at least to my boyhood self) Felicity Kendall as a couple looking to escape the rat race by running their own farm in the middle of suburbia, in order to realise their ambition of becoming self-sufficient; and their neighbours, played by Penelope Keith and Paul Eddington, who weren't only very much part of the rat race, but appeared to be winning it too.

Nearby there's a **B&B** right on the LOOP called ***Leafy Suburban*** (🖥 leafy suburbanbedandbreakfast.com; 1S/1D en suite, 2D shared facilities) suggesting that a) the producers chose the correct location for their filming; and b) the locals round here are happy to poke gentle fun at themselves.

MOOR PARK   **[Map 28, pp146-7]**
Situated in Hertfordshire, Moor Park is of course named after the mansion (see opposite), the grounds of which are now occupied by the golf course that the LOOP passes right through.

Facilities within easy walking distance of the LOOP are few, though by the station there is a small **store**, Moor Park Fine Foods (Mon-Sat 10am-5pm) with its own **hot-drinks machine**. When I visited, the **post office** nearby was operating limited hours (Mon-Fri 1.30-5.30pm) due to Coronavirus.

Transport   **[see map pp42-3]**
Moor Park station is on a branch of the Metropolitan line of the London Underground, with regular services to central London but also to Watford in one direction, and Amersham/Chesham in the other.

STAGE 14: MOOR PARK TO HATCH END   [MAPS 28-29]

This is another stage where you'll spend much of your time sheltering under a woodland canopy, for a large part of this 3¾-mile stage **(6km; C & A/C 1hr 35mins to 1hr 55mins)** is spent in enticing **Oxhey Woods**, a 98-hectare (242-acre) nature reserve divided into three tracts by two busy roads, Prestwick Rd and Oxhey Drive. The trail passes through all three parts of the wood and performs a complete traverse of them, from north-west to south-east.

Woodland on the LOOP is nothing special, of course, but parts of Oxhey Woods are rather special. For it's believed that certain sections are properly ancient, having been continuously wooded for several hundred years, and possibly several thousand years – and maybe even as far back as the last Ice Age, 11,500 years ago.

There are a couple of other highlights to this stage. Near the end there's the Victorian author **Edward Bulwer-Lytton's lovely house**, which can be glimpsed from the LOOP through the trees. And just before Oxhey Woods is **South Oxhey Playing Fields**, a large open expanse of meadow and woodland that is an ideal location for a picnic, particularly as just before it you can buy the ingredients from the stage's only **supermarket** and **baker**.

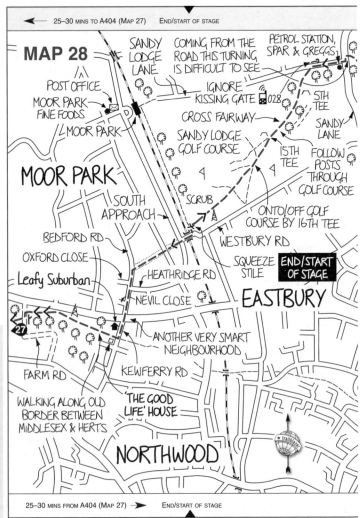

The A4125, Northwood

There's a 24hr petrol station and **Spar supermarket** with a *Gregg's* (Mon-Fri 6.30am-3.30pm, Sat from 7am, Sun 8am-3pm) and an **ATM** on the corner of the A4125 and Sandy Lodge Lane (named after the golf club that you will have walked through if you started this stage at Moor Park).

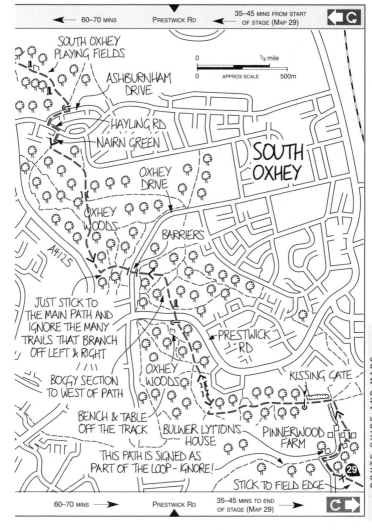

← 60-70 MINS   PRESTWICK RD   ←   35-45 MINS FROM START
OF STAGE (MAP 29)

SOUTH OXHEY
PLAYING FIELDS

ASHBURNHAM
DRIVE

0   ¼ mile
0   APPROX SCALE   500m

HAYLING RD
NAIRN GREEN

SOUTH
OXHEY

OXHEY
DRIVE

OXHEY
WOODS

A4125

BARRIERS

JUST STICK TO
THE MAIN PATH AND
IGNORE THE MANY
TRAILS THAT BRANCH
OFF LEFT & RIGHT

PRESTWICK
RD

BOGGY SECTION
TO WEST OF PATH

OXHEY
WOODS

KISSING GATE

BENCH & TABLE
OFF THE TRACK

BULWER LYTTON'S
HOUSE

PINNERWOOD
FARM

THIS PATH IS SIGNED AS
PART OF THE LOOP - IGNORE!

STICK TO FIELD EDGE

29

60-70 MINS →   PRESTWICK RD   35-45 MINS TO END
OF STAGE (MAP 29) →

ROUTE GUIDE AND MAPS

South Oxhey Playing Fields

The name for this 7.2-hectare (18 acres) of semi-natural woodland, wildflower meadow and manicured lawn is a bit misleading, for playing fields actually form a relatively minor part of it. The LOOP describes an arc round the south-western corner of the fields, brushing against the edge of several woodland patches, and, temptingly, several benches too.

Oxhey Woods Local Nature Reserve

You'll need to follow the signs closely, and the map on p147, to negotiate your way through these massive 98-hectare (242-acre) woods. Your route through the woods is divided into three by two fast roads. If you negotiate the woods correctly, at the end you'll reach the woods' south-eastern corner, the border of London and some horse fields.

Bulwer-Lytton's house

There is a huddle of large and attractive houses to the south-east of Oxhey Woods. The centrepiece is Pinnerwood House, one-time home of Victorian author and MP Edward Bulwer-Lytton. Celebrated and successful in his day, his books are now little-read, though his best-known phrases are still common currency. Expressions such as '*the great unwashed*' and '*the pen is mightier than the sword*' are all from the pen of Bulwer-Lytton. However, his reputation has not held up well, to the extent that there's now an annual competition, named in his honour and organised by San Jose University (USA), which is given to the contestant who can come up with the *worst* opening sentence – possibly because Bulwer-Lytton himself penned the line '*It was a dark and stormy night*'.

Between the house and the end of the stage, the latter marked by a signpost, stile and path that leads to Hatch End, there are several **horse fields** which can be very muddy after heavy rain.

HATCH END   [Map 29, pp150-1]

As you make your way to the station from the LOOP, along Grimsdyke Rd and onto the A40, you'll come to several shops that may be of interest.

Services

There's a **post office** opposite the end of Grimsdyke Rd, and Village **Pharmacy** (Mon, Tue & Thur 9am-6.15pm, Wed & Fri to 6pm, Sat to 5.30pm) a little further along.

Still further along, across the road, is a **Tesco Express** (daily 7am-11pm), while nearer the station is a Wetherspoons pub, ***The Moon and Sixpence*** (☎ 020-8420 1074, 🖥 jdwetherspoon.com; food daily 8am-9pm); as with all Wetherspoons pubs, food is served all day and is very good value, but no dogs are allowed across the threshold.

Transport   [see map pp42-3]

Hatch End station is in Zone 6 and a stop on the London Overground (Euston to Watford **railway** line; see p47).

Bus-wise, services travelling west along Uxbridge Rd are heading to South Harrow; H12 (Stanmore to South Harrow via Rayners Lane, Pinner & Harold Weald; daily 4-6/hr) or H14 (to Harrow via Harold Weald & Headstone; daily 4-6/hr).

STAGE 15: HATCH END TO ELSTREE & BOREHAMWOOD
[MAPS 29-31]

I found it remarkably easy to lose my way on this **8¾ mile stage (14.1km; C & A/C 3hrs 10mins to 3hrs 40mins)**. The woods of **Grim's Dyke** are dark and overgrown, the path is rarely straight, the signposts infrequent, and there are plenty of alternative paths to tempt you away from the correct one. I've done my best to provide comprehensive instructions on the map but don't be surprised if you find yourself stumbling around in the undergrowth for a few minutes on today's trail. Staggering around lost in unfamiliar surroundings is always quite unsettling, of course, and it doesn't help that these woods have an eerie, sombre atmosphere, and a certain amount of infamy, too, given that this was the place where a high-profile Victorian celebrity lost his life in a tragic accident. Should you, too, lose your way, perhaps you can distract yourself by musing on the as-yet unknown origins and purpose of the **Iron Age earthwork** that runs through these woods, and after which they are named.

The rest of the stage can't quite match up to Grim's Dyke in terms of drama, consisting as it does not of one but two **golf courses**, the rather neglected **Aldenham Reservoir** and some lengthy stretches of **road walking**. Indeed, the whole stage rather dribbles on and then peters out in pretty unspectacular fashion. Still, there's a good **pub** on Old Redding Rd where you can sit and savour some great views, and places where you can catch a **bus** or **train** away from the LOOP altogether.

B4542/Little Oxhey Lane
One of the longer and more tedious sections of road walking on the LOOP is at least brightened by the presence of a **Carpenders Park Garden Centre** and its *Evergreen Café* (☎ 020-8420 1959, 🖥 carpenders.co.uk/evergreen-cafe; 🐕 on lead; Mon-Sat 9am-4.30pm, Sun 10am-3.30pm), a welcome shelter on a rainy day. The centre sits at the eastern end of Little Oxhey Lane, at the junction with Oxhey Lane.

Grim's Dyke Golf Course
Grim's Dyke Golf Course straddles both London and Hertfordshire, so on this course it really is possible to hit a ball into the next county. Those in charge here insist you follow the white posts through their land, but these posts are intermittent to say the least. Still, as long as you follow the hedge on the course's northern side (ie on your left if you're walking the LOOP clockwise) you'll be on the right track.

Grim's Dyke
Consisting of an old mud bank and a ditch, this earthwork, perhaps more commonly called **Grim's Ditch**, was built in around 300BC during the Iron Age. Its purpose, like many similar earthworks across the south-east of England, is unknown. The LOOP actually walks on top of the bank, with the ditch on your right if you're walking the LOOP clockwise and have just come from the golf course that shares the Dyke's name.

These woodlands form part of Grim's Dyke Estate, once owned by lyricist William Schwenck Gilbert, of Gilbert & Sullivan fame. It was Gilbert who installed the boating lake that you see as you walk through the woods. Unfortunately, his decision to build the lake proved fateful. In 1911 a teenager, Ruby Preece, got into trouble while swimming in the water. Gilbert raced to save her, but in doing so had a heart attack and drowned. In almost every description of the Dyke and the grounds of the house today the writers talk about how there is a melancholy air to the place and it's hard to disagree. The

dark, brooding atmosphere of the lake and woods clearly pervaded into the house, as several **Hammer House of Horror films** were shot in the property. The lake is dark and still and the whole place is overgrown and neglected.

The very secluded house is now ***Grim's Dyke Hotel*** (☎ 020-8385 3100, 🖥 grimsdyke.com; 🐕; main building 9D all en suite; garden lodge 38/D or Tw all en suite), part of the Best Western (Plus) chain. In the main property, one room boasts a four-poster bed. Rates are either Saver (from £72.90 inc breakfast) which are paid at the time of booking, or Flexible (from £90) paid at the hotel;

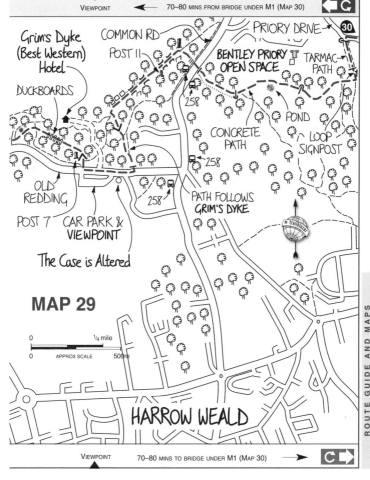

single occupancy is the room rate. Regular performances of Gilbert & Sullivan operettas are held at the hotel.

Old Redding
If you manage to find your way out of the woods – no guarantee, whichever direction you're coming from! – you land up at a road called Old Redding, where there's a great **viewpoint** overlooking Harrow on the Hill, Wembley Stadium and Heathrow, and a pub with a curious name, *The Case is Altered* (☎ 020-8954 1002, 🖳 thecaseisaltered.co.uk; 🐾; food Mon-Sat noon-9pm, Sun to 8pm); apparently this is a legal phrase and a name that is common to several pubs in England, though what the exact change in circumstances was that merited the name in this instance is uncertain.

Common Road
It's easy to get lost when taking the path through the wood between Old Redding and Common Rd, largely because signs are scarce (at least they were at the time of research); once again, follow the instructions on Map 29 (see pp150-51) carefully to keep to the trail.

From Common Rd you can catch **bus** No 258 (daily approx 4/hr) heading north to Bushey and Watford Junction stations and south to South Harrow via Harrow & Wealdstone & Harrow.

Bentley Priory Open Space
You largely follow a tarmac path running along the top of the slope through this SSSI. The park is named after **Bentley Priory**, built in the late 18th century, though only after demolishing the original Augustinian priory which had existed since the 12th century. However, it is its associations with the RAF that give this impressive creamy-yellow building – the one with the clocktower on top – it's main claim to fame. The RAF were installed there in 1926, soon after they had been formed, and by 1936 it was the headquarters of Fighter Command. So it was from here that the RAF, under Air Chief Marshal Hugh Dowding, plotted their successful defence of this island in 1940 during the Battle of Britain; a victory that is celebrated in the small **museum** (🖳 bentleypriorymuseum .org.uk; Wed & Sat 10am-4.30pm; £8, prebooked tickets only at time of research) within the house (though off the LOOP).

Stanmore Hill & Cricket Club   [Map 30]
Stanmore Cricket Club is one of the oldest in the county, having been established in the middle of the 19th century. The path passes close to the pitch and by a couple of **brewers ponds**, used as a reservoir for the local 18th-century Stanmore Brewery.

Upper and Lower Spring Pond
These two ponds just off the road in Stanmore Little Common have been here since the Romans; indeed, Upper Spring Pond is often called Caesar's Pond (though he wouldn't have come here).

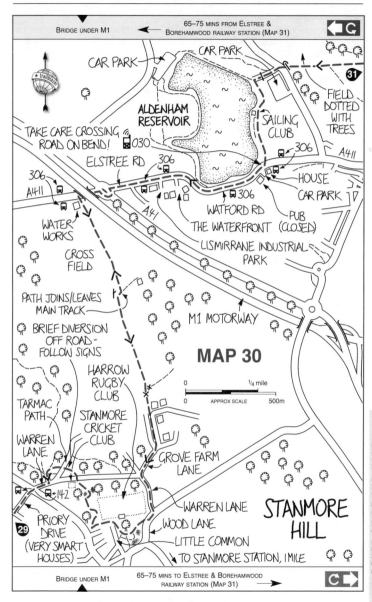

BRIDGE UNDER M1

65–75 MINS FROM ELSTREE & BOREHAMWOOD RAILWAY STATION (MAP 31)

31

CAR PARK

CAR PARK

CAR PARK

ALDENHAM RESERVOIR

SAILING CLUB

FIELD DOTTED WITH TREES

A411

TAKE CARE CROSSING ROAD ON BEND! 030

ELSTREE RD 306

306

A411

306

306

HOUSE

CAR PARK

WATER WORKS

WATFORD RD

THE WATERFRONT

PUB (CLOSED)

CROSS FIELD

LISMIRRANE INDUSTRIAL PARK

PATH JOINS/LEAVES MAIN TRACK

M1 MOTORWAY

BRIEF DIVERSION OFF ROAD - FOLLOW SIGNS

MAP 30

HARROW RUGBY CLUB

0 ¼ mile

0 APPROX SCALE 500m

TARMAC PATH

STANMORE CRICKET CLUB

WARREN LANE

142

GROVE FARM LANE

29

PRIORY DRIVE (VERY SMART HOUSES)

WARREN LANE

WOOD LANE

LITTLE COMMON

TO STANMORE STATION, 1 MILE

STANMORE HILL

BRIDGE UNDER M1

65–75 MINS TO ELSTREE & BOREHAMWOOD RAILWAY STATION (MAP 31)

ROUTE GUIDE AND MAPS

Link path to Stanmore station

There is a link from the ponds to Stanmore underground station, heading off through **Stanmore Country Park**. However, the station is just shy of a mile away, so unless you have a pressing reason to leave the path at this point, I would stay on it until the end of the stage. The link, which is partially sign-posted, takes you down Dennis Lane and then into Stanmore Country Park.

All being well, by following the fingerpost along a broad track you should emerge onto Kerry Avenue; follow this to Kerry Court – the station is on the southern side.

Stanmore is the northernmost station on the **Jubilee Underground line** (daily 15-20/hr) to Stratford through the centre of the capital (see map pp42-3).

The No 142 **bus** (Watford Junction to Brent Cross via Bushey, Stanmore & Edgware; daily 4-7/hr) stops near the junction of Warren Lane and Priory Drive.

Elstree Road

There are (non-TfL) **bus** services along Elstree Rd and given how unpleasant it is to walk along this fast road, it's quite tempting to jump on one, regardless of where it's going. The bus is Sullivan's No 306 (Mon-Sat 2-3/hr, Sun 4-5/day) and it travels between Watford and Borehamwood via Bushey and Elstree & Borehamwood. Note that TfL Travelcards aren't valid.

Aldenham Reservoir

The LOOP walks along the lake's eastern shore; the reservoir was originally dug by French prisoners from the Napoleonic War at the end of the 18th century. Unfortunately, perhaps because they were giving their labour unwillingly, their work was not perfect. In particular, the clay dam they built on the reservoir's northern side has needed constant repairs for much of the subsequent 200 years. The reservoir is now in private hands, but its long-term future remains uncertain.

Watling Street   [Map 31]

When you cross **Elstree Hill North** and the adjacent Radlett Park **Golf Course**, you once again encounter the line of the old Roman road, Watling Street, which, if you're walking the LOOP clockwise and started in Erith, you would have last encountered way back at Crayford (see p68), and again at the playing fields of Sparrow's Den (p91). Since then, the Street has made its way towards central London. It actually disappears at Southwark, south of the Thames, re-emerging again north of Hyde Park, near Marble Arch, at the western end of Oxford St. So nobody is quite sure exactly what route it took through the heart of modern London. What I do know is that after Elstree, it heads via the Midlands towards the Welsh border; making it, at 240 miles, the longest Roman road in Britain, as well as the first road they built on the island.

There's a **bus** stop on Allum Lane and also further along at Fir Tree Close from where you can catch the No 107 (daily 2-4/hr) to New Barnet via Elstree & Borehamwood & High Barnet or, across the road, to Edgware. Alternatively take the 306 (Mon-Sat 2-3/hr, Sun 4-5/day) to Elstree & Borehamwood station or west to Watford via Aldenham Reservoir but this is operated by Sullivan's and since it goes to Watford (Herts) TfL Travelcards aren't valid.

ELSTREE & BOREHAMWOOD
[Map 31]
This odd union of two neighbouring towns always raises more questions than it answers, the two main ones being a) why have the two places been joined together like this? and b) where does Elstree end and Borehamwood begin? Well, the Borehamwood faction actually gets a pretty raw deal out of their relationship.

Though the whole suburb is best known as the home of **Elstree Studios**, all but one of those studios were really in Borehamwood (and the other one was actually in Aldenham, which is separated from Elstree by a reservoir). The railway station is also in Borehamwood, which is actually by far the bigger place, though it has to accept equal billing with Elstree on the station's name, even though the centre of Elstree village is 1¼ miles away.

Services
Facility-wise, there's a Sainsbury's local **supermarket** (daily 7am-11pm) by the roundabout very close to the station.

Round the corner on Theobald St is **The Wellington** (☎ 020-8191 9366, 🖳 the wellingtonborehamwood.co.uk; 🐾; food Mon-Fri noon-2.30pm & 6-8.30pm, Sat noon-9pm, Sun noon-6pm).

Shenley Sandwich Bar & Bakery (☎ 020-8953 4967, 🖳 shenleysandwichbar.co .uk; Mon-Sat 6.30am-4pm) is the best of the eateries near the station.

The shops tend to get smarter and shinier as you move away from the station, and (off Map 31) you can find branches of both **Starbucks** (Mon-Sat 6.30am-6.30pm, Sun 8am-6pm) and **Caffè Nero** (Mon-Sat 7am-4.30pm, Sun 8am-4.30pm) coffee chains. Beyond is Gilbert's (Mon-Thur

❏ **ELSTREE FILM STUDIOS**

A quick scuttle round the railway station's forecourt and adjacent bus terminus will bring you to various information boards dedicated to the careers of Dirk Bogarde, Barbara Windsor, Cliff Richard et al, all of whom owe a great deal to Elstree. But there isn't actually one Elstree Studios. Instead, it's an umbrella term for no fewer than seven studios, past and present, that were based in this Hertfordshire settlement.

The first studios established here were Eldon Avenue Studios, opened by Neptune Film Company way back in 1914. The most famous, however, were either **Elstree Studios** on Borehamwood's Shenley Rd, where the first British talking movie, Alfred Hitchcock's *Blackmail*, was shot in 1929, as well as the first five films in the *Star Wars* franchise and all the *Indiana Jones* films; or **MGM British Studios**, again in Borehamwood, where *2001: A Space Odyssey* was filmed. Indeed, the director Stanley Kubrick, who was notorious for always running over-schedule and over-budget on nearly all his movies, is sometimes blamed for the demise of the studios.

Other hit movies that were created at Elstree include the *Pink Panther* series with Peter Sellers, *The Shining*, *Labyrinth*, *The King's Speech* and *Paddington*. The influence that Elstree Studios has had on the history of film-making cannot be over-estimated. Indeed, Cliff Richard said that the films he made at Elstree were important in helping him to break America. (I know what he means. I watched *Summer Holiday* last night and it almost broke me.)

What is less well-known, perhaps, is the fact that the studios are also used by TV companies: shows such as *Strictly Come Dancing*, *The Voice*, *The Chase*, *Pointless*, *Have I Got News For You?* and *Eastenders* are all made at Elstree.

9am-6.30pm, Fri & Sat to 6pm), a **chemist**. There are lots of hotels in the area catering for everyone involved in the studios; two economical options, on Shenley Rd (but off the map), are **Ibis London Elstree Borehamwood** (🖳 all.accor.com), near the studios, and a bit further away a branch of **Premier Inn** (London Elstree/ Borehamwood; 🖳 premierinn.com).

Transport [see map pp42-3]
Elstree & Borehamwood railway station is one of the more interesting on the LOOP, thanks largely to the way it celebrates its associations with the film industry. If you have to hang around waiting for a train or bus you can read all about the stars of the big and small screen who have worked at Elstree. It's on the Thameslink line (St Albans to Sutton); see p48 for details.

On the eastern side of the station there are **bus** stops for the No 107 (Edgware to New Barnet & High Barnet; daily 2-4/hr); 292 (Colindale to Borehamwood via Edgware; daily 2-3/hr) and 306 (Watford to Borehamwood via Bushey & Elstree; Mon-Sat 2-3/hr, Sun 4-5/day).

❏ **IMPORTANT NOTE – WALKING TIMES**

Unless otherwise specified, **all times in this book refer only to the time spent walking**. You will need to add 20-30% to allow for rests, photography, checking the map, drinking water etc. When planning the day's hike count on 5-7 hours' actual walking.

STAGE 16: ELSTREE & BOREHAMWOOD TO COCKFOSTERS
[MAPS 31-34]

Though this, the longest stage **(11 miles, 17.7km; C: 4hrs 25 mins to 5¼hrs, A/C: 4½hrs to 5hrs 20mins)** of them all, starts off in unpromising fashion, there are a couple of real gems. For one thing, this hike contains perhaps my favourite stretch of walking on the LOOP's northern half. **Totteridge Fields** is a series of former hay meadows, a part of which has become a nature reserve, and *all* of which is an absolute haven of tranquillity surrounded by the otherwise ceaseless din of Barnet. You don't stay in the fields for long, but I advise you to spend as long as you can there, at least if the weather's good, and possibly stop for a picnic too – you'll be glad you did.

What's more, I think this 16th stage has the prettiest and most intriguing village on the entire trail: **Monken Hadley** may only be small but can boast an ancient church, several magnificent properties and a few famous former residents too. What's more, there are some lengthy rolls of green, **King George's Fields** and **Hadley Woods/Folly Farm**, that unfurl down the hillside on either side of the village, and through which you must walk.

True, before you get to any of these treasures you have some lengthy trudging to do, both right at the start, from the station, and **along the A1**. (I have in fact followed here an alternative and far superior route that is suggested by Colin Saunders in his Aurum Press Guide, and which saves a lot of pavement pummelling.) And while the A1/Barnet Way can't be avoided, there is at least some pleasant strolling to be had either side of it, through **Scratchwood** and **Moat Mount Open Space**.

And if the thought of completing an 11-mile hike in one go is unconscionable, you can always divide it by diverting off to the **underground station** at High Barnet (or the railway station at New Barnet), or take a **bus** from Monken Hadley. There are also **refreshments** and **shops** in New Barnet.

Deacon's Hill Rd [Map 31, p155; Map 32, p158]
The official route from Elstree takes you back onto Deacon's Hill Rd and from there onto rapid Barnet Lane and then to Scratchwood (see p158).

Woodcock Hill Village Green alternative route
This alternative route (suggested by Colin Saunders, see above) takes you through a village green that almost definitely will be quite unlike any other green you may have seen before; Woodcock Hill Village Green is actually quite a wild and fairly steep slope of long grass and scrub, through which paths have been mown for walkers to use. The route is perfect for those starting from the station but is also an easy continuation if already on the LOOP,

At the top of the slope, on the path that runs parallel to Barnet Lane, you'll find the **Armada Beacon** (Map 32, p158), so-called because it was one of a chain of beacons that ran all along the south coast and, from there, inland, to warn people of the approaching Spanish Armada in the 16th century (the same Armada that was eventually defeated by Francis Drake – after he'd finished his game of bowls, of course – in 1588). The beacon, which is not an Elizabethan original but stands on a site where the original may have stood, was last lit in 2016 to celebrate the 90th birthday of the Queen.

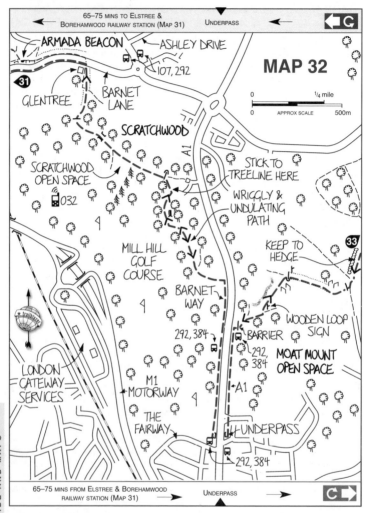

ARMADA BEACON   ASHLEY DRIVE

MAP 32

107, 292

GLENTREE   BARNET LANE

SCRATCHWOOD

0   ¼ mile
0   APPROX SCALE   500m

A1

STICK TO TREELINE HERE

SCRATCHWOOD OPEN SPACE

WRIGGLY & UNDULATING PATH

032

KEEP TO HEDGE

33

MILL HILL GOLF COURSE

WOODEN LOOP SIGN

BARNET WAY

292, 384   BARRIER

292, 384   MOAT MOUNT OPEN SPACE

LONDON GATEWAY SERVICES

M1 MOTORWAY

A1

THE FAIRWAY   UNDERPASS

292, 384

Scratchwood   [Map 32]

It's an unpromising location, squeezed between the M1 and the A1 (not to mention frantic Barnet Lane to the north), but Scratchwood is a **nature reserve** and, if you can block out the drone of traffic, quite the haven. Its gargantuan northern entrance makes it clear that there are deer in the 57-hectare (141-acre) reserve, but there's plenty more besides, including bird species such as nuthatch, lesser whitethroat and the increasingly rare cuckoo. The LOOP takes a fairly meandering course, crossing between Hertfordshire and London at the northern end of the park, where a farm track crosses the path. You also pass along the edge of **Scratchwood Open Space**, also known as **Model Aeroplane Field**.

The No 107 (Edgware station to New Barnet via Elstree & Borehamwood & High Barnet stations; daily 2-4/hr) and 292 (Colindale to Borehamwood via Edgware & Elstree & Borehamwood; daily 2-3/hr) stop on Furzehill Rd; the stop is called Ashley Drive.

Barnet Way/A1

It's with no enthusiasm that walkers find themselves once more having to negotiate a hectic multi-lane thoroughfare, though this one is particularly irritating as there is, like the A30 at Hatton (Map 21, p127), no safe place to cross it where the LOOP emerges, so walkers face a lengthy, stultifying trudge along the pavement to reach a subway to the south. The entire detour is around 1.5km, or just under a mile, and it's a serious contender for the least pleasant mile on the entire LOOP.

There are **bus** stops on the way for the No 292 (see above) and No 384 (Edgware to Cockfosters via High Barnet & New Barnet; daily 2-4/hr).

Moat Mount Open Space

The sign by the entrance to this 'Open Space' indicates that this is the place to join **Dollis Valley Greenwalk**; this walk follows the Dollis Valley and connects at Hampstead Garden Suburb with Stage 11 of the Capital Ring (see box below) so in effect provides a connecting path between the two walks.

If you're walking the LOOP clockwise this is the first time you encounter the waterway that will be your companion for so much of this stage. But for the moment you must satisfy yourself with this sample of the 'greenwalk', which does actually pass by the pond that is the Dollis's source.

❏ THE CAPITAL RING

If the LOOP is proving to be a bit too, well, long for you, its concentric cousin the Capital Ring could be just the trail you're seeking and if you follow the Dollis Valley Greenwalk (see above) you could join it.

Covering 78 miles, the Capital Ring describes a circle around London, just like the LOOP, with the official starting and finishing points located right by the Thames. However, unlike the LOOP the Ring describes a *complete* circle, with Woolwich Foot Tunnel under the Thames allowing walkers to complete their circumambulation of the capital. (Next door to the tunnel entrance is the free Woolwich Ferry, which is an alternative way for Ring Walkers to traverse the Thames, and it has been operating for the small matter of 800 years!)

Where the LOOP tends to hang about in Zones 5 and 6, the Capital Ring prefers to stick to Zones 3 to 4. Highlights include (listed clockwise, from the tunnel) the Thames Barrier, the open expanses of Streatham, Wandsworth and Wimbledon commons, the deer of Richmond Park, the views from Horsenden Hill, the genteel beauty of Hampstead Garden Suburb, Clissold Park, and the River Lee Navigation (a part of which the LOOP also visits – see box on p173). The logo on the signposts is a depiction of Big Ben encircled by a ring of arrows.

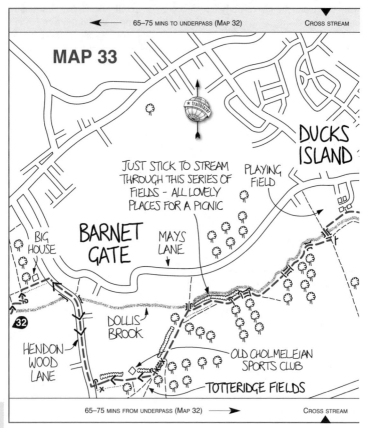

Incidentally, the fields you walk beside here belong to Mote End Farm, another property with connections to William Wilberforce (see pp86-7), who lived at Mote End (1826-33) for the final years of his life.

The Old Cholmeleians   [Map 33]

If you're coming from Elstree, it's with no small amount of relief that you finally arrive at a signboard announcing that you are now outside **The Old Cholmeleians Sports Club and Ground** – and thus can leave Hendon Wood Lane behind. This rather curious name is derived from Roger Cholmeley, who founded Highgate School as a charity way back in 1565; the Old Cholmeleians are the former pupils of this independent school.

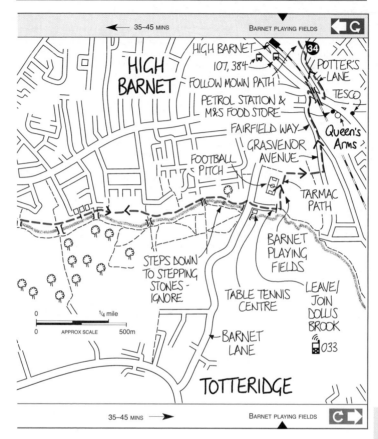

HIGH BARNET

HIGH BARNET
107, 384
FOLLOW MOWN PATH
PETROL STATION &
M&S FOOD STORE
FAIRFIELD WAY
GRASVENOR
AVENUE
FOOTBALL
PITCH

34
POTTER'S
LANE
TESCO
Queen's
Arms
TARMAC
PATH

STEPS DOWN
TO STEPPING
STONES -
IGNORE

BARNET
PLAYING
FIELDS

TABLE TENNIS
CENTRE

LEAVE/
JOIN
DOLLIS
BROOK
033

BARNET
LANE

TOTTERIDGE

0   ¼ mile
0   APPROX SCALE   500m

Totteridge Fields

It's below the sports pitches where the real joy lies. Maybe I just caught these fields at the right time, with the sun blazing and the wind gently caressing the meadow grass, but I think the western end of this stretch, as you join the Dollis, is one of the lovelier parts of the whole LOOP.

The tranquillity, the lack of any crowds or traffic, the birdsong – it's rather blissful, and a lovely location for a picnic. These are Totteridge Fields, which cover 97 hectares (240 acres) in total, including a 7-hectare (17-acre) nature reserve that the LOOP passes right through, which is made up of three fields that had for centuries been farmed as hay meadows. Mature hawthorn and blackthorn hedgerows separate the fields.

ROUTE GUIDE AND MAPS

Dollis Brook through Barnet

If you're walking the LOOP clockwise you'll find the path eventually crossing the Dollis to the outskirts of Barnet and an area known as **Ducks Island**, where, it's fair to say, the river loses some of its charm, though it's still an uncomplicated, easy stroll, this time through mown fields and along tarmac paths.

At the eastern end of the stroll beside the Dollis, the path enters **Barnet Playing Fields**. Dollis Valley Greenwalk continues its riparian wanderings but the LOOP takes a more northerly direction now.

HIGH BARNET & NEW BARNET
[Map 33, pp160-1]

High Barnet station lies about 500m north of where Fairfield Way meets the A411. If you're heading there, you'll find a parade of shops opposite the station subway.

If, however, you turn right (ie continue along the trail) instead of left, officially you come to **New Barnet**. Just a few metres ahead, off the trail, there's a petrol station with a 24hr **M&S store**. If they don't have what you want, there's a **Tesco Express** (daily 6am-11pm) a little further ahead at the junction.

Between the two is the *Queens Arms* (☎ 020-8449 0156, 🖥 mcmullens.co.uk /queensarms; food Mon-Fri noon-3pm & 5-8pm, Sat & Sun noon-6pm). Note that they don't accept dogs.

Transport
[see map pp42-3]

● **High Barnet** This is the northernmost terminus for the High Barnet branch of the Northern **underground** line; the line provides a frequent service to central London.

There are **bus** stops for the No 107 (Edgware to New Barnet via Elstree & Borehamwood, Borehamwood & High Barnet; daily 2-4/hr) & 384 (Edgware to Cockfosters via High Barnet & New Barnet; daily 2-4/hr) outside the station.

The No 184 (Chipping Barnet to Turnpike Lane via New Barnet, Arnos Grove & Wood Green; daily 2-7/hr) and 383 (to Woodside Park via New Barnet, Whetstone & Friern Barnet; daily 2/hr) travel along Meadway (see Map 34) which is a short walk north of High Barnet station.

● **New Barnet** This station is south of the LOOP but is a stop on Great Northern's **rail** services between Moorgate and Welwyn Garden City (see pp46-7 for details).

The No 184 and 383 **buses** (see above) provide a convenient service between the stations.

King George's Fields, Barnet
[Map 34, pp164-5]

This 28-hectare (69-acre) quilt of fields, with their grassy meadows knitted together with hedgerows, offers several benches to weary walkers on the LOOP as they struggle up the slope. While taking in the views south and east on the benches, you may also care to gaze skywards to see if you can spy sparrowhawks, doves, willow warblers and the uncommon chimney sweeper moth, all of which make their home in the fields. The name, incidentally, refers to **King George V**, and is one of about twenty such playing fields in London that were dedicated to his memory following his death in 1936.

There are bus stops on Meadway (King Edward Rd) near the southern entrance to the Fields, served by bus No 184 (Chipping Barnet to Turnpike Lane via High Barnet, New Barnet, Arnos Grove & Wood Green; daily 2-7/hr) and 383 (High Barnet to Woodside Park via New Barnet; Whetstone & Friern Barnet; daily 2/hr) respectively.

❑ **THE BATTLE OF BARNET**

In 1470 the reigning monarch, Edward IV, from the House of York, was overthrown by supporters of the Lancastrian Henry VI, led by the Earl of Warwick, Richard Neville (who had previously supported the claims of Edward before switching sides).

Having fled in fear of his life to France, Edward rallied his troops for a counter-attack and the two sides clashed here on 14 April, 1471. It was to be Neville's last stand; there's an obelisk to the north of the LOOP supposedly marking the spot where he fell. Nevertheless, the Lancastrians had the last laugh.

Though the House of York went on to rule for 12 years, Henry Tudor, a Lancastrian, eventually overcame the Yorkists at the Battle of Bosworth Field in 1485. Henry went on to found the Tudor Dynasty, while his opponent, Richard III, ended up beneath a car park in Leicester.

Hadley Green

Hadley Green is best known as a possible location for the **Battle of Barnet**, one of the most important battles in the War of the Roses – a fight for supremacy between the two most powerful houses in England at the time, the House of Lancaster and the House of York.

Monken Hadley

In the introduction to this book I state that one of the joys of the LOOP is the chance it offers walkers to visit places that they had heard of but never before had reason to visit; even if, on occasion, the place itself if not as interesting as one might have originally hoped. Well, Monken Hadley is quite the opposite – a place we'd never heard of, but really should have done! The prettiest village on the LOOP, at least in this author's opinion, Monken Hadley is clustered around the handsome 15th-century **St Mary the Virgin Church**.

But it's the houses of Monken Hadley that stick in the memory, all but erad-icating from one's mind the relentless din of traffic that does its best to blight the village, as it does pretty much every other place on the trail. Some of these houses are so grand, historical and important that they have their own Wikipedia page. Places such as **Livingstone Cottage**, so-named because the famous explorer, David Livingstone, lived here on his return from Africa in 1857. Or magnificent **Hadley Hurst**, a Grade II-listed building, which was reputedly designed by Christopher Wren.

Finally, though the path heads into the woods opposite Hadley Hurst, you may want to keep to the road for just a bit longer to visit a side road called The Crescent; the red-brick Victorian pile halfway down the street at No 15 is called **Monkenhurst** and was once the home of Spike Milligan.

Sullivan's No 399 (Chipping Barnet to Hadley Wood station; Mon-Sat 1/hr) **bus** stops by the church on a Hail and Ride basis. Note also that this is not a TfL service so the only valid passes are the Freedom Pass or English National Concessionary Travel Scheme bus pass.

Hadley Wood **railway** station is a stop on Great Northern services between Moorgate (London) and Welwyn Garden City (see box on pp46-7).

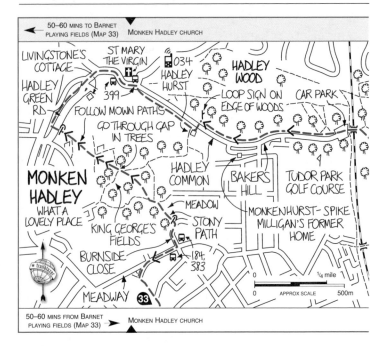

50–60 MINS TO BARNET PLAYING FIELDS (MAP 33) MONKEN HADLEY CHURCH

LIVINGSTONE'S COTTAGE
ST MARY THE VIRGIN
034
HADLEY WOOD
HADLEY GREEN RD
399
HADLEY HURST
LOOP SIGN ON EDGE OF WOODS
CAR PARK
FOLLOW MOWN PATHS
GO THROUGH GAP IN TREES
MONKEN HADLEY
WHAT A LOVELY PLACE
HADLEY COMMON
BAKERS HILL
TUDOR PARK GOLF COURSE
MEADOW
MONKENHURST – SPIKE MILLIGAN'S FORMER HOME
KING GEORGE'S FIELDS
STONY PATH
BURNSIDE CLOSE
184, 383
MEADWAY 33

trailblazer

0   ¼ mile
0   APPROX SCALE   500m

50–60 MINS FROM BARNET PLAYING FIELDS (MAP 33) → MONKEN HADLEY CHURCH

Hadley Wood

At the foot of the bridleway that runs between Monken Hadley and Cockfosters, just across the **bridge** over the Great Northern railway line (whose services stop at Hadley Wood station, see p163, which is just north of the LOOP) – and the East Coast main line (whose services don't) – the trail passes through a dappled grove of oak and beech. This is the former location of Folly Farm, a 17th-century farm that became, between the two World Wars, the home of a funfair and tearoom. Another part of the farm, not on the trail, is now the home of the Jewish Community Secondary School.

COCKFOSTERS [Map 34]

Though the etymology is uncertain, there is a theory that Cockfosters' unusual name may have originally come from the fact that the 'cock forester', or chief forester, of Epping Chase, had his home here. You won't find any evidence of that today, of course, though just beyond the station there are some useful facilities, including a **Co-op** (daily 7am-10pm), a **post office** (Mon-Fri 9am-5pm) with **ATM**, and several

restaurants, and there are more shops and **cafés** further down the street.

Coming from Monken Hadley, you'll pass *The Cock Inn* (☎ 020-8449 7160, ☐ thecockinncockfosters.co.uk; 🐾 in main bar area only; food daily 10am-9pm), a gastro-pub, opened at the end of the 18th century.

A branch of *Premier Inn* (London Southgate; ☐ premierinn.com) is one stop away on the tube line.

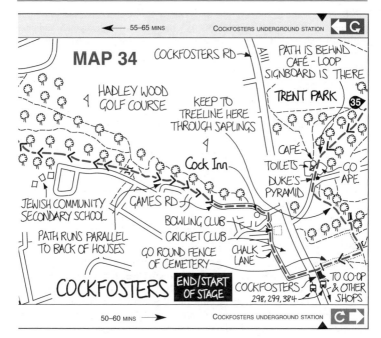

MAP 34   COCKFOSTERS RD →

PATH IS BEHIND CAFÉ - LOOP SIGNBOARD IS THERE

TRENT PARK

HADLEY WOOD GOLF COURSE

KEEP TO TREELINE HERE THROUGH SAPLINGS

Cock Inn

CAFÉ

TOILETS

DUKE'S PYRAMID

GO APE

JEWISH COMMUNITY SECONDARY SCHOOL

GAMES RD

BOWLING CLUB

CRICKET CLUB

PATH RUNS PARALLEL TO BACK OF HOUSES

GO ROUND FENCE OF CEMETERY

CHALK LANE

COCKFOSTERS   END/START OF STAGE   COCKFOSTERS 298, 299, 384

TO CO-OP & OTHER SHOPS

Transport   **[see map pp42-3]**
Cockfosters is one of the few places where the **London Underground** network manages to reach the LOOP, with Cockfosters being the north-eastern terminus of the **Piccadilly line**.

Buses from the station include the No 298 (Arnos Grove to Potters Bar via Southgate; daily 2-3/hr), and 299 (to Muswell Hill via Southgate; daily 2-4/hr) as well as the 384 (to Edgware via New Barnet & High Barnet; daily 2-4/hr).

STAGE 17: COCKFOSTERS TO ENFIELD LOCK   [MAPS 34-37]

This **8½-mile stage (13.7km; C & A/C 3hrs to 3hrs 25mins)** begins with a delightful march through popular **Trent Park**, and it's a rare walker who doesn't cite this as the highlight of the stage. But it's unassuming **Salmon's Brook**, that you follow immediately afterwards that is, in this author's opinion, the stage's real delight: a peaceful, lonely walk alongside a trickling stream with nothing but birdsong and brambles for company. You won't however, actually see any salmon in Salmon's Brook – but then neither will you find any turkeys bathing in **Turkey Brook**, which you follow for nearly all the rest of the stage to Enfield Lock. It's a waterway that will take you through the lovely parkland of **Hilly Fields** and past **Forty Hall**, yet another country house with associations with Henry VIII and the Tudors.

Regarding the facilities on the trail, Turkey Brook also runs past a **pub** that can boast of associations with the country's most famous highwayman, and busy **Enfield Wash**, with its **cafés** and **shops**. And if you plan to stop before the end, the easiest way to get back to central London is via **train** from Turkey Street station, right on the trail, or there are **buses** from Clay Hill and Enfield Wash.

Enfield Chase

Since Monken Hadley you have been walking largely within the boundary of Enfield Chase. This was the royal hunting ground for Plantagenet kings – 'chase', or 'chace', was a tract of ground for breeding wild animals, usually for hunting purposes. It appears that there has been hunting in the woods round here since at least the Norman Conquest, though it only officially became known as Enfield Chase in the 14th century. Princess Elizabeth, later Elizabeth I, was just one member of the Tudor royals who hunted in the Chase. In 1777, however, Enfield Chase, now almost 35 sq km, was broken up and the forests were largely cleared as a consequence. **Trent Park** remains one of the few patches of the trace without significant development. Its name lives on, however, as a railway station (off the trail), tennis club and in the name of the former hotel on this stage, The Royal Chace (see p169).

Trent Park   [Map 34, pp164-5; Map 35, pp168-9]

Previously part of the Enfield Chase (see above), the history of Trent Park really begins not in England but in northern Italy, where, in 1777, the royal physician Sir Richard Jebb saved the life of George III's brother, the Duke of Gloucester. To show his gratitude, George leased 385 acres (156 hectares) of Enfield Chase to Sir Richard, who built a small house on it and named the estate after the Italian city, Trentino, where he had attended to the duke. That house was largely pulled down, and those bits that survived were extensively altered and added to in the early 20th century by Sir Philip Sassoon. Sir Philip, who had inherited the estate from his father in 1912, and who was a cousin of the World War I poet Siegfried, had a reputation as a generous host and party-thrower supreme, as this quote from the period confirms:

'a dream of another world – the white-coated footmen serving endless courses of rich but delicious food, the Duke of York coming in from golf... Winston Churchill arguing over the teacups with George Bernard Shaw, Lord Balfour dozing in an armchair, Rex Whistler absorbed in his painting... while Philip himself flitted from group to group, an alert, watchful, influential but unobtrusive stage director – all set against a background of mingled luxury, simplicity and informality, brilliantly contrived...'

With Sassoon's death in 1939, however, the British government requisitioned the house to accommodate captured German pilots, equipping the rooms with secret microphones so they could listen in on the pilots' conversations in the hope of discovering useful information. Post-war it's been a teacher-training facility, then a student campus for Middlesex University, with annexes added that, inevitably, had none of the style or flair of Sir Philip's. In 2015 the site was sold to developers, with many of the historic buildings now repurposed as flats.

The house itself lies off the LOOP, though there are several of the park's attractions that you do pass by, in addition to the *café* (Mon-Thur 8.30am-4pm, Fri-Sun to 4.30pm) and **toilets** at the southern end of the park.

The Trent Park memorials Just by the car park, toilets and café at the southern end of Trent Park is a memorial known as **Duke's Pyramid**. It was built to commemorate the passing of Henry Grey, who died on 5th June 1740. This is the first of two memorials that the LOOP passes on its way through Trent Park (see also the Sassoon Obelisk, below). It should be noted, however, that neither was originally built for these grounds but instead both were transferred over in 1934 by Sir Philip Sassoon from Wrest Park (Silsoe, Beds), where they were first erected. It is believed that Sir Philip bought them to impress two very special guests of his, Prince George and Princess Marina, who spent part of their honeymoon at the park in December of that year. The pair had recently been given the titles of the Duke and Duchess of Kent, so Sir Philip thought it appropriate to decorate the grounds with memorials to an earlier (albeit non-royal) Duke and Duchess of Kent.

Another memorial, the 'Pineapple' which lies to the north off the trail, was also transferred from Wrest Park at the behest of Sir Philip. This memorial is dedicated to the wife of Henry Grey, Jemima, who died in 1728. Though the marriage was a happy one, Jemima had been unable to provide a male heir for Henry, producing only daughters. It was largely for this reason, so it is believed, that Henry married again following her death. His new wife, Sofia, did indeed produce the longed-for male heir, whom they christened George. The obelisk is a celebration of this event, which happened in 1732 (though mysteriously the obelisk says it happened in 1702). Tragically, George died while still in infancy the following year, thus extinguishing Grey's family line. The 20m-tall obelisk, officially titled the **George Grey, Earl of Harold Obelisk** although also known as the **Sassoon Obelisk** after the man who brought it to Trent Park, dwarfs the surrounding trees.

Camlet Moat So what is this 70m-long moat of water, lying near the top of **Ferny Hill**, hidden in the woods to the side of the path, where the surrounding trees are, on occasion, festooned by ribbons and other lucky charms? Could it really be Camelot, the legendary castle of King Arthur? No, probably not, though this does explain why the trees are decorated so, and you'll find plenty of online bloggers trying to convince their readers otherwise. Or maybe it's the home of the ghost of Geoffrey de Mandeville, then Earl of Sussex and Hertfordshire and Constable of the Tower of London, who was arrested for treason but not before hiding much of his wealth down a very deep well somewhere near here? Well, whether you think that's true depends largely on where you stand on ghosts, though believers will point to the fact that the well has never been found, largely because, so they say, those who get close to finding it are usually frightened off by an apparition of Geoffrey himself.

Or could it be, rather more prosaically, the site of a mediaeval manor house, demolished in 1429, with the materials then used to help fund the repairs to Hertford Castle? Well, if we're to believe various historical records and the odd

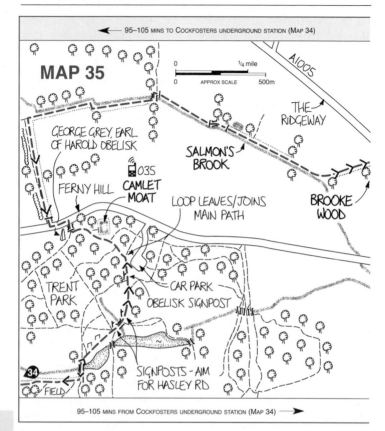

archaeological dig that has taken place over the last hundred years, the only conclusion one can draw is that is exactly what it is. Excavations also revealed that the moat was crossed by a wooden drawbridge, though these days there's a causeway on its eastern side.

Salmon's Brook [Map 35]

Rather an unsung part of the stage, but rather a lovely one too methinks, as you drop off Ferny Hill (assuming, of course, you've come from Trent Park) to stroll along Salmon's Brook. True, your chances of seeing any actual salmon are zero – unless you've got one as a pet, of course, and have brought it along for the afternoon – as the name comes from the local 13th-century Salemon family, rather than the fish. But it's a joy skipping along the meadows, once part – as so much of the LOOP is around these parts – of Enfield Chase. It's certainly serene and scenic enough that you may feel a picnic coming on.

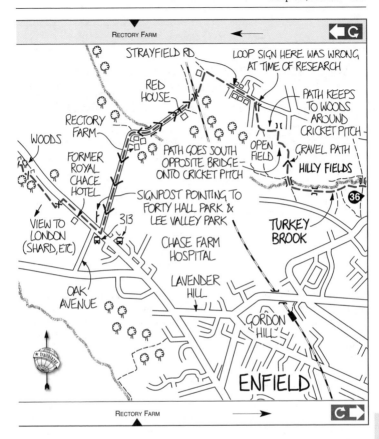

The Ridgeway, Enfield

Between Salmon's and Turkey Brooks, the path now veers from one aeroplane-menu option to the other via the aptly named Ridgeway, nothing to do with the National Trail of the same name but instead a high-level and busy road where the ground slopes away on either side. It's here that you find the former **Royal Chace Hotel**); this grand property sits on the Ridgeway (aka the A1005), though the house is set back from the noise of the road, and is right on the LOOP. There are great views out the back and front of the property. The hotel was run for over 40 years by the same family, but the gates near the main entrance that read '1891' suggest there is a whole lot more past to uncover.

The No 313 (Chingford station to Potters Bar station via Enfield Town & Enfield Chase stations; daily 2-3/hr) **bus** stops here on The Ridgeway (Roundhedge Way).

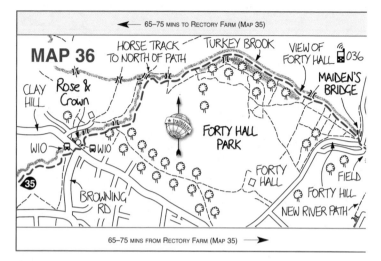

← 65–75 MINS TO RECTORY FARM (MAP 35)

MAP 36

HORSE TRACK TO NORTH OF PATH

TURKEY BROOK

VIEW OF FORTY HALL 🗼036

CLAY HILL

Rose & Crown

MAIDEN'S BRIDGE

trailblazer

FORTY HALL PARK

W10

W10

35

BROWNING RD

FORTY HALL

FIELD

FORTY HILL NEW RIVER PATH

65–75 MINS FROM RECTORY FARM (MAP 35) →

Turkey Brook & Hilly Fields

As with Salmon's Brook (see p168), the source of the name is unexpected, coming neither from the country nor the bird but from an eminent local family, the Tokes. If you are coming from Cockfosters you will have already been introduced to the brook near Rectory Farm, to the north of the Ridgeway. But it is at **Hilly Fields**, yet another ribbon of green saved from the developers' diggers and now providing an essential clump of countryside for locals and LOOP walkers, that you become better acquainted. Turkey Brook is a tributary of the Lee, and the path follows it for its entire time through Hilly Fields.

Clay Hill, Enfield [Map 36]

The brook and LOOP cross Clay Hill, with the 17th-century *Rose & Crown* (☎ 020-8366 0864; **fb**; 🐾; food Thur-Sun noon-8pm) – a pub that claims Dick Turpin's grandparents as previous landlords – nearby.

The W10 **bus** (Enfield to Enfield Town via Forty Hill; Mon-Sat 4-7/day) operates on a Hail and Ride (see p203) basis here.

Forty Hall Park

The Brook continues through Forty Hall Park. The 17th-century **Forty Hall** is visible in the distance to the south through an avenue of lime trees, and is built on, or very near, the site of Elysing Palace, the third of Henry VIII's palaces, after Nonsuch and Hampton Court, encountered en route (and you'll bump into one or two more before the LOOP's end too).

The palace is perhaps most famous for the fact that Henry's daughter, Elizabeth, found out her father had died while residing here in 1547. After she'd ascended the throne, however, Elysing Palace was seldom used and was eventually demolished in 1608. (Indeed, so thoroughly was it destroyed that its exact

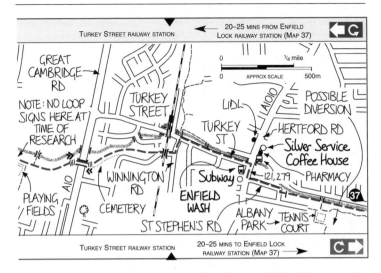

location was only rediscovered in the 1960s.) The **two fishing lakes** you also pass by were probably the fishponds of the original palace.

Maiden's Bridge

Though the path doesn't actually cross this bridge, it's only a few steps away from it. It also has one major claim to fame. For it was here, supposedly, that Walter Raleigh performed perhaps the single most famous act of chivalry by anyone, ever, when he allegedly draped his cloak across a puddle so that Queen Elizabeth didn't get her feet wet. Whether it actually happened, and whether it actually worked, are both moot points, and there are several other places that claim to be the location of this gallantry. Perhaps, however, the fact that Elizabeth did at least reside close by for a period gives this bridge's claim more credibility than others. Even if it *is* the spot, however, the bridge itself is not a Tudor original but dates only from the 19th century.

Turkey Street link

Unusually, the LOOP goes right past the entrance to this **railway station** even though it's not the end of the stage. Turkey Street is a stop on London Overground's Liverpool Street to Cheshunt line (see p47 and map pp42-3).

ENFIELD WASH (HERTFORD ROAD) [Map 36]

Probably known as Enfield Wash as this was an area that was prone to flooding, the area is centred around noisy, multilingual, multi-cultural Hertford Rd, where you'll find most services.

Services

Head north away from the LOOP and you'll see a Lidl **supermarket** (Mon-Sat 8am-10pm, Sun 11am-5pm) ahead of you, just 100m from the trail; opposite is Ronchetti **Pharmacy** (Mon-Fri 9am-7pm, Sat to

6pm) and next door to that is *Silver Service Coffee House* (☎ 01992-712816, 🖳 silver servicecoffeehouse.com; Mon-Fri 9am-7pm, Sat to 6pm, Sun 9am-5pm).

There's no need to leave the LOOP for sustenance, however, for there's a branch of the sandwich chain *Subway* (Mon-Fri 7am-10pm, Sat from 8am, Sun from 9am) opposite St Stephen's Rd, where you turn off

Hertford St, and several **Turkish cafés** serving dark, rich, thick coffee.

Transport   **[see map pp42-3]**
Bus services travelling through the mayhem include the No 121 (Turnpike Lane to Enfield Lock/Enfield Island Village; daily 4-5/hr) and 279 (Manor House to Waltham Cross; daily 4-10/hr).

Albany Park

Named after the youngest son of Victoria, Leopold, the Duke of Albany, who died in 1884 (and thus was outlived by his mother) Albany Park separates Enfield Wash from Enfield Lock. The park has been enlarged several times, the last time in 1935 as part of the King George's Fields programme (see p162).

ENFIELD LOCK   **[Map 37]**

There are few facilities at Enfield Lock itself – you need to return to Hertford Rd/ Enfield Wash for that – but there is a hot drinks wagon, *The Daily Grind* (☎ 07961 445661; Mon-Sat 6am-1pm), and on the corner is *The Railway Inn* (☎ 01992-718566; bar Mon-Fri 3-10pm, Sat & Sun 2-10pm), a real atmospheric back-street

boozer. However, at the time of writing they weren't offering food or accommodation and it wasn't certain whether they would again so check in advance. Alternatively there is a branch of *Premier Inn* (London Enfield; 🖳 premierinn.com) about a mile from the station.

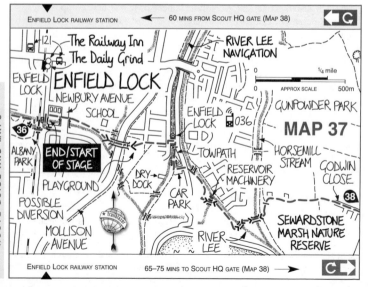

Transport [see map pp42-3]
There are **trains** (Greater Anglia) from here south to both Liverpool Street and Stratford and north to Hertford East and Bishops Stortford; see p46.

The No 121 **bus** (Turnpike Lane to Enfield Island Village via Enfield Wash; daily 4-5/hr) travels along Ordnance Rd, in front of the station.

STAGE 18: ENFIELD LOCK TO CHINGFORD [MAPS 37-39]

Considering much of the first half of this **4¾-mile stage (7.6km; C: 1hr 40mins to 2hrs, A/C: 1hr 40mins to 1hr 50 mins)** is spent walking over land that was previously a no-go area, thanks to the amount of ordnance that once lay scattered hereabouts, it's remarkable how pretty this walk appears today.

Enfield has always been synonymous with a major arms manufacturer, and many of their new weapons were initially tested on the ground that you'll be walking on throughout this stage. But where bullets once flew over, today it's the birdlife of **Sewardstone Marsh Nature Reserve**. Nor is this the only attraction of this 18th stage. The **River Lee** (also spelt **River Lea**) is interesting, the **Sewardstone Hills** offer some panoramic views and, for the final 45 minutes of the stage, you walk through epic **Epping Forest**.

Facility-wise, if you need a break on the way there's a **café-cum-restaurant** at around the halfway point, at Sewardstone, and another **café** right at the end of the trail.

Enfield Lock

The lock sits on an 'improvement' to the River Lee, known as River Lee Navigation – about which, see box below. The lock dates back only to 1922, though there was a lock on the actual river, a few steps away, by 1725, which therefore pre-dates the Navigation. Indeed, there are records that show that this area was called Norhtlok in 1325, and suggesting that there was some sort of lock here many centuries before.

River Lee and marshland

Unassuming though it may be, the Lee is perhaps London's second most important river, behind only the Thames. The river runs for 42 miles (68km), rising in the Chilterns near Luton before emptying, finally, at Bow Creek and the Limehouse Cut, across the Thames from the O2. The river also doubles up, in

---

❏ **RIVER LEE NAVIGATION**

It may be called River Lee Navigation, but this stretch of man-made waterway is, in effect, London's first canal. It runs all the way between Hertford and Bromley-by-Bow and was cut largely at the behest of the 18th-century brewing industry. Barley, that had been malted in Hertford, was shipped via the River Lee to the brewers of London, but it was becoming increasingly difficult to navigate the river, particularly when water was being 'siphoned off' as drinking water for London. The brewers joined together in 1739 to campaign for improvements to the river in order to make it more navigable, and the Navigation, dug between 1767 and 1770, is the result.

places, as a border between London and both Hertfordshire and Essex. Note, however, that for most of your time on this section, you aren't actually walking by the main body of the Lee, but a **side channel** built to provide water for the huge **George V Reservoir**, whose feeder channel you cross over on a bridge by a large piece of reservoir machinery.

Sewardstone Marsh Nature Reserve & Gunpowder Park

To the east of the channel, across **Horsemill Stream**, which marks the border of Greater London and Essex, is an area of marshland known as **Sewardstone Marsh**. This wonderful wetland habitat is, remarkably, one of the main reasons why arms factories were built in Enfield in the first place. The marshes were used to test weaponry, firing over a large and sparsely inhabited area. It was also used for quarrying gravel, and for dumping rubbish. However, having been acquired by Lee Valley Park (🖳 visitleevalley.org.uk), the gravel pits were converted into fantastic habitats for aquatic creatures such as water voles, snipe and various species of dragonfly. It's really quite delightful.

Sewardstone   [Map 38]

Sewardstone, a hamlet of Waltham Abbey, holds a unique distinction of being the only place outside London with a London postcode. LOOP walkers will probably find the place unremarkable though there is a place to eat, *Farmhouse* (☎ 020-8616 2191, 🖳 thefarmhouseessex.com; Mon-Fri 9am-5pm, Sat & Sun to 6pm).

Sewardstone Hills

Behind The Farmhouse are the Sewardstone Hills. The LOOP crosses the **Meridian** in a field that, on a Sunday between spring and summer, is the venue for Netherhouse Farm Car Boot Sales. When they're happening (see their Facebook page for dates and times), crossing this field can be rather tricky and more than a little dangerous.

Incidentally, if you're walking the LOOP in a clockwise direction and started at Erith, this is the second time you've crossed the Meridian, having previously done so way back at Coney Hall Park (see pp90-1) on Stage 4; unlike there, however, there is no marker to show whereabouts you actually cross over.

On **Daws Hill** you can look west to see the huge George V Reservoir that the path passes so close to – too close, actually, to be visible, as it's hidden behind the bank of the reservoir.

Gilwell Park

This is the **worldwide headquarters of the Scouting movement** (🖳 gilwell park.co.uk), with camping spaces for up to 3000 people, all centred round an 18th-century farmhouse. The place also used to host weddings and offered hotel accommodation, but all that had to stop permanently due to COVID-19.

Epping Forest

If you're coming from Enfield Lock you will already have entered Epping Forest (🖳 visiteppingforest.org) at the top of Sewardstone Hills, before crossing the road to the Scouts HQ. The forest was once part of the Forest of Essex, a hunting forest in the 11th century for the kings of the day that would once

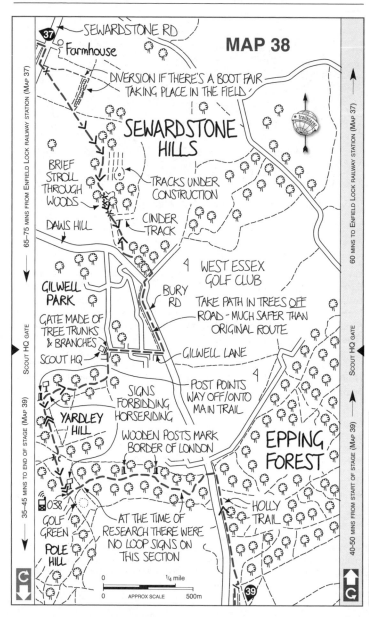

MAP 38

SEWARDSTONE RD

Farmhouse

37

DIVERSION IF THERE'S A BOOT FAIR
TAKING PLACE IN THE FIELD

SEWARDSTONE
HILLS

BRIEF
STROLL
THROUGH
WOODS

TRACKS UNDER
CONSTRUCTION

CINDER
TRACK

DAWS HILL

GILWELL
PARK

BURY
RD

WEST ESSEX
GOLF CLUB

GATE MADE OF
TREE TRUNKS
& BRANCHES

SCOUT HQ

TAKE PATH IN TREES OFF
ROAD - MUCH SAFER THAN
ORIGINAL ROUTE

GILWELL LANE

SIGNS
FORBIDDING
HORSERIDING

POST POINTS
WAY OFF/ONTO
MAIN TRAIL

YARDLEY
HILL

WOODEN POSTS MARK
BORDER OF LONDON

EPPING
FOREST

038

GOLF
GREEN

POLE
HILL

AT THE TIME OF
RESEARCH THERE WERE
NO LOOP SIGNS ON
THIS SECTION

HOLLY
TRAIL

0   ¼ mile
0   APPROX SCALE   500m

39

← 65-75 MINS FROM ENFIELD LOCK RAILWAY STATION (MAP 37)

◄ SCOUT HQ GATE

35-45 MINS TO END OF STAGE (MAP 39) ↓

60 MINS TO ENFIELD LOCK RAILWAY STATION (MAP 37) →

SCOUT HQ GATE ►

40-50 MINS FROM START OF STAGE (MAP 39) →

ROUTE GUIDE AND MAPS

have covered almost the entire county. Gradually parcelled up and sold off over the intervening centuries, it was only local pressure in the 19th century that ensured that this stretch of woodland remained undeveloped, leading to Epping Forest Act of 1878, protecting the 2476 hectares (6118 acres) of forest that still remains today. You'll need to follow my instructions on Map 38 (p175) to navigate your way through the forest. The trail visits **Yardley** and **Pole Hills** in the forest, as well as the broad **Holly Trail** on the other side of Bury Rd.

At the corner of Chingford Plain, and at the end of the stage too, there's *Holly Trail Café* (☎ 020-8529 6080; **fb**; Mon-Fri 7.30am-4pm, Sat & Sun to 5pm) with its large menu.

CHINGFORD   [Map 39]
The precise etymology of Chingford is uncertain, though there is a widespread belief that 'Ching' is old English for 'King' (see also Kingston-upon-Thames, p116). Given how keen royalty has been to hunt in this area, and given that there are several rivers that need fording around here, it's not such a stretch of the imagination to think that hereabouts was a 'king's ford'. The place was big enough to merit a mention in the Domesday Book as '*Cingefort*'. But pretty much all of what you see today, save for the hunting lodge and Butler's Retreat (see p178), dates back only as far as the 20th century.

What it lacks in visible history, however, it does make up for in terms of facilities. Though many LOOP walkers may choose to continue onto the next stage, and thus miss out on the centre of Chingford altogether, it's only a short stroll to the station, and just beyond is a **post office** (Mon-Fri 9am-5.30pm, Sat 9am-12.30pm), the decent *Café Delice* (☎ 020-8523 9660; daily 9.30am-4.30pm), and still further up is a **Tesco** (daily 6am-11pm).

There is a branch of *Premier Inn* and also a *Brewer's Fayre* in Chingford Plain (see p178).

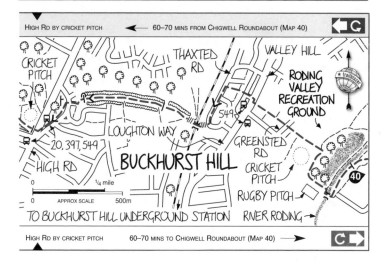

THAXTED RD

VALLEY HILL

CRICKET PITCH

RODING VALLEY RECREATION GROUND

549

LOUGHTON WAY

GREENSTED RD

20, 397, 549

BUCKHURST HILL

HIGH RD

CRICKET PITCH

0   ¼ mile

RUGBY PITCH

0   APPROX SCALE   500m

TO BUCKHURST HILL UNDERGROUND STATION   RIVER RODING →

40

Transport   **[see map pp42-3]**
Chingford station is in Zone 5 and on the London Overground **railway** line to Liverpool Street station (see p47).

A large number of **bus** services (for details see p210) stop in the station or just outside on Station Rd but probably the most useful for LOOP walkers is the No 397 (daily 2-3/hr) to Debden via Buckhurst Hill (Epping New Rd) & Loughton.

STAGE 19: CHINGFORD TO CHIGWELL   [MAPS 39-40]

As with several previous stages, this is another relatively short walk of **4 miles (6.4km; C & A/C 1hr 25mins to 1hr 40mins)**. Today, you'll be continuing the exploration of **Epping Forest** that you began in Stage 18. Epping is not only a glorious forest, it's a historical one too, and on this hike you'll be walking past a **Tudor hunting lodge-cum-museum**. The other highlight is **Roding Valley Recreation Ground** and its lovely lake, a positive consequence from the construction of the M11 that roars along nearby.

Facility-wise there is a **café** and **pub** on the eastern side of Chingford Plain near the hunting lodge and a second **pub** on the **A104**, along which you can also catch a **bus**. Overall then, it may not soar to the heights of other stages but it lacks any obvious faults too, and as the venue for an uncomplicated, leisurely afternoon's stroll it's hard to beat, either as a walk in its own right or combined with a neighbouring stage for a more testing full day's hike.

Chingford Plain

Chingford Plain was once as densely wooded as the rest of Epping Forest, before Henry VIII ordered the clearance of this section as part of his improvements to the hunting grounds (see also Nonsuch Park, pp108-10; Bushy Park, pp120-1; and

Elysing Palace, p170). A shelter for spectators to watch the hunting, known as a '**standing**', was built here on his orders. The plain, and indeed the whole hunting ground, fell out of favour during Henry's lifetime, but the trees never came back, and today it's a lovely open expanse of grassland, popular largely with golfers and sunbathers. The standing is still here, though it's now known as **Queen Elizabeth's Hunting Lodge** and houses a **museum** dedicated to the Tudor age.

Next door to the Lodge is **Epping Forest Visitor Centre** and nearby are two places to eat: right on the path is *Butler's Retreat* (☎ 020-7998 7858, 🖳 larderlondon.co.uk/the-larder-at-butlers-retreat; food mid Mar-Oct Mon-Fri 9am-3pm, Sat & Sun to 4pm, Oct-mid Mar daily 9am-3pm) while back near the Visitor Centre is a *Brewer's Fayre* (☎ 020-8523 7246, 🖳 brewersfayre.co.uk; breakfast Mon-Fri 6.30-10.30am, Sat & Sun 7-11am, lunch & dinner noon-8.30pm). Attached to the latter is a *Premier Inn* (London Chingford Hotel; 🖳 premierinn.com).

Hatch Forest
The trail largely parallels Rangers Rd through this strip of forest, crossing as it does so the tiny **River Ching**, marking the border between London and Essex, as the road sign ('Welcome to Essex') proves.

Epping New Rd/A104 & the High Road
At the eastern end of the forest in **Buckhurst Hill** is Epping New Rd/A104, where you'll find a 24-hr **petrol station** with a few supplies and a pub, *Warren Wood* (☎ 020-8505 3737; **fb**; daily noon-9pm). Indeed, the whole forest immediately east of Chingford was once known by this name, denoting the fact that there used to be a huge rabbit warren here.

Separating the A104 from the High Road is a strip of woodland and a cricket pitch. **Buses** travelling along High Rd, include the: No 13 (Epping to Waltham Cross bus station; Mon-Fri 9/day); 20 (Debden to Walthamstow Central via Loughton tube station, Woodford Green & Whipps Cross; daily 2-4/hr); No 397 (Chingford railway station to Debden via Loughton tube station; daily 2-3/hr) and No 549 (Loughton to South Woodford via Buckhurst Hill & Woodford tube stations; Mon-Sat 1/hr).

The LOOP crosses the Central Line and Buckhurst Hill tube station can be reached by taking the No 167 bus south from the stops on Loughton Way.

Roding Valley Recreation Ground
Not for the first time on the LOOP, a lovely area of cricket pitches and playing fields, centred on a pair of **large lakes** beloved by birdlife, was born out of unpromising circumstances. The lake, for example, is yet another former gravel pit (as on the previous stage at Sewardstone Marsh), the gravel this time going into the construction of the M11 in the 1970s. The lake is popular with waterfowl, of course, but anglers often wax lyrical about the fish that live in the lakes too, including pike, mirror carp and common carp.

River Roding runs along the eastern side of the lakes, forming a nature reserve called **Roding Valley Meadows**, home to the song thrush, blackcap and whitethroat, that thrive in the hedgerows that interlace the reserve.

CHIGWELL [Map 40, pp180-1]

"...the greatest place in the world ... Such a delicious old inn opposite the churchyard ... such beautiful forest scenery ... such an out of the way rural place..."

Charles Dickens in a letter to his friend and biographer, John Forster.

Whether you feel the same as Dickens about Chigwell after you've visited is, I suppose, a moot point, though it's a pleasant enough place and clearly, given the average price of a house around here, a lot of people do love the place.

The most attractive part is at the top of the hill, which the LOOP passes right through, though pretty much everything else is at the bottom, including a Mace **convenience store** (Mon-Sat 7.30am-10.30pm, Sun 8am-10pm), **post office** (daily 6am-8pm), and **chemist** (Brook House Pharmacy; Mon-Fri 9am-7pm, Sat to 5.30pm).

There's also an **Italian restaurant**, a **chippy** and a **deli** (daily 7.45am-4pm), while across the road and the first establishment you come to from the LOOP is a pub, *King William IV* (☎ 020-8500 4122, 🖥 www.thekingwilliamiv.co.uk; 🐕; food daily noon-8.30pm).

There is a branch of *Travelodge* (London Chigwell; 🖥 travelodge.co.uk) south of the station on High Rd.

Transport [see map pp42-3]
The **underground station** lies a few metres beyond the parade of shops, and for only the second time on the trail you've encroached into Zone 4. Chigwell is on the Hainault loop of the Central Line (daily approx 3/hr to Central London).

The No 167 **bus** (Loughton to Ilford via Buckhurst Hill; daily 2-3/hr) calls here.

STAGE 20: CHIGWELL TO HAVERING-ATTE-BOWER
[MAPS 40-42]

The centrepiece of this **7-mile stage (11.3km; C: 2½hrs to 2hrs 50mins, A/C: 2hrs 25 mins to 2¾hrs)** is **Hainault Forest** and its accompanying lake, meadows and golf course. Together they form a habitat for a remarkable 158 bird species and it'll take you about an hour to get from one side to the other. Indeed, once you've passed the attractive settlements of **Upper Chigwell** and **Chigwell Row** you're in countryside for pretty much the whole time on this stage, including a rather spectacular final stroll beneath the giant sequoias of **Havering Country Park**.

When it comes to facilities, being so rural, the only option for refreshment is the **café** in Hainault Forest and there aren't many places where you can catch public transport: note that the bus services between Havering-Atte-Bower at the end of the stage and the rest of the world are scant, and non-existent on Sundays, so this is another place where, time and energy willing, you may want to continue onto the next stage (which – Hallelujah! – finishes at a railway station).

SYMBOLS USED IN TEXT
🐕 Dogs allowed; see pp34-5 for more information
fb signifies places that have a Facebook page (for latest opening hours)
C = walking clockwise   A/C = walking anti-clockwise

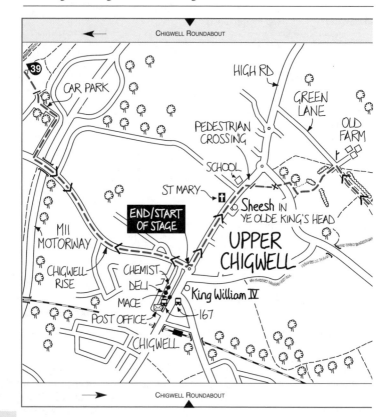

Upper Chigwell

Not much in the way of facilities here but there are a few buildings of note. The comely **St Mary Church** has features dating back to antiquity, including the 12th-century southern aisle and chancel. Next door, the early 17th-century **grammar school** was originally set up for 'poor scholars'; William Penn, the founder of Pennsylvania, was educated here.

Opposite both is **Ye Olde King's Head** pub, which features as a location in Charles Dickens' novel *Barnaby Rudge* (though in the book it is rechristened

❏ **IMPORTANT NOTE – WALKING TIMES**

All times in this book refer only to the time spent walking. You will need to add 20-30% to allow for rests, photography, checking the map, drinking water etc.

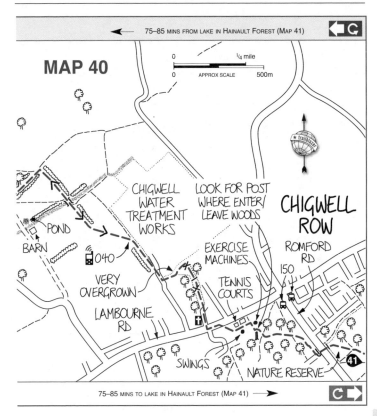

MAP 40

75–85 MINS FROM LAKE IN HAINAULT FOREST (MAP 41)

0   ¼ mile
0   APPROX SCALE   500m

CHIGWELL WATER TREATMENT WORKS

LOOK FOR POST WHERE ENTER/ LEAVE WOODS

CHIGWELL ROW

POND

BARN

040

VERY OVERGROWN

LAMBOURNE RD

EXERCISE MACHINES

TENNIS COURTS

ROMFORD RD

150

SWINGS

NATURE RESERVE

41

75–85 MINS TO LAKE IN HAINAULT FOREST (MAP 41) →

'The Maypole'). Winston Churchill was also said to have been a regular here. The pub is now a smart Turkish restaurant called **Sheesh** (🖳 sheeshrestaurant .co.uk) owned by entrepreneur and star of TV's *The Apprentice*, Alan Sugar. There is a tunnel, now blocked up, that runs from the pub to the grammar school. Rumour has it that it was built as an escape route by the Roundheads, who would meet at the inn during the Civil War.

Chigwell Row

For walkers Chigwell Row will consist of little more than a **water treatment works**, the **recreation ground** and **Chigwell Row Wood Local Nature Reserve**, a remnant of the woodland that would have once covered this whole area, before it was developed in the middle of the 19th century.

Bus No 150 runs from Lambourne Rd to Becontree via Hainault & Ilford (daily 3-5/hr).

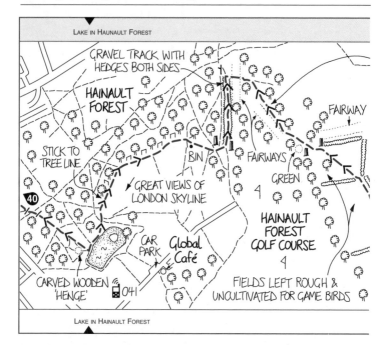

In the map:

LAKE IN HAUNAULT FOREST

GRAVEL TRACK WITH HEDGES BOTH SIDES

HAINAULT FOREST

FAIRWAY

STICK TO TREE LINE

BIN

FAIRWAYS

GREEN

40

GREAT VIEWS OF LONDON SKYLINE

HAINAULT FOREST GOLF COURSE

CAR PARK

Global Café

CARVED WOODEN 'HENGE'   041

FIELDS LEFT ROUGH & UNCULTIVATED FOR GAME BIRDS

LAKE IN HAINAULT FOREST

Hainault Forest [Map 41]

Once again you need to keep your wits – and Maps 40-41 – about you if you're going to negotiate this former hunting forest. Despite heavy depredation by developers over the centuries, the rump of the Forest of Essex that remains is an SSSI and one of the best examples of a pollarded oak and hornbeam forest. Within the forest you cross between Essex and London. If you're doing the LOOP clockwise, it's London you'll be in for most of the rest of the trail now.

At the bottom of the forest the trees give way to parkland surrounding a man-made lake, dug at the beginning of the last century as a job-creation scheme for unemployed men from the East End. There's *Global Café* (daily 9.30am-4pm) on the eastern side of the lake by the car park (though the path keeps to the lake's western side). As you walk along the edge of the woods above the lake, do look westwards to see one of the best views of the London skyline.

Hainault Forest Golf Course
You'll no doubt be delighted to know that, if you're walking the LOOP clockwise, this is the last golf course you'll see on the trail. Even better, the path does a good job of separating golfer from walker, with the latter tracing a route that sticks within the trees, following the yellow-painted marks on trees, crossing fairway only when unavoidable.

ROUTE GUIDE AND MAPS

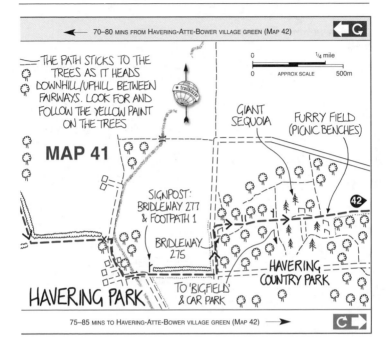

—THE PATH STICKS TO THE TREES AS IT HEADS DOWNHILL/UPHILL BETWEEN FAIRWAYS. LOOK FOR AND FOLLOW THE YELLOW PAINT ON THE TREES

★ trailblazer

MAP 41

GIANT SEQUOIA

FURRY FIELD (PICNIC BENCHES)

SIGNPOST: BRIDLEWAY 277 & FOOTPATH 1

BRIDLEWAY 275

42

HAVERING COUNTRY PARK

HAVERING PARK

TO 'BIGFIELD' & CAR PARK

Note that the path through the trees is different to the one marked on OS maps. Note, too, that the copse of trees you've been walking through actually marks the border between the boroughs of Redbridge and Hillingdon.

Havering Country Park   [Map 41; Map 42, pp184-5]

It takes no more than 20 minutes to pass through this stretch of woodland along the LOOP, but it's quite an interesting 20 minutes, for the trail is lined for much of its length by giant sequoia trees, *Sequoiadendron giganteum*, amongst the largest tree species on the planet.

The conditions in England aren't as perfect for the sequoia as they are in California, where they can grow to almost 100m, but they can still reach a height of over 50m here, far taller than any native species. (It should also be pointed out that the sequoia in the UK tend to date only as far back as the 1860s at the earliest, when they were first imported after being discovered during the Great Gold Rush, whereas some American sequoias are over 3200 years old!)

The rough, unmetalled track that takes you through the eastern half of the park is called **Wellingtonia Avenue** after the trees (an alternative name for the trees and one that honours the Duke of Wellington).

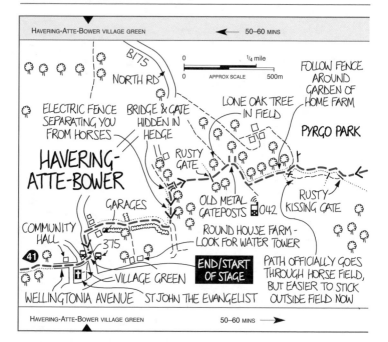

HAVERING-ATTE-BOWER village green   ← 50–60 MINS

B/75
NORTH RD

0   ¼ mile
0   APPROX SCALE   500m

FOLLOW FENCE
AROUND
GARDEN OF
HOME FARM

ELECTRIC FENCE
SEPARATING YOU
FROM HORSES

BRIDGE & GATE
HIDDEN IN
HEDGE

LONE OAK TREE
IN FIELD

PYRGO PARK

HAVERING-
ATTE-BOWER

RUSTY
GATE

RUSTY
KISSING GATE

GARAGES

OLD METAL
GATEPOSTS   042

COMMUNITY
HALL

375

41

ROUND HOUSE FARM -
LOOK FOR WATER TOWER

END/START
OF STAGE

PATH OFFICIALLY GOES
THROUGH HORSE FIELD,
BUT EASIER TO STICK
OUTSIDE FIELD NOW

VILLAGE GREEN

WELLINGTONIA AVENUE   ST JOHN THE EVANGELIST

HAVERING-ATTE-BOWER village green   50–60 MINS →

HAVERING-ATTE-BOWER [Map 42]

Though the name may speak of an ancient past – the unusual suffix Atte-Bower (locally pronounced Atty-Bower) means '*at the royal residence*' and refers to **Havering Palace**, which was built near here by William the Conqueror in the same year as his victory – there's little of antiquity to this village now. The metal on the stocks and whipping post on the village green are said to be ancient, though the wood itself is a modern replacement. Still, the fact that a village feels so rural yet sits in the boundaries of the capital is reason enough to celebrate, and this is the best place to do so in Havering.

You may find yourself spending longer there than you hoped, however, with the bus service for Havering rather dire, and, on a Sunday, non-existent. Small wonder that most walkers treat Havering as a staging post on a longer walk, tackling the next stage of the LOOP as well, rather than as a final destination for a day's walk.

Transport   [see map pp42-3]
That **bus**, incidentally, is the No 375 (Mon-Sat 8/day) between Romford and Passingford Bridge; it stops on Havering Green. Note that **the 375 does not run on Sunday**.

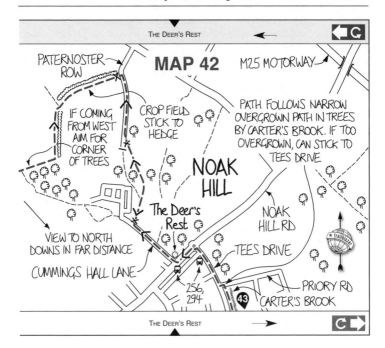

THE DEER'S REST ←

PATERNOSTER ROW

MAP 42

M25 MOTORWAY

IF COMING FROM WEST AIM FOR CORNER OF TREES

CROP FIELD STICK TO HEDGE

PATH FOLLOWS NARROW OVERGROWN PATH IN TREES BY CARTER'S BROOK. IF TOO OVERGROWN, CAN STICK TO TEES DRIVE

NOAK HILL

The Deer's Rest

NOAK HILL RD

VIEW TO NORTH DOWNS IN FAR DISTANCE

CUMMINGS HALL LANE

TEES DRIVE

256, 294

43 CARTER'S BROOK

PRIORY RD

THE DEER'S REST →

STAGE 21: HAVERING-ATTE-BOWER TO HAROLD WOOD
[MAPS 42-43]

This **5¼-mile stage (8.5km; C & A/C 1¾hrs to 2hrs 5mins)** can be seen as the archetypal LOOP walk, with many of the features that have been repeated time and again over the last 20 stages resurfacing once more here. This isn't the first occasion, for example, that you've encountered a former property of Henry VIII along the trail, as you do here at **Pyrgo Park**. Nor is it the first time the route has followed the course of a stream, as you do here along **Carter's Brook** and **Paine's Brook**. Impressively large and unexpected municipal park with children's playground and games court? Yep, that's here too, in the form of **Central Park**.

In addition, there's also a **pub** and decent **bus** connections at **Noak Hill** and **Harold Hill**.

Pyrgo Park

A pair of rusting **old gateposts** in a field may not immediately conjure up images of regal splendour, but these corroding bits of ironmongery are one of the few indications that Pyrgo Park once stood here. Remarkably, this is yet another property of Henry VIII. Even more remarkably, perhaps, it's yet another one that he 'appropriated' from a member of his staff, with this one originally belonging

ROUTE GUIDE AND MAPS

to his steward Brian Tuke. Nothing remains of the buildings today. Further east, in the **horse field** that you walk either through (the official route) or round (the unofficial, but less complicated, trail), you get great views across the various bumps and dips in the land and beyond to the grey silhouette of the North Downs. These views perhaps give you some idea why a palace was once built here and why Henry wanted it for himself.

There's a big riding school near the path so you may well find yourself accompanied by riders along the way; as such, dogs do need to be kept on a lead.

Paternoster Row
The simple turn onto this street marks the point where the LOOP takes a more southerly turn to head more directly to the Thames (and, of course, the end of the path). The name, of course, means 'Our Father' – the start of the Lord's Prayer.

NOAK HILL (ROMFORD)
[Map 42, pp184-5]

The LOOP passes a big noisy pub, *The Deers Rest* (☎ 07768 314040, 🖥 deersrest pub.co.uk; 🐾) on Noak Hill Rd. They normally serve food daily noon-8pm but at the time of research the hours were limited so check before you go.

Transport   [see map pp42-3]

The No 256 (to Hornchurch via Harold Hill & Harold Wood; daily 3-6/hr) and 294 (to Havering Park via Harold Hill, Harold Wood station & Romford; daily 3-5/hr) **bus** services stop on Tees Drive (by Wincanton Rd).

Carter's Brook   [Map 42, pp184-5; Map 43]
Most people walk on the grassy sward above this tree-choked gully, which begins (for those tackling the LOOP clockwise) at Priory Rd. However, it is worth trying to stumble your way through on the banks if you can, if only because, when I did, I encountered a dozen-strong herd of **deer** mooching about amongst the branches. It should also be noted that if you were somehow to launch a (presumably tiny) boat into the water here and let it drift downstream all the way to the confluence with the Ingrebourne, and continued to follow *that* river as it flowed into the Thames, in theory you would eventually arrive at the LOOP's end at Purfleet-on-Thames, and on much the same route as the LOOP takes too.

South of Whitchurch Rd, the path is much easier to follow; it is a clear tarmac trail heading south to Dagnam Park Drive.

Bus No 256 (to Hornchurch via Harold Hill & Harold Wood; daily 3-6/hr) and the 294 (Havering Park to Noak Hill via Romford, Harold Wood & Harold Hill; daily 3-5/hr) run along Tees Drive and stop at its southern end (near Whitchurch Rd).

The No 174 (to Dagenham via Romford; daily 4-5/hr) and 294 (see above) **bus** services stop on Dagnam Park Drive.

Paine's Brook   [Map 43]
South of Dagnam Park Drive, Carter's Brook turns into Paine's Brook; it's the same body of water, just with a new name.

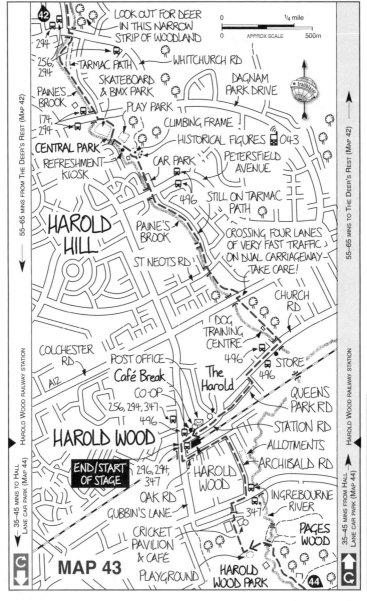

Central Park

Central Park is an impressive facility-filled recreation ground with BMX track, skateboard park, sport's court, a children's playground (the best on the LOOP), parkour, outdoor gym, **refreshment kiosk** and plenty of benches for weary walkers to rest their fatigued feet.

By one of the benches are the **metal silhouettes of three notable 'locals'** – namely Henry VIII, Dick Bouchard (who dedicated his life to teaching music to children, and founded Romford Drum and Trumpet Corps) and Harry Eccleston, whose name may not be familiar but whose work you probably will be aware of if you're of a certain age, for throughout the '70s he designed several of the Bank of England banknotes including those featuring Florence Nightingale (£10), Isaac Newton (£1) and William Shakespeare (£20). These sculptures were installed by walking and cycling charity Sustrans and similar figures can be found all over the country, often in groups of three, to celebrate well-known local heroes.

HAROLD HILL   [Map 43, p187]

The name of this suburb – and the suburb at the end of this stage too, of course – both celebrate their connections to **King Harold**, the loser in the Battle of Hastings in 1066 (and who, indeed, died on the field of battle, perhaps, as the Bayeux Tapestry suggests, from an arrow to the eye, though this is now largely dismissed as a misinterpretation).

Harold owned the estate of Havering-Atte-Bower – an estate that was subsequently taken over by his conqueror, William.

Transport   [see map pp42-3]
The No 496 (Harold Wood to Romford station; daily 3-4/hr) **bus** stops on Petersfield Avenue (Paines Brook Way).

HAROLD WOOD   [Map 43, p187]

Yet another place name that, along with Harold Hill, celebrates **King Harold**'s rule over this part of the country (in fact, given that the roads that you pass on the LOOP name-check both Athelstan and Ethelburga, it's clear that the local developers have quite a penchant for Anglo-Saxon royalty).

Services

There's also 19th-century **The Harold** (☎ 01708-345078, 🖳 theharold.wixsite.com/theharold; 🐾; food daily noon-5pm) that you pass on the LOOP.

Up the road a little are all the essential facilities, including a **post office** (Mon-Fri 10am-4.30pm), a **Co-op supermarket** (daily 6am-10pm), and the decent **Café Break** (☎ 01708-376313; Mon-Sat 6am-5pm, Sun 8am-5pm).

Accommodation is available in Romford, a train journey away. Options

there include branches of a **Travelodge** (🖳 travelodge.co.uk) and a **Premier Inn** (🖳 premierinn.com); both are about a 5- to 10-minute walk from Romford station.

Transport   [see map pp42-3]
The LOOP has the decency to pass right in front of the **railway station** door, from where you can catch a TfL train (Liverpool Street to Shenfield); see p48.

As for **buses**, the No 256 (Noak Hill to Hornchurch via Harold Hill; daily 3-6/hr), 294 (Havering Park to Noak Hill via Romford & Harold Hill; daily 3-5/hr) and 347 (Romford to South Ockenden via Upminster; Mon-Sat 4/day) stop on Gubbin's Lane and Station Rd by the railway station. The No 496 (to Romford via Harold Hill; daily 3-4/hr) leaves from outside the Co-op on Station Rd and also stops on Church Rd (Firham Park Ave).

STAGE 22: HAROLD WOOD TO UPMINSTER BRIDGE
[MAPS 43-45]

Two adjacent parks form the greater part of this **4¼-mile stage (6.8km; C & A/C 1½hrs to 1hr 50mins)**. The first is **Harold Wood**, a cheerful world of children's play areas, sports pitches and tree-lined boulevards. A short hop across the **Ingrebourne**, and providing a neat juxtaposition to Harold Wood Park, is calmer, quieter **Pages Wood**, a haven for cyclists, hikers and those who just want to escape the constant hubbub of metropolitan life. As with several other places on the LOOP, this park is the result of what can happen once man has stopped despoiling a place, and nature (with a little help from us) is allowed to reclaim it. (Sewardstone Marsh Nature Reserve, see p174, is another such place that springs to mind, and you'll encounter an even more famous one, Rainham Marshes, on Stage 24.) It's a lovely spot, and a real high point on this stage.

As far as **facilities** go on this stage, there are **refreshments** to be had at Harold Wood Park, but there is only one **bus service**, on Hall Lane, that would allow you to escape the trail once you're on it; thankfully, this stage is short enough that you shouldn't need to anyway.

Harold Wood Park
Visit this park on a sunny Sunday afternoon when the cricket and football matches are in full swing and it can feel like the entire population of Harold Wood has descended on this place. Happily, there are plenty of benches along the trail and there are certainly worse things to do than visit the Co-op supermarket by the railway station for picnic items and spend a happy hour enjoying a sumptuous al-fresco lunch on the boundary's edge.

The pavilion by the park's entrance also has a small *café* and **toilets**. In fact, if it wasn't for the cricket pitches there may not be a park at all, for the farmer who donated the land to the council did so only on condition that it be dedicated to the sport.

Pages Wood   [Map 43, p187; Map 44, p190]
At the bottom of the park the path joins Pages Wood, the dividing line being the **Ingrebourne**, to which the LOOP sticks for much of this stretch. Though the river is actually invisible in the undergrowth, it's still a wonderful amble, with **wooden sculptures** of the local wildlife lining the sandy-coloured gravel path.

These woods are part of the Thames Chase Project, a cross-borough initiative aimed at improving an area of 100 sq km of green belt, including much land that had been left derelict. The ambition was not only to improve recreation opportunities for local residents and increase access, but also to improve the conditions for wildlife, and increase tree cover too. Whilst it must be recognised that the programme still has several years left of its original 40-year mandate, and several of their targets have yet to be met, nevertheless if appearances are anything to go by it seems they've done a marvellous job thus far. According to their website (🖳 thameschase.org.uk), over 13 million trees have been planted since 1990, leading to an increase in woodland cover of 70% over the same period.

Hall Lane   [Map 44]

Another lengthy stretch of roadside rambling defines the middle section of this stage, this time along noisy Hall Lane.

There are bus stops along the way; the No 347 (Romford to South Ockenden via Harold Wood & Upminster; Mon-Sat 4/day) travels along Hall Lane. The 248 (Romford to Cranham via Upminster Bridge & Upminster; daily 3-9/hr) stops on Avon Rd (Severn Drive) and Hall Lane (River Drive).

The Ingrebourne

If you're walking the LOOP clockwise it's hard to avoid the conclusion that, after Pages Wood, the stage rather deteriorates in quality, with some lengthy walking on busy roads. Respite of sorts comes at the end of River Drive where an overgrown woodland path brings you to a reunion with the Ingrebourne,

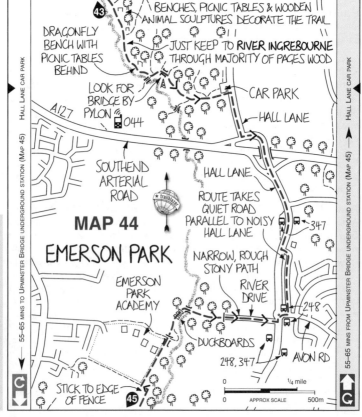

which you follow past Emerson Park Academy and several crop fields. You leave the stream again to head to Upminster Bridge.

UPMINSTER BRIDGE [Map 45, p192]

There's been a bridge across the Ingrebourne here since 1375, though the current 'Upminster Bridge', a brick and mortar affair, dates only from the end of the 19th century. The bridge is easy to miss – it's the one that carries the modern A124 across the Ingrebourne, and lies immediately east of The Windmill pub; the pub is named after the (currently sail-less) **windmill** you can see from the bridge across the railway, and which is one of only seven left standing in London.

Services

Between the bridge and the station are most of the facilities you may need, including a Co-op **supermarket** (daily 7am-11pm), and a Londis (Mon-Sat 5.30am-8.30pm, Sun 6am-4pm). Just the other side of the station, on the other side of the road, is the post office (Mon-Fri 6am-8pm, Sat 7am-8pm, Sun 7am-5pm), while opposite is *Café 122* (daily 7am-4pm); or for something heartier there's the pub, *The Windmill* (☎ 01708-442657, 💻 greene king-pubs.co.uk; food daily noon-9pm).

Transport [see map pp42-3]

Upminster Bridge **underground station** (note the swastika design on the floor) is at the end of the District Line; it's the penultimate stop before the line's terminus at Upminster.

Both the No 248 (daily 3-9/hr) and 370 (daily 2-4/hr) **buses** go to Romford, Hornchurch & Upminster, but in the other direction the 248 goes to Cranham and the 370 to South Ockendon and Lakeside Shopping Centre. They both depart from outside the station.

STAGE 23: UPMINSTER BRIDGE TO RAINHAM [MAPS 45-47]

This penultimate, **4½-mile stage (7.3km; C & A/C 1½hrs to 1hr 50mins)** improves the further you get into it.

Having joined the **Ingrebourne River** round the back of a football club car park, you stick with it, with only the occasional diversion, all the way to Rainham. At times this means you'll essentially be walking on a narrow ribbon of green and blue round the back housing estates, such as at the '**Parkways**'; while at other times the landscape opens out and you'll find yourself walking in some lovely countryside, such as in the wonderful **Hornchurch Country Park**, another haven for animals and birdlife. At the end of it, the Ingrebourne deposits you in Rainham, by the railway station, with only one more stage standing between you and glory.

As for facilities, there's a good **café** by the **visitor centre** in Hornchurch Country Park, and you can catch a **bus** on Rainham Rd – though it's only a few minutes from there to the railway station at Rainham anyway.

'The Parkways'

The 2.5km **riverside walk** that begins behind Hornchurch Football Club (nickname: 'The Urchins') is christened The Parkways. In fact, it's made up of three 'parkways', named, from north to south, as follows: **Gaynes Parkway**, where you cross the Inglebourne near Hacton Lane; **Hacton Parkway**; and, the most untamed of the lot, **Sutton Parkway**. This last one is now part of Ingrebourne Valley Local Nature Reserve.

ROUTE GUIDE AND MAPS

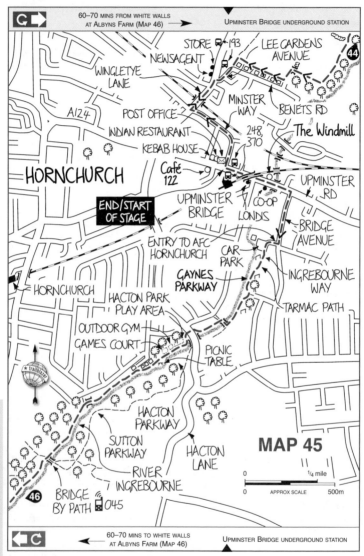

Hornchurch Country Park   [Map 46]

With its own **visitor centre** (Ingrebourne Valley Visitor Centre; Wed-Mon 10am-5pm) including *café* (same hours) and a large children's play area, Hornchurch Country Park is a very popular spot for locals to come and enjoy

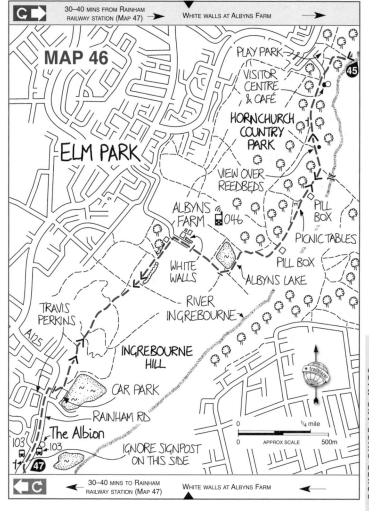

the sun, particularly at weekends. Do take time to walk a few steps off the path to the **viewpoints** over the marshes and bird lakes, where lapwings swoop and soar in unison above the water while rarities such as spotted crake and bittern stalk the reed beds below. Pause, too, to read about the park's surprising past, when the lakes were just gravel pits and the land you stand on was an airfield during both World Wars; some of the vehicle tracks, as well as a couple of pill-boxes, still line the trail today.

At the park's southern end is **Albyns Lake**, next to the upmarket walled development of Albyns Farm.

Ingrebourne Hill

Like neighbouring Hornchurch Country Park, this hill is part of the Thames Chase project. Similarly, it too is made up of detritus from a gravel excavation, but has been restored and landscaped and is now home to a 2km **mountain-bike circuit**. The bikes can whizz past at unnerving speed so do keep your wits about you. Just by the car park on South End Rd is a **fake runway complete with lights** – one last reference to this area's previous incarnation.

The Albion (🖥 greeneking-pubs.co.uk/pubs/essex/albion; daily 11am-10pm) serves food (till 9pm).

On Rainham Rd, the busy road running along the western side of the hill, the No 103 (Rainham to Chase Cross via South Hornchurch, Dagenham & Romford; daily 3-6/hr) **bus** runs north towards Dagenham and beyond.

RAINHAM   [Map 47]

Rainham is often called **Rainham Essex**, to differentiate it from its namesake in Kent – even though today, of course, it's actually in London.

The town's existence is largely due to the crossing of the Ingrebourne, which today, on the LOOP, you do via **Red Bridge**, though there's been some sort of bridge across the water here since at least 1357. The town, however, had already been in existence for several centuries before then.

In the centre of Rainham, right by the trail, is **St Helen and St Giles Church**, a properly squat Norman edifice with round-headed arches. The church was built between 1160 and 1170 on the orders of Richard de Lucy, which must have earned him great credit in Heaven, before helping to instigate the murder of that Archbishop of Canterbury, Thomas à Becket in 1170, which presumably didn't.

Next door is the grand but discreet **Rainham Hall**, a Grade II Queen-Anne style property now owned and run by the National Trust. The view of the house looks much better from the rear, overlooking the sweeping lawns.

However, man has been settling in this area for millennia, as a hoard of Bronze Age (900-800BC) treasures, known as the **Havering Hoard**, attests. The trove of 453 objects, including spear heads, axe heads, knives, daggers and woodwork tools, is the largest Bronze-Age find ever discovered in London – and the third largest in Britain.

Services

Next door to Red Bridge and right on the LOOP on the way into town is a Tesco **superstore** (Mon-Sat 6am-midnight, Sun 10am-4pm).

The rest of the facilities lie either to the east of the church away from the trail or to the north, such as *Delight Café* (☎ 01708-526937; daily generally 8am-4pm but the hours can vary).

Accommodation is available at a branch of *Premier Inn* (London Rainham; 🖥 premierinn.com), about a two-mile walk from the station.

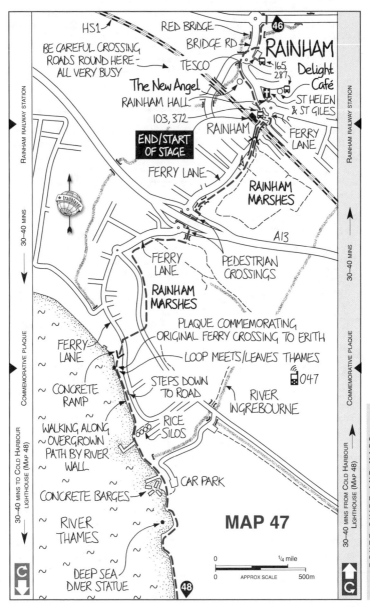

HS1

RED BRIDGE

BRIDGE RD

RAINHAM

46

BE CAREFUL CROSSING
ROADS ROUND HERE -
ALL VERY BUSY

TESCO

165
287

Delight
Café

The New Angel

RAINHAM HALL

ST HELEN
& ST GILES

103, 372

RAINHAM

FERRY
LANE

END/START
OF STAGE

FERRY LANE

RAINHAM
MARSHES

A13

FERRY
LANE

PEDESTRIAN
CROSSINGS

RAINHAM
MARSHES

PLAQUE COMMEMORATING
ORIGINAL FERRY CROSSING TO ERITH

FERRY
LANE

LOOP MEETS/LEAVES THAMES

047

STEPS DOWN
TO ROAD

RIVER
INGREBOURNE

CONCRETE
RAMP

WALKING ALONG
OVERGROWN
PATH BY RIVER
WALL

RICE
SILOS

CONCRETE BARGES

CAR PARK

MAP 47

RIVER
THAMES

0   ¼ mile

0   500m
APPROX SCALE

DEEP SEA
DIVER STATUE

48

RAINHAM RAILWAY STATION

30-40 MINS

COMMEMORATIVE PLAQUE

30-40 MINS TO COLD HARBOUR
LIGHTHOUSE (MAP 48)

RAINHAM RAILWAY STATION

30-40 MINS

COMMEMORATIVE PLAQUE

30-40 MINS FROM COLD HARBOUR
LIGHTHOUSE (MAP 48)

ROUTE GUIDE AND MAPS

Transport   **[see map pp42-3]**
The bus and railway stations, however, are both right on the LOOP. C2C **trains** (see p46) head west to Fenchurch Street and east to Grays via Purfleet-on-Thames.

For **buses**, at the station/Station Interchange you have the No 103 (to Chase Cross via South Hornchurch, Dagenham & Romford; daily 3-6/hr), 372 (Hornchurch to Lakeside Shopping centre; daily 2-3/hr). The No 165 (to Romford via Hornchurch; daily 3-5/hr) and 287 (to Barking via Dagenham; daily 3-4/hr) stop on Upminster Rd South.

STAGE 24: RAINHAM TO PURFLEET-ON-THAMES   [MAPS 47-48]

And so you come to the final **4¾-mile/7.6km stage (C & A/C 1¾hrs to 2¼hrs)** on the LOOP, and what a lovely way to finish your walk it is. Viewed from above, the area hugging the Thames around these parts can be viewed as a bit of a wasteland, and it's true that there is both plenty of noisy industry here and some smelly waste-processing facilities that deal with the rubbish emanating from the capital and beyond.

❑ **FLOOD ALERT!**

The river here is liable to flooding at very high tides. If you find the path under water outside the rice silos (**Map 47**) follow the lane (Ferry Lane) by the factory up to Coldharbour Lane taking it to cross the River Ingrebourne and then go back down again to the car park by the concrete barges.

  If you want to check tide tables in advance, when the figure for Coldharbour Point is higher than 8m it's likely the path will be flooded.

But there is also plenty of interest here too, including the wonderful **Rainham Marshes** – perhaps the most famous, and vital, bird sanctuary in the South-East; and a **riverfront walk** along the Thames to finish the LOOP that takes you past **sculpture**, **concrete barge** and **lighthouse**.

There are also **marker posts** on the riverside walk that count down your progress every 200m, showing how far you've come (and how far you've still got to go). Some joker has also decorated the trail with various rhymes, limericks and jokes, all on a vaguely pirate theme, that helps to pass the time and, perhaps, distract you from the tiredness you may now be feeling.

As for **facilities** on this last stage, there's no public transport, and the only source of refreshments before the end of the walk is at the **RSPB Visitor Centre** and **café** on the edge of Purfleet-on-Thames.

And as for the actual end, well the LOOP finally stops outside a **hotel in Purfleet-on-Thames**, as low-key a finish to your hike as the start was at Erith. It's a gentle, friendly finish, to what has been a pretty gentle – if lengthy! – trail.

Rainham Marshes

You encounter the marshes both at the beginning of the stage and at the end. But the LOOP's route through them is rather disappointing. Not only is the encounter rather brief, but the path never delves deeply into the reserve's interior, preferring instead to keep alongside the (often noisy) roads that run along its perimeter.

The Thames riverfront
The ferry plaque If you've been tackling the LOOP clockwise you'll climb up to the wall that runs alongside the river via a ramp on Ferry Lane. A few steps along from the top of the ramp, a **plaque** commemorates the 800th anniversary of the old Erith to Rainham Ferry, which ran from 1199.

While it's nice to see the old ferry being celebrated in this way, it would be even nicer to see the old ferry back in action, ferrying passengers from one side of the river to the other – and enabling LOOP walkers, of course, to complete the circle. Incidentally, the ferry never actually went from here but from a point further downstream (see box below).

The concrete barges There are 16 concrete barges here, made in the 1940s, and though they sound about as useful as chocolate teapots, they actually played a vital role in 1944's Normandy landings of World War II.

Though it seems illogical, they can actually float, and were used to transport fuel to other ships during the invasion (though they couldn't propel themselves so were towed by other craft). They also acted as supports for the pontoon bridges and as temporary harbour arms. Most of these concrete (actually, ferro-concrete as they have an iron frame) barges were lost at sea, but these 16 were towed up the Thames to act as flood defences.

The Diver: Regeneration Standing an impressive 460cm high, this piece of public art looks, at first glance, like just another twisted scrap of waste metal emerging from the mud. It's only as you continue along the path that you realise it has a very definite, deliberate shape and, on closer studying, is a really rather impressive **sculpture of a deep-sea diver**. It's the work of the admirably self-taught artist John Kaufman, in tribute to his grandfather who was a diver in the Thames. The work was installed here in 2000, just a couple of years before Kaufman's death.

❏ RAINHAM MARSHES
The RSPB acquired 850 acres (344 hectares) of these Essex marshes in 2000 from the Ministry of Defence, who had previously used them as a firing range. Prior to their ownership, the area had largely been used as grazing land by the monks of nearby Lessness Abbey. There was also a ferry here from at least the 1500s, patronised largely by pilgrims to cross the Thames on their way to Canterbury. (This is how Ferry Lane, which the LOOP visits, gets its name.)

The marshes today aren't just one of the largest RSPB reserves, but also one of the most important thanks to the wealth of wildlife they support. And it's not just birdlife either: the threatened water vole, water shrew, stoat, weasel, grass snake, as well as numerous insects including butterflies, bees, crickets, dragonflies and damselflies – all make their home in the marshes. But it's undoubtedly the avifauna that is the main draw, from the raptors – the buzzards, sparrow hawks and peregrines – to the owls (both barn owls and short-eared owls can be seen here) and the more glamorous and/or rarer members of the bird world, such as the kingfisher, woodlark, Cetti's warbler and very rare sociable lapwing.

ROUTE GUIDE AND MAPS

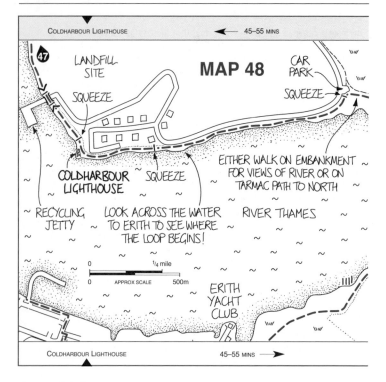

A recycling jetty At one point the path crosses the gangway of a jetty (Map 48), on which stands a large hangar. This jetty collects a lot of the rubbish that is brought here by boat to be either recycled or deposited in the adjacent massive landfill site.

According to the company's website, there's been a dump here for almost the last two centuries. Gases that are released by the rubbish escapes through the tubes that protrude from the ground, though some of that gas is also captured and used to generate electricity that's sold to the national grid.

Apparently, the dumping of rubbish at this landfill site is due to finish in 2024, after which, so it is hoped, it will be returned to nature as part of Rainham Marshes.

Coldharbour Lighthouse There are nine small lighthouses on the Thames, each placed on the riverbank in the 19th century to warn shipping of the various bends in the river. This is a fine example, placed here in 1885 and little-changed since.

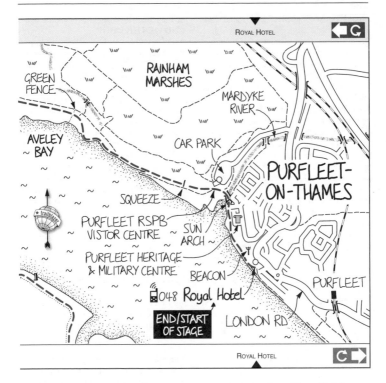

Aveley Bay There's a choice of paths around Aveley Bay. The official route follows the tarmac path. However, the more popular option is to stick to the top of the embankment so as to enjoy further views of the river, with the Dartford Crossing, soaring impressively above the river, looming ahead.

Along the bay you cross, maybe for the last time on the LOOP, the border of Greater London. There are several places where the two paths reunite, most conveniently at the bay's eastern end by the **RSPB Visitor Centre** (☎ 01708-899840, 🖳 rspb.org.uk/reserves-and-events/reserves-a-z/rainham-marshes; Thur-Sun 9.30am-5pm) with *café* (Thur-Sun 10am-4pm). In 2021 they hope to be able to open daily (the hours will be the same though). Opposite the centre you cross **Mardyke River** on a bridge, at the far end of which is the '**Sun Arch**' – your gateway to Purfleet-on-Thames.

PURFLEET-ON-THAMES [Map 48]

In 2020 Purfleet added '-on-Thames' to its name to advertise the fact that it lies on Britain's most important river. The idea is

that, by doing this, the town will attract more visitors and hopefully emulate its late Victorian heyday when 1500 people a day would flock to Purfleet and spend their money here. (While sceptics may sneer, such a name change did work for Staines who also added '-on-Thames' to their name in 2011, and reaped the economic benefits as a consequence.)

To be fair, Purfleet-on-Thames has plenty to celebrate. Not only is there the brilliant **RSPB Visitor Centre** (see p199), but the town, which was first mentioned in 1285 (the name means 'Purta's stream', presumably referring to the Mardyke), was the main storage and testing facility for gunpowder in the 19th century; one of the five magazines that stored the gunpowder is still standing and is now a museum, **Purfleet Heritage & Military Centre** (🖳 purfleet-heritage.com; Thur, Sun & Bank holiday Mon 10am-3pm; £3). When the magazine was in its heyday Britain's most celebrated artist, JMW Turner, was making sketches of the town that are now part of the collection at Tate Britain.

The song *Amazing Grace* was also inspired by Purfleet – or, rather, the composer, the Rev John Newton, was inspired to write it after a near-death boating accident close to the town. And in Bram Stoker's most famous novel, *Dracula*, the count buys the fictional Carfax Abbey which is based in Purfleet.

Services
There aren't too many facilities in the town but **Purfleet General Stores** (daily 8am-10pm) has an **ATM** and is close to the station. But for most people, the entire focus

of their time in Purfleet-on-Thames is the **END OF THE LOOP**.

The end lies just a few steps back from the riverfront outside *Royal Hotel* (☎ 01708-860852, 🖳 theroyalpurfleet.co.uk). There's no plaque to tell you it's the end – just as there was nothing in Erith. So you'll just have to make do with a photo or two, as well as a sense of satisfaction, relief – and possibly a little smugness – that comes with a job well done. The hotel of course offers accommodation; they have about 50 rooms (S/D & Tw, all en suite; room from £45, sgl occ room rate; breakfast £6.95) though at the time of writing (and because of COVID-19) they were only offering about 20 rooms. They also weren't serving food except breakfast for guests.

Transport [see map pp42-3]
Purfleet is on C2C's Fenchurch Street to Grays (in Essex) railway line (see p46).

Fenchurch Street station is by the Tower of London. For connections to other mainline rail stations Tower Hill (District line) tube station is a 2-minute walk and Aldgate (Circle Line) a 5-minute walk from Fenchurch Street rail station.

Should you want to feel you have completed the circuit the No 44 **bus** (Mon-Sat 2/hr, Sun 1/hr) goes from Grays to Lakeside shopping centre via Purfleet railway station. At Lakeside pick up an X80 (Chafford Hundred to Bluewater; daily 1/hr) bus to Bluewater and then the No 428 to Erith.

APPENDIX A: GPS WAYPOINTS

Each GPS waypoint below was taken on the route at the reference number marked on the map as below. This list of GPS waypoints is also available to download from the Trailblazer website – 🖳 trailblazer-guides.com.

WAYPOINT	MAP	OS GRID REF	DESCRIPTION
001	Map 1	N51.48163° E0.17549°	Start of trail at Erith railway station
002	Map 2	N51.44866° E0.17003°	Small post just in treeline (Hall Place Park)
003	Map 3	N51.42647° E0.13102°	Five Arches Bridge, Foots Cray Meadows
004	Map 4	N51.41031° E0.09726°	Remains of Scadbury moated manor
005	Map 5	N51.37950° E0.06374°	Bridge in Crofton Wood
006	Map 6	N51.34860° E0.04613°	View of Holwood House from LOOP
007	Map 7	N51.36725° W0.00000°	Meridian marker
008	Map 8	N51.36304° W0.05923°	Addington Hills viewing platform
009	Map 9	N51.33863° W0.03795°	Junction with Baker Boy Lane
010	Map 10	N51.32272° W0.08461°	Sharp turn in trail in Sanderstead to Whyteleafe Countryside Area
011	Map 11	N51.29479° W0.12189°	Double bench in Happy Valley
012	Map 12	N51.33216° W0.17087°	Stile into/out of Mayfield Lavender Farm
013	Map 13	N51.33208° W0.20937°	End/start of stage by signpost on Banstead Downs
014	Map 14	N51.35159° W0.24224°	Banqueting House of Nonsuch Park
015	Map 15	N51.36020° W0.26512°	Packhorse Bridge over the Hogsmill
016	Map 16	N51.38241° W0.26109°	St John's Church, Old Malden
017	Map 17	N51.41403° W0.33772°	Woodland Gardens entrance/exit, Bushy Park
018	Map 18	N51.41322° W0.34679°	Gate on Ash Walk (Bushy Park)
019	Map 19	N51.43743° W0.37136°	Leave/join Twickenham Rd
020	Map 20	N51.45578° W0.38149°	Junction of paths on Hounslow Heath, for the LOOP turn south
021	Map 21	N51.47061° W0.41117°	End/start of stage
022	Map 22	N51.50043° W0.40861°	Helter-skelter ramps at junction of LOOP and the Grand Union Canal
023	Map 23	N51.50795° W0.43896°	Stockley Park entrance/exit
024	Map 24	N51.52930° W0.48847°	Sculpture by B470
025	Map 25	N51.56922° W0.48179°	Bridge to/from Denham Quarry
026	Map 26	N51.58824° W0.48334°	Barrier by Moorhall Rd
027	Map 27	N51.61399° W0.48376°	Stile off/onto Plough Lane, Harefield
028	Map 28	N51.63170° W0.41800°	Ignore kissing gate (Sandy Lodge Lane)
029	Map 29	N51.62177° W0.35819°	Grim's Dyke monument
030	Map 30	N51.64398° W0.30815°	Road crossing on bend of A411 (Elstree Rd)
031	Map 31	N51.64939° W0.29636°	Kissing gate off/onto Allum Lane
032	Map 32	N51.64096° W0.26258°	Scratchwood Open Space
033	Map 33	N51.64193° W0.19307°	Leave/join Dollis Brook in Barnet Playing Fields

WAYPOINT	MAP	OS GRID REF	DESCRIPTION
034	Map 34	N51.65913° W0.18818°	Turn off road opposite Hadley Hurst
035	Map 35	N51.66745° W0.13962°	Camlet Moat
036	Map 36	N51.67357° W0.06519°	View of Forty Hall from LOOP
037	Map 37	N51.66707° W0.01819°	Enfield Lock
038	Map 38	N51.64076° E0.00130°	Sharp turn near top of Pole Hill
039	Map 39	N51.63481° E0.01872°	Obelisk Fountain near Butler's Retreat
040	Map 40	N51.62220° E0.10146°	Chigwell Water Treatment Works
041	Map 41	N51.61483° E0.12473°	Carved wooden 'henge'
042	Map 42	N51.62128° E0.19484°	Old metal gateposts in Pyrgo Park
043	Map 43	N51.60725° E0.22854°	Historical figures (sculptures)
044	Map 44	N51.58234° E0.24736°	Bridge in undergrowth by pylon in Pages Wood
045	Map 45	N51.54516° E0.22105°	Bridge by path in Hornchurch Country Park
046	Map 46	N51.53337° E0.20285°	Albyns Farm
047	Map 47	N51.50497° E0.17883°	LOOP meets/leaves River Thames
048	Map 48	N51.48289° E0.23153°	End/start of trail by Royal Hotel, Purfleet-on-Thames

APPENDIX B: MAP KEY

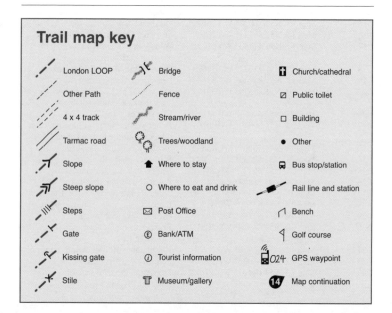

Trail map key

London LOOP · Bridge · Church/cathedral

Other Path · Fence · Public toilet

4 x 4 track · Stream/river · Building

Tarmac road · Trees/woodland · Other

Slope · Where to stay · Bus stop/station

Steep slope · O Where to eat and drink · Rail line and station

Steps · Post Office · Bench

Gate · Bank/ATM · Golf course

Kissing gate · Tourist information · O24 GPS waypoint

Stile · Museum/gallery · 14 Map continuation

APPENDIX C: BUS SERVICES

The services listed below are only a few of the many available in London. Only the locations most relevant for LOOP walkers are included and places in **bold text** are on, or near, the LOOP. Note that in quiet rural areas a few services operate on a '**hail and ride**' basis ie there are no fixed stops and drivers will stop where it is safe either for you to get on or off.

For full details of the services check the TfL website or app (see p41).

Erith
99 Woolwich High St to Bexleyheath via Woolwich Arsenal station, **Erith** railway station, **Slade Green** & **Barnehurst** railway station; daily 2-5/hr
229 Thamesmead to Sidcup via **Erith** (West St), **Barnehurst** railway station & **Bexley**; daily 4-6/hr
428 Bluewater Shopping Centre to Erith via **Crayford** & Dartford; daily 2-4/hr
469 Erith to Woolwich Arsenal via Abbey Wood & Plumstead stations; daily 4-8/hr

Crayford
428 Bluewater Shopping Centre to Erith via **Crayford** & Dartford; daily 2-4/hr
492 Sidcup railway station to Bluewater via **Foots Cray**, **Bexley**, **Bexleyheath**, **Barnehurst**, **Crayford** & Dartford railway stations; daily 1-2/hr

Bexley
132 Bexleyheath to North Greenwich via **Bexley** (for Bexley railway station), Eltham station/Lassa Rd; daily 2-6/hr
229 Thamesmead to Sidcup via **Erith** (West St), **Barnehurst** railway station & **Bexley**; daily 3-5/hr
492 Sidcup railway station to Bluewater via **Foots Cray**, **Bexley**, **Bexleyheath**, **Barnehurst**, **Crayford** & Dartford railway stations; daily 1-2/hr

Foots Cray
51 Woolwich High St to Orpington via Woolwich Arsenal station, **Sidcup** station & **Foots Cray** (Sidcup Hill); daily 2-6/hr
233 Swanley to Eltham bus station via **New Eltham** station & **Foots Cray**; daily 2-3/hr
321 Foots Cray Tesco to New Cross Gate via Sidcup High St/Station Rd, **New Eltham** station, Eltham, Blackheath Park & Lewisham station; daily 2-5/hr

Foots Cray (cont'd)
492 Sidcup railway station to Bluewater via **Foots Cray**, **Bexley**, **Bexleyheath**, **Barnehurst**, **Crayford** & Dartford railway stations; daily 2/hr
R11 Sidcup to Green Street Green via **Foots Cray**, St Mary Cray railway station & **Orpington**; daily 2-5/hr

Sidcup
51 Woolwich High St to Orpington via Woolwich Arsenal station, **Sidcup** station & **Foots Cray** (Sidcup Hill); daily 2-6/hr
160 Sidcup to Catford via Chislehurst, New Eltham & Eltham; daily 3-4/hr
229 Thamesmead to Sidcup via **Erith** (West St), **Barnehurst** railway station & **Bexley**; daily 3-5/hr
269 Bromley North to Bexleyheath via Chislehurst & **Sidcup**; daily 4-5/hr
286 Sidcup to Greenwich via Eltham & Kidbrooke, daily 3-5/hr
321 Foots Cray Tesco to New Cross Gate via **Sidcup** High St/Station Rd, **New Eltham** station, Eltham, Blackheath Park, Lewisham & New Cross Gate railway stations; daily 2-5/hr
492 Sidcup railway station to Bluewater via **Foots Cray**, **Bexley**, **Bexleyheath**, **Barnehurst**, **Crayford** & Dartford railway stations; daily 2/hr
R11 Sidcup to Green Street Green via **Foots Cray**, St Mary Cray railway station & **Orpington**; daily 2-5/hr

Petts Wood & Jubilee Country Park
208 Lewisham station to Orpington station via Bromley South & **Petts Wood**; daily 4-5/hr
273 Petts Wood station to Lewisham station via St Mary Cray & Lee railway stations; daily 2-3/hr
R3 Orpington station to Locksbottom via **Petts Wood** (Station Sq); daily 2-3/hr

Petts Wood & Jubilee Country Park *(cont'd)*
R7 Chislehurst to Chelsfield via Petts Wood & Orpington station; daily 1-2/hr

Farnborough
358 Crystal Palace to Orpington via Beckenham Road tram stop, Clock House station, Beckenham, Shortlands & Bromley South stations & Farnborough; daily 2-4/hr

Holwood Farm Shop (Keston)
146 Bromley North station to Downe via Bromley South & Hayes stations, Keston (The Fox) & Holwood Farm; daily 1/hr

Keston
146 Bromley North station to Downe via Bromley South & Hayes stations, Keston (The Fox) & Holwood Farm; daily 1/hr
246 Bromley North to Westerham via Hayes railway station, Coney Hall, Keston (The Fox); daily 1-2/hr

Coney Hall
138 Bromley North station to Coney Hall via Bromley South & Hayes railway stations, daily 1-3/hr
246 Bromley North to Westerham via Hayes railway station, Coney Hall, Keston (The Fox); daily 1-2/hr
314 New Addington tram stop to Eltham bus station via Coney Hall, Hayes station, Bromley South station, New Eltham station & Eltham station; daily 2-5/hr

Hayes
119 Bromley North station to South Croydon via Bromley South, Hayes station, West Wickham, Shirley & East Croydon station; daily 2-4/hr
138 Bromley North station to Coney Hall via Bromley South & Hayes railway stations, daily 1-3/hr
146 Bromley North station to Downe via Bromley South & Hayes stations, Keston (The Fox) & Holwood Farm; daily 1/hr
246 Bromley North to Westerham via Hayes railway station, Coney Hall, Keston (The Fox); daily 1-2/hr
314 New Addington tram stop to Eltham bus station via Coney Hall and Hayes railway station, Bromley South railway station,

New Eltham station & Eltham station; daily 2-5/hr

Shirley
119 Bromley North station to South Croydon via Bromley South, Hayes station, West Wickham (Swan), Shirley & East Croydon station; daily 2-4/hr
130 New Addington to Thornton Heath via Gravel Hill, Coombe Lane tram stop, Shirley (Upper Shirley Rd) & Norwood Junction railway station; daily 2-5/hr
466 Addington Village to Caterham-on-the-Hill via Gravel Hill & Coombe Lane tram stops, Shirley, Sandilands, East Croydon station, South Croydon, Purley & Coulsdon Common; daily 2-6/hr

Coombe Lane
130 New Addington to Thornton Heath via Gravel Hill, Coombe Lane tram stop, Shirley (Upper Shirley Rd) & Norwood Junction railway station; daily 2-5/hr
466 Addington Village to Caterham-on-the-Hill via Gravel Hill & Coombe Lane tram stops, Shirley, Sandilands, East Croydon station, South Croydon, Purley & Coulsdon Common; daily 2-6/hr

Selsdon
64 New Addington to Thornton Heath via Selsdon (Ashen Vale/Pixton Way & Peacock Gardens), South Croydon, East Croydon station & West Croydon bus station; daily 2-7/hr
359 Addington Village to Purley via Gravel Hill, Selsdon (Sorrel Bank & Peacock Gardens) & Sanderstead; daily 1-2/hr
433 Addington Village to East Croydon station via Selsdon (Sorrel Bank & Peacock Gardens) & South Croydon; daily 4-5/hr

Hamsey Green
403 West Croydon to Warlingham via Sanderstead & Hamsey Green; daily 3-5/hr

Whyteleafe and Upper Warlingham
407 Sutton to Caterham Valley station via Carshalton, West Croydon bus, rail & tram stations, Purley station, Warlingham (Godstone Rd), Whyteleafe & Upper Warlingham railway stations; daily 3-6/hr

Whyteleafe & Upper Warlingham *(cont'd)*
434 Coulsdon Town to Whyteleafe South railway station via Warlingham (New Barn Lane) & Whyteleafe & Upper Warlingham railway stations; daily 2/hr

Coulsdon Common
404 Coulsdon Town to Caterham-on-the-hill via Coulsdon South railway station & Coulsdon Common; daily 2/hr
466 Addington Village to Caterham-on-the-Hill via Gravel Hill & Coombe Lane tram stops, Shirley, Sandilands, East Croydon station, South Croydon, Purley & Coulsdon Common; daily 2-6/hr

Coulsdon/Coulsdon South
166 Epsom/Banstead to West Croydon via Woodmansterne station & Coulsdon Town station; daily 2-5/hr – Mon-Sat 1-2/hr continue(s) to/start(s) in Epsom.
404 Coulsdon Town to Caterham-on-the-hill via Coulsdon South railway station & Coulsdon Common; daily 2/hr
405 Redhill to Croydon via Coulsdon South & Coulsdon Town stations; daily 2-4/hr
463 Coulsdon South to Pollards Hill via Coulsdon, Woodmansterne station, Therapia Lane & Beddington Lane tram stops; daily 2-4/hr

Clock House Village/Woodmansterne
166 Epsom/Banstead to West Croydon via Woodmansterne station & Coulsdon Town station; daily 2-5/hr – Mon-Sat 1-2/hr continue(s) to/start(s) in Epsom.
463 Coulsdon South to Pollards Hill via Coulsdon Town station, Woodmansterne station, Clock House Village (The Mount), Therapia Lane & Beddington Lane tram stops; daily 2-4/hr

Banstead
166 Epsom/Banstead to West Croydon via Woodmansterne station & Coulsdon Town station; daily 2-5/hr – Mon-Sat 1-2/hr continue(s) to/start(s) in Epsom.

Nonsuch Park
470 Colliers Wood station to Epsom via Sutton, Cheam, Nonsuch Park, Ewell & Ewell East station; Mon-Sat 2/hr

Ewell
293 Epsom to Morden via Ewell & North Cheam; daily 2-3/hr
406 Epsom to Kingston-upon-Thames via The Spring (Bourne Hall Park) Ewell, Worcester Park Road (A240) & Tolworth station; daily 2-3/hr
467 Epsom to Hook via Ewell, Ewell West station & Chessington; Mon-Sat 1/hr
470 Colliers Wood station to Epsom via Sutton, Cheam, Nonsuch Park, Ewell & Ewell East station; Mon-Sat 2/hr

Malden Manor
K1 New Malden to Kingston-upon-Thames via Malden Manor & Surbiton stations; Mon-Fri 6-8/hr, Sat 3-6/hr, Sun 2-4/hr

Malden Way/Kingston Bypass
265 Tolworth to Putney Bridge via New Malden (Malden Way) & Barnes; daily 4-6/hr
K1 New Malden station to Kingston-upon-Thames via Malden Manor station, Malden Way/Kingston Bypass (Southwood Drive/Elmbridge Ave) & Surbiton station; Mon-Fri 6-8/hr, Sat 3-6/hr, Sun 2-4/hr

Berrylands
K2 Hook to Norbiton via Tolworth, Berrylands & Surbiton stations & Kingston-upon-Thames; daily 3-6/hr

Kingston-upon-Thames
71 Chessington to Kingston-upon-Thames via Hook; daily 4-6/hr
85 Kingston-upon-Thames to Putney (last stop Kingston Hall Rd); daily 2-6/hr
111 Heathrow Airport to Kingston-upon-Thames via Cranford, Hounslow East bus station, Hounslow, Whitton, Hanworth, Hampton station, Hampton Court & Hampton Wick; daily 4/hr
213 Kingston-upon-Thames to Sutton via New Malden & Worcester Park stations; daily 2-3/hr
216 Kingston-upon-Thames to Staines via Hampton Wick (Church Grove), Hampton Court, Hampton station, Sunbury & Ashford; daily 2-3/hr

Kingston-upon-Thames *(cont'd)*

281 Tolworth to Hounslow via Kingston-upon-Thames, Hampton Wick, Fulwell & Twickenham stations; daily 5-7/hr

285 Heathrow Airport to Kingston-upon-Thames via Hatton Cross station, Great South West Rd, Feltham station, Hampton Hill, Teddington & Hampton Wick station; daily 2-3/hr

371 Kingston-upon-Thames (Kingston Hall Rd) to Richmond; daily 4/hr

406 Epsom to Kingston-upon-Thames via The Spring (Bourne Hall Park) Ewell, Worcester Park Road (A240) & Tolworth station; daily 2-3/hr

411 Kingston-upon-Thames to West Molesey via Hampton Wick (Church Grove) & Hampton Court; daily 2-4/hr

481 Isleworth to Kingston-upon-Thames via Whitton, Fulwell, Teddington & Hampton Wick; daily 1-2/hr

K1 New Malden to Kingston-upon-Thames via Malden Manor & Surbiton stations; Mon-Fri 6-8/hr, Sat 3-6/hr, Sun 2-4/hr

K2 Hook to Norbiton via Tolworth, Berrylands & Surbiton stations & Kingston-upon-Thames; daily 3-6/hr

X26 West Croydon bus station to Heathrow Central bus station via Worcester Park station, New Malden, Kingston-upon-Thames & Hatton Cross stations; daily 2/hr

Hampton Wick & Bushy Park

111 Heathrow Airport to Kingston-upon-Thames via Cranford, Hounslow East bus station, Hounslow, Whitton, Hanworth, Hampton station, Hampton Court & Hampton Wick; daily 4/hr

216 Kingston-upon-Thames to Staines via Hampton Wick (Church Grove), Hampton Court, Hampton station, Sunbury & Ashford; daily 2-3/hr

285 Heathrow Airport to Kingston-upon-Thames via Hatton Cross station, Great South West Rd, Feltham station, Hampton Hill, Teddington & Hampton Wick station; daily 2-3/hr

406 Epsom to Kingston-upon-Thames via The Spring (Bourne Hall Park) Ewell, Worcester Park Road (A240) & Tolworth station; daily 2-3/hr

Hampton Wick & Bushy Park *(cont'd)*

411 Kingston-upon-Thames to West Molesey via Hampton Wick (Church Grove) & Hampton Court; daily 2-4/hr

481 Isleworth to Kingston-upon-Thames via Whitton, Fulwell, Teddington & Hampton Wick; daily 1-2/hr

Hampton Hill

285 Heathrow Airport to Kingston-upon-Thames via Hatton Cross station, Great South West Rd, Feltham station, Hampton Hill, Teddington & Hampton Wick station; daily 2-3/hr

R70 Hampton to Richmond station via Hampton Hill & Fulwell; daily 3-6/hr

Fulwell

110 Hounslow to Isleworth via Whitton Corner (Hospital Bridge Rd), Fulwell (Sixth Cross Rd) & Twickenham station; daily 3/hr

281 Tolworth to Hownslow via Kingston-upon-Thames, Hampton Wick, Fulwell (Sixth Cross Rd & station) & Twickenham stations; daily 5-7/hr

290 Twickenham to Staines via Fulwell (Sixth Cross Rd), Hanworth, Sunbury & Ashford; daily 2-4/hr

R70 Hampton to Richmond station via Hampton Hill & Fulwell (station & Sixth Cross Rd); daily 3-6/hr

Whitton Corner

110 Hounslow to Isleworth via Whitton Corner (Hospital Bridge Rd), Fulwell (Sixth Cross Rd) & Twickenham station; daily 3/hr

Hanworth Road

111 Heathrow Airport to Kingston-upon-Thames via Cranford, Hounslow East bus station, Hounslow, Whitton, Hanworth Rd, Hampton station, Hampton Court & Hampton Wick; daily 4/hr

Great South West Rd/Hatton/Hatton Cross

90 Feltham to Northolt via Great South West Rd, Hatton Cross underground station, Hayes & Harlington railway station; daily 3-5/hr

Great South West Rd/Hatton/Hatton Cross (cont'd)

203 Staines to Hounslow via Ashford, Great South West Rd, Hatton Cross & Hounslow West stations; daily 2-3/hr

285 Heathrow Airport to Kingston-upon-Thames via Hatton Cross station, Great South West Rd, Feltham station, Hampton Hill, Teddington & Hampton Wick station; daily 2-3/hr

423 Heathrow Airport Terminal 5 to Hounslow via Hatton Cross station & Hounslow West; daily 2-3/hr

482 Southall to Heathrow Airport via Hounslow West, Cranford (The Parkway) & Hatton (Great South West Road) & Hatton Cross station; daily 2-3/hr

490 Richmond station to Heathrow Airport via Fulwell, Feltham, Hatton (Great South West Rd) & Hatton Cross station; daily 2-6/hr

X26 West Croydon bus station to Heathrow Central bus station via Worcester Park station, New Malden, Kingston-upon-Thames & Hatton Cross stations; daily 2/hr

Cranford

81 Slough bus station to Hounslow via Langley, Harmondsworth & Cranford; daily 4-5/hr

105 Heathrow to Greenford via Cranford & Southall; daily 4-5/hr

111 Heathrow Airport to Kingston-upon-Thames via Cranford, Hounslow East bus station, Hounslow, Whitton, Hanworth Rd, Hampton station, Hampton Court & Hampton Wick; daily 4/hr

222 Uxbridge station to Hounslow via Yiewsley (High St), West Drayton, Cranford & West Hounslow; daily 5-6/hr

482 Southall to Heathrow Airport via Hounslow West, Cranford (The Parkway) & Hatton (Great South West Road) & Hatton Cross station; daily 2-3/hr

E6 Greenford to Cranford (Bulls Bridge) via Hayes town, Hayes & Harlington station; daily 4-5/hr

Hayes & Harlington

90 Feltham to Northolt via Great South West Rd, Hatton Cross station, Hayes & Harlington station; daily 3-5/hr

Hayes & Harlington (cont'd)

140 Hayes & Harlington to Harrow & Wealdstone station via Northolt & South Harrow stations; daily 4-7/hr

195 Brentford station to Hillingdon Heath via Southall station, Hayes & Harlington station & North Hillingdon; daily 5/hr

350 Hayes & Harlington to Heathrow Terminal 5 via Iron Bridge Rd (Stockley Park), Horton Rd (Yiewsley) & West Drayton station; daily 3/hr

E6 Greenford to Cranford (Bulls Bridge) via Hayes town, Hayes & Harlington station; daily 4-5/hr

H98 Hounslow to Hayes End via Hounslow West station & Great West Road, Cranford, Hayes, Hayes & Harlington station; daily 4-6/hr

U4 Hayes to Uxbridge via Hayes & Harlington station; daily 4-6/hr

U5 Hayes & Harlington to Uxbridge via Iron Bridge Rd (Stockley Park), West Drayton station & Yiewsley (High St); daily 4-5/hr

Stockley Park

350 Hayes & Harlington to Heathrow Terminal 5 via Iron Bridge Rd (Stockley Park), Horton Rd (Yiewsley) & West Drayton station; daily 3/hr

A10 Uxbridge to Heathrow Airport via Iron Bridge Rd (Stockley Park); daily 2-3/hr

U5 Hayes & Harlington to Uxbridge via Iron Bridge Rd (Stockley Park), West Drayton station & Yiewsley (High St); daily 4-5/hr

West Drayton

222 Uxbridge station to Hounslow via Yiewsley (High St), West Drayton, Cranford & West Hounslow; daily 5-6/hr

350 Hayes & Harlington to Heathrow Terminal 5 via Iron Bridge Rd (Stockley Park), Horton Rd (Yiewsley) & West Drayton station; daily 3/hr

U1 West Drayton station to Ruislip via Yiewsley (High St), Uxbridge station, Ickenham & West Ruislip; daily 2-3/hr

U3 Uxbridge station to Heathrow Airport via Yiewsley (High St), West Drayton station & Harmondsworth; daily 3-5/hr

U5 Hayes & Harlington to Uxbridge via

Iron Bridge Rd (Stockley Park), West Drayton station & Yiewsley (High St); daily 4-5/hr

Yiewsley
222 Uxbridge station to Hounslow via Yiewsley (High St), West Drayton, Cranford & West Hounslow; daily 5-6/hr
350 Hayes & Harlington to Heathrow Terminal 5 via Iron Bridge Rd (Stockley Park), Horton Rd (Yiewsley) & West Drayton station; daily 3/hr
U1 West Drayton station to Ruislip via Yiewsley (High St), Uxbridge station, Ickenham & West Ruislip; daily 2-3/hr
U3 Uxbridge station to Heathrow Airport via Yiewsley (High St), West Drayton station & Harmondsworth; daily 3-5/hr
U5 Hayes & Harlington to Uxbridge via Iron Bridge Rd (Stockley Park), West Drayton station & Yiewsley (High St); daily 4-5/hr

Uxbridge
222 Uxbridge station to Hounslow via Yiewsley (High St), West Drayton, Cranford & West Hounslow; daily 5-6/hr
331 Ruislip to Uxbridge via Northwood, Batchworth Heath, South Harefield (Broadwater Lock/Grand Union Canal) & Denham (Station Parade/Moorfield Rd); daily 2-3/hr
A10 Uxbridge to Heathrow Airport via Iron Bridge Rd (Stockley Park); daily 2-3/hr
U1 West Drayton station to Ruislip via Yiewsley (High St), Uxbridge station, Ickenham & West Ruislip; daily 2-3/hr
U3 Uxbridge station to Heathrow Airport via Yiewsley (High St), West Drayton station & Harmondsworth; daily 3-5/hr
U4 Hayes to Uxbridge via Hayes & Harlington station; daily 4-6/hr
U5 Hayes & Harlington to Uxbridge via Iron Bridge Rd (Stockley Park), West Drayton station & Yiewsley (High St); daily 4-5/hr
U9 Uxbridge to Harefield (Mount Pleasant) via Ickenham; Mon-Sat 3/hr, Sun 1/hr

South Harefield
331 Ruislip to Uxbridge via Northwood, Batchworth Heath, South Harefield (Broadwater Lock/Grand Union Canal) & Denham (Station Parade/Moorfield Rd); daily 2-3/hr

West Harefield/Harefield
U9 Uxbridge to Harefield (Mount Pleasant) via Ickenham; Mon-Sat 3/hr, Sun 1/hr

Batchworth Heath
331 Ruislip to Uxbridge via Northwood, Batchworth Heath, South Harefield (Broadwater Lock/Grand Union Canal) & Denham (Station Parade/Moorfield Rd); daily 2-3/hr

Hatch End
H12 Stanmore to South Harrow via Rayners Lane, Pinner, Hatch End & Harold Weald; daily 4-6/hr
H14 Hatch End to Harrow via Harrow Weald & Headstone; daily 4-6/hr

Common Road
258 Watford Junction station to South Harrow via Bushey station, Bushey Heath (Common Rd), Stanmore, Harrow & Wealdstone station & Harrow bus station; daily approx 4/hr

Stanmore Hill
142 Watford Junction station to Brent Cross shopping centre via Bushey station, The Common/Priory Drive (Stanmore Hill), Stanmore station & Edgware station; daily 4-7/hr

Elstree Road/Aldenham Reservoir
306 Watford to Borehamwood via Bushey, Borehamwood (Elstree Hill North), Barham Ave (Fir Tree Close), Aldenham Reservoir and Elstree & Borehamwood railway station; Mon-Sat 2-3/hr, Sun 4-5/day
(Note: service is operated by Sullivan's and TfL Travelcards are not valid on it)

Watling Street/Elstree

107 Edgware station to New Barnet station via Elstree Hill North, Barham Ave (Fir Tree Close), Elstree & Borehamwood station, Stirling Corner (Barnet Lane) & High Barnet station; daily 2-4/hr

306 Watford to Borehamwood via Bushey, Elstree Hill North, Barham Ave (Fir Tree Close) and Elstree & Borehamwood station; Mon-Sat 2-3/hr, Sun 4-5/day

(Note: service is operated by Sullivan's and TfL Travelcards are not valid on it)

Elstree & Borehamwood

107 Edgware station to New Barnet station via Elstree Hill North, Barham Ave (Fir Tree Close), Elstree & Borehamwood station, Scratchwood (Ashley Drive) & High Barnet station; daily 2-4/hr

292 Colindale to Borehamwood via Edgware station, The Fairway (Mill Hill), Moat Mount Park, Scratchwood (Ashley Drive) & Elstree & Borehamwood station; daily 2-3/hr

306 Watford to Borehamwood via Bushey, Elstree Hill North, Barham Ave (Fir Tree Close) and Elstree & Borehamwood station; Mon-Sat 2-3/hr, Sun 4-5/day

(Note: service is operated by Sullivan's and TfL Travelcards are not valid on it)

Scratchwood

107 Edgware station to New Barnet station via Elstree Hill North, Barham Ave (Fir Tree Close), Elstree & Borehamwood station, Scratchwood (Ashley Drive) & High Barnet station; daily 2-4/hr

292 Colindale to Borehamwood via Edgware station, The Fairway (Mill Hill), Moat Mount Park, Scratchwood (Ashley Drive) & Elstree & Borehamwood railway station; daily 2-3/hr

Barnet Way/A1/Moat Mount Open Space

292 Colindale to Borehamwood via Edgware station, The Fairway (Mill Hill), Moat Mount Park, Scratchwood (Ashley Drive) & Elstree & Borehamwood station; daily 2-3/hr

384 Edgware to Cockfosters via The Fairway (Mill Hill), Moat Mount Park, High Barnet & New Barnet stations; daily 2-4/hr

High Barnet & New Barnet

107 Edgware station to New Barnet station via Elstree Hill North, Barham Ave (Fir Tree Close), Elstree & Borehamwood station, Scratchwood (Ashley Drive) & High Barnet station; daily 2-4/hr

184 Chipping Barnet to Turnpike Lane station via High Barnet station, Meadway (King Edward Rd), New Barnet station (Station Rd), Arnos Grove station & Alexandra Palace station; daily 2-7/hr

383 High Barnet station to North Finchley bus station via Meadway (King Edward Rd), New Barnet station, Whetstone High Rd (Friern Barnet Lane) & Woodside Park station; daily 2/hr

384 Edgware station to Cockfosters via The Fairway (Mill Hill), Moat Mount Park, High Barnet station & New Barnet Station (Station Rd); daily 2-4/hr

King George's Fields

184 Chipping Barnet to Turnpike Lane station via High Barnet station, Meadway (King Edward Rd), New Barnet station (Station Rd), Arnos Grove station & Alexandra Palace station; daily 2-7/hr

383 High Barnet station to North Finchley bus station via Meadway (King Edward Rd), New Barnet station, Whetstone High Rd (Friern Barnet Lane) & Woodside Park station; daily 2/hr

Monken Hadley/Hadley Wood

399 Chipping Barnet to Hadley Wood station via Monken Hadley; Mon-Sat 1/hr

(Note: service is operated by Sullivan's and TfL Travelcards are not valid on it)

Cockfosters

298 Arnos Grove to Potters Bar via Cockfosters station; daily 2-3/hr

299 Cockfosters to Muswell Hill via Southgate station; daily 2-4/hr

384 Edgware to Cockfosters via The Fairway (Mill Hill), Moat Mount Park, High Barnet station & New Barnet Station (Station Rd); daily 2-4/hr

The Ridgeway

313 Chingford station to Potters Bar station via Enfield Town & Enfield Chase stations & The Ridgeway (Roundhedge Way); daily 2-3/hr

Clay Hill

W10 Enfield (Golf Ride) to Enfield Town station via Clay Hill; Mon-Sat 4-7/day

Enfield Wash (Hertford Rd)

121 Turnpike Lane bus station to Enfield Lock station via Enfield Chase and Enfield Town stations & Hertford Rd (for Turkey Street station); daily 4-5/hr

279 Manor House station to Waltham Cross bus station via Seven Sisters, White Hart Lane & Edmonton Green stations & Hertford Rd (for Turkey Street station); daily 4-10/hr

Enfield Lock

121 Turnpike Lane bus station to Enfield Lock station via Enfield Chase and Enfield Town stations & Hertford Rd (for Turkey Street station); daily 4-5/hr

Chingford

97 Chingford to Stratford via Walthamstow; daily 8-10/hr

179 Chingford to Ilford via Woodford Green; daily 3-5/hr

212 Chingford to Walthamstow via Highams Park station, Mon-Sat 4-6/hr, Sun 1-4/hr

313 Chingford station to Potters Bar station via Enfield Town & Enfield Chase stations & The Ridgeway (Roundhedge Way); daily 2-3/hr

397 Chingford to Debden via Epping High Rd (Cricket Ground) & Loughton; daily 2-3/hr

444 Chingford to Turnpike Lane station via Edmonton; daily 3-5/hr

Epping High Rd/Buckhurst Hill

13 Epping to Waltham Cross bus station via Epping High Rd; Mon-Fri 9/day

20 Debden to Walthamstow Central via Loughton station, Epping High Rd (Cricket Ground), Woodford Green, Upper Walthamstow & Whipps Cross; daily 2-4/hr

167 Loughton tube station to Ilford via Buckhurst Hill (Pentlow Way & Buckhurst Hill tube station) & Chigwell station; daily 2-3/hr

397 Chingford to Debden via Epping High Rd (Cricket Ground) & Loughton; daily 2-3/hr

549 Loughton to South Woodford via Epping High Rd (Cricket Ground), Buckhurst Hill station & Woodford station; Mon-Sat 1/hr

Chigwell

167 Loughton tube station to Ilford via Buckhurst Hill (Pentlow Way & Buckhurst Hill tube station) & Chigwell station; daily 2-3/hr

Chigwell Row

150 Becontree to Chigwell Row via Hainault underground station & Ilford; daily 3-5/hr

Havering-atte-Bower

375 Romford station to Passingford Bridge via Havering-atte-Bower (Havering Green); Mon-Sat 8/day

Noak Hill

256 Noak Hill (Wincanton Rd) to Hornchurch station via Harold Hill (Whitchurch Rd/Troopers Drive) & Harold Wood station; daily 3-6/hr

294 Havering Park to Noak Hill (Wincanton Rd) via Romford bus garage, Romford station, Harold Wood station & Harold Hill (Dagnam Park Drive, Brookside School); daily 3-5/hr

Carter's Brook (Whitchurch Rd & Dagnam Park Drive)

174 Dagenham Heathway station to Harold Hill (Dagnam Park Square) via Romford station & Dagnam Park Drive (Brookside School); daily 4-5/hr

256 Noak Hill (Wincanton Rd) to Hornchurch station via Harold Hill (Whitchurch Rd/Troopers Drive) & Harold Wood station; daily 3-6/hr

294 Havering Park to Noak Hill via Romford bus garage, Romford station, Harold Wood station & Harold Hill (Dagnam Park Drive/Brookside School); daily 3-5/hr

Harold Hill (Petersfield Ave)

496 Harold Wood (Co-op) to Romford station via Church Rd (Firham Park Ave) & Harold Hill (Paines Brook Way, Petersfield Avenue); daily 3-4/hr

Harold Wood

256 Noak Hill (Wincanton Rd) to Hornchurch station via Harold Hill (Whitchurch Rd/Troopers Drive) & Harold Wood station; daily 3-6/hr

294 Havering Park to Noak Hill via Romford bus garage, Romford station, Harold Wood station & Harold Hill (Dagnam Park Drive, Brookside School); daily 3-5/hr

347 Romford to South Ockendon via Harold Wood station, Hall Lane (Wylie Veterinary Centre & River Drive) & Upminster station; Mon-Sat 4/day

496 Harold Wood (Co-op) to Romford station via Church Rd (Firham Park Ave) & Harold Hill (Paines Brook Way, Petersfield Avenue); daily 3-4/hr

Hall Lane

248 Romford to Cranham via Hornchurch, Upminster Bridge & Upminster stations, Hall Lane (The Fairway & Severn Drive); daily 3-9/hr

347 Romford to South Ockendon via Harold Wood station, Hall Lane (Wylie Veterinary Centre & River Drive) & Upminster station; Mon-Sat 4/day

Upminster Bridge

248 Romford to Cranham via Hornchurch, Upminster Bridge & Upminster stations; daily 3-9/hr

370 Romford station to Lakeside shopping centre via Hornchurch, Upminster Bridge & Upminster stations & South Ockendon; daily 2-4/hr

Rainham

103 Rainham Interchange (station) to Chase Cross via Rainham Rd (Dovers Corner), South Hornchurch, Dagenham East station & Romford station; daily 3-6/hr

165 Rainham to Romford via Hornchurch; daily 3-5/hr

287 Rainham to Barking via Dagenham; daily 3-4/hr

372 Hornchurch to Lakeside Shopping centre via Rainham; daily 2-3/hr

Purfleet-on-Thames

44 Grays to Lakeside shopping centre bus station via Purfleet railway station; Mon-Sat 2/hr, Sun 1/hr

Purfleet-on-Thames to Erith

44 Grays to Lakeside shopping centre bus station via Purfleet railway station; Mon-Sat 2/hr, Sun 1/hr

X80 Chafford Hundred to Bluewater via Lakeside, Dartford & Greenhithe railway station; daily 1/hr

428 Bluewater Shopping Centre to Erith via Crayford & Dartford; daily 2-4/hr

	Erith	Crayford	Bexley	Petts Wood	Farnborough	Keston	Coney Hall	Shirley	Hamsey Green	Godstone Road	Coulsdon South	Clock House Village	Banstead	Ewell	Malden Manor link	Berrylands	Kingston-upon-Thames
Erith	0																
Crayford	5.7																
Bexley	8.2	2.5															
Petts Wood	15.5	9.7	7.2														
Farnborough	18.5	12.7	10.2	3													
Keston	22.2	16.5	14	6.7	3.7												
Coney Hall	23.5	17.7	15.2	8	5	1.2											
Shirley	26.7	21	18.5	11.2	8.2	4.5	3.2										
Hamsey Green	32.2	26.5	24	16.7	13.7	10	8.7	5.5									
Godstone Road	33.7	28	25.5	18.2	15.2	11.5	10.2	7	1.5								
Coulsdon South	38.7	33	30.5	23.2	20.2	16.5	15.2	12	6.5	5							
Clock House Village	40	34.2	31.7	24.5	21.5	17.7	16.5	13.2	7.7	6.2	1.2						
Banstead	43.5	37.7	35.2	28	25	21.2	20	16.7	11.2	9.7	4.7	3.5					
Ewell	47	41.2	38.7	31.5	28.5	24.7	23.5	20.2	14.7	13.2	8.2	7	3.5				
Malden Manor link	50.7	45	42.5	35.2	32.2	28.5	27.2	24	18.5	17	12	10.7	7.2	3.7			
Berrylands	52.2	46.5	44	36.7	33.7	30	28.7	25.5	20	18.5	13.5	12.2	8.7	5.2	1.5		
Kingston-u-Thames	54.2	48.5	46	38.7	35.7	32	30.7	27.5	22	20.5	15.5	14.2	10.7	7.2	3.5	2	
Fulwell High St	57.7	52	49.5	42.2	39.2	35.5	34.2	31	25.5	24	19	17.7	14.2	10.7	7	5.5	3.5
A30/Hatton Cross	63.7	58	55.5	48.2	45.2	41.5	40.2	37	31.5	30	25	23.7	20.2	16.7	13	11.5	9.5
Cranford	64.5	58.7	56.2	49	46	42.2	41	37.7	32.2	30.7	25.7	24.5	21	17.5	13.7	12.2	10.2
Hayes & Harlington	67.2	61.5	59	51.7	48.7	45	43.7	40.5	35	33.5	28.5	27.2	23.7	20.2	16.5	15	13
West Drayton	70.2	64.5	62	54.7	51.7	48	46.7	43.5	38	36.5	31.5	30.2	26.7	23.2	19.5	18	16
Uxbridge	74.5	68.7	66.2	59	56	52.2	51	47.7	42.2	40.7	35.7	34.5	31	27.5	23.7	22.2	20.2
West Harefield	79.5	73.7	71.2	64	61	57.2	56	52.7	47.2	45.7	40.7	39.5	36	32.5	28.7	27.2	25.2
Moor Park	84.2	78.5	76	68.7	65.7	62	60.7	57.5	52	50.5	45.5	44.2	40.7	37.2	33.5	32	30
Hatch End	88	82.2	79.7	72.5	69.5	65.7	64.5	61.2	55.7	54.2	49.2	48	44.5	41	37.2	35.7	33.7
Stanmore Hill	92.7	87	84.5	77.2	74.2	70.5	69.2	66	60.5	59	54	52.7	49.2	45.7	42	40.5	38.5
Elstree & B'wood	96.7	91	88.5	81.2	78.2	74.5	73.2	70	64.5	63	58	56.7	53.2	49.7	46	44.5	42.5
Great North Rd	104.2	98.5	96	88.7	85.7	82	80.7	77.5	72	70.5	65.5	64.2	60.7	57.2	53.5	52	50
Cockfosters	107.7	102	99.5	92.2	89.2	85.5	84.2	81	75.5	74	69	67.7	64.2	60.7	57	55.5	53.5
Turkey Street	115.5	109.7	107.2	100	97	93.2	92	88.7	83.2	81.7	76.7	75.5	72	68.5	64.7	63.2	61.2
Enfield Wash/Lock	116.2	110.5	108	100.7	97.7	94	92.7	89.5	84	82.5	77.5	76.2	72.7	69.2	65.5	64	62
Chingford	121	115.2	112.7	105.5	102.5	98.7	97.5	94.2	88.7	87.2	82.2	81	77.5	74	70.2	68.7	66.7
Chigwell	125	119.2	116.7	109.5	106.5	102.7	101.5	98.2	92.7	91.2	86.2	85	81.5	78	74.2	72.7	70.7
Havering-a-Bower	132	126.2	123.7	116.5	113.5	109.7	108.5	105.2	99.7	98.2	93.2	92	88.5	85	81.2	79.7	77.7
Harold Wood	137.2	131.5	129	121.7	118.7	115	113.7	110.5	105	103.5	98.5	97.2	93.7	90.2	86.5	85	83
Upminster Bridge	141.5	135.7	133.2	126	123	119.2	118	114.7	109.2	107.7	102.7	101.5	98	94.5	90.7	89.2	87.2
Rainham	146	140.2	137.7	130.5	127.5	123.7	122.5	119.2	113.7	112.2	107.2	106	102.5	99	95.2	93.7	91.7
Purfleet-on-Thames	150.7	145	142.5	135.2	132.2	128.5	127.2	124	118.5	117	112	110.7	107.2	103.7	100	98.5	96.5

London LOOP
DISTANCE CHART

Erith to Purfleet-on-Thames

(MILES)

Fulwell High St	A30/Hatton Cross	Cranford	Hayes & Harlington	West Drayton	Uxbridge	West Harefield	Moor Park	Hatch End	Stanmore Hill	Elstree & Borehamwood	Great North Road	Cockfosters	Turkey Street	Enfield Wash & Enfield Lock	Chingford	Chigwell	Havering-atte-Bower	Harold Wood	Upminster Bridge	Rainham	Purfleet-on-Thames
6																					
6.7	0.7																				
9.5	3.5	2.7																			
12.5	6.5	5.7	3																		
16.7	10.7	10	7.2	4.2																	
21.7	15.7	15	12.2	9.2	5																
26.5	20.5	19.7	17	14	9.7	4.7															
30.2	24.2	23.5	20.7	17.7	13.5	8.5	3.7														
35	29	28.2	25.5	22.5	18.2	13.2	8.5	4.7													
39	33	32.2	29.5	26.5	22.2	17.2	12.5	8.7	4												
46.5	40.5	39.7	37	34	29.7	24.7	20	16.2	11.5	7.5											
50	44	43.2	40.5	37.5	33.2	28.2	23.5	19.7	15	11	3.5										
57.7	51.7	51	48.2	45.2	41	36	31.2	27.5	22.7	18.7	11.2	7.7									
58.5	52.5	51.7	49	46	41.7	36.7	32	28.2	23.5	19.5	12	8.5	0.7								
63.2	57.2	56.5	53.7	50.7	46.5	41.5	36.7	33	28.2	24.2	16.7	13.2	5.2	4.7							
67.2	61.2	60.5	57.7	54.7	50.5	45.5	40.7	37	32.2	28.2	20.7	17.2	9.2	8.7	4						
74.2	68.2	67.5	64.7	61.7	57.5	52.5	47.7	44	39.2	35.2	27.7	24.2	16.2	15.7	11	7					
79.5	73.5	72.7	70	67	62.7	57.7	53	49.2	44.5	40.5	33	29.5	21.5	21	16.2	12.2	5.2				
83.7	77.7	77	74.2	71.2	67	62	57.2	53.5	48.7	44.7	37.2	33.7	25.7	25.2	20.5	16.5	9.5	4.2			
88.2	82.2	81.5	78.7	75.7	71.5	66.5	61.7	58	53.2	49.2	41.7	38.2	30.2	29.7	25	21	14	8.7	4.5		
93	87	86.2	83.5	80.5	76.2	71.2	66.5	62.7	58	54	46.5	43	35	34.5	29.7	25.7	18.7	13.5	9.2	4.7	

	Erith	Crayford	Bexley	Petts Wood	Farnborough	Keston	Coney Hall	Shirley	Hamsey Green	Godstone Road	Coulsdon South	Clock House Village	Banstead	Ewell	Malden Manor link	Berrylands	Kingston-upon-Thames
Erith	0																
Crayford	9.4																
Bexley	13.4	4															
Petts Wood	25.1	15.7	11.7														
Farnborough	30	20.6	16.6	4.9													
Keston	36	26.6	22.6	10.9	6												
Coney Hall	38	28.6	24.6	12.9	8	2											
Shirley	43.3	33.9	29.9	18.2	13.3	7.3	5.3										
Hamsey Green	52.1	42.7	38.7	27	22.1	16.1	14.1	8.8									
Godstone Road	54.5	45.1	41.1	29.4	24.5	18.5	16.5	11.2	2.4								
Coulsdon South	62.5	53.1	49.1	37.4	32.5	26.5	24.5	19.2	10.4	8							
Clock House Village	64.5	55.1	51.1	39.4	34.5	28.5	26.5	21.2	12.4	10	2						
Banstead	70.1	60.7	56.7	45	40.1	34.1	32.1	26.8	18	15.6	7.6	5.6					
Ewell	75.7	66.3	62.3	50.6	45.7	39.7	37.7	32.4	23.6	21.2	13.2	11.2	5.6				
Malden Manor link	81.8	72.4	68.4	56.7	51.8	45.8	43.8	38.5	29.7	27.3	19.3	17.3	11.7	6.1			
Berrylands	84.2	74.8	70.8	59.1	54.2	48.2	46.2	40.9	32.1	29.7	21.7	19.7	14.1	8.5	2.4		
Kingston-u-Thames	87.5	78.1	74.1	62.4	57.5	51.5	49.5	44.2	35.4	33	25	23	17.4	11.8	5.7	3.3	
Fulwell High St	93.1	83.7	79.7	68	63.1	57.1	55.1	49.8	41	38.6	30.6	28.6	23	17.4	11.3	8.9	5.6
A30/Hatton Cross	102.8	93.4	89.4	77.7	72.8	66.8	64.8	59.5	50.7	48.3	40.3	38.3	32.7	27.1	21	18.6	15.3
Cranford	104	94.6	90.6	78.9	74	68	66	60.7	51.9	49.5	41.5	39.5	33.9	28.3	22.2	19.8	16.5
Hayes & Harlington	108.5	99.1	95.1	83.4	78.5	72.5	70.5	65.2	56.4	54	46	44	38.4	32.8	26.7	24.3	21
West Drayton	113.3	103.9	99.9	88.2	83.3	77.3	75.3	70	61.2	58.8	50.8	48.8	43.2	37.6	31.5	29.1	25.8
Uxbridge	120.2	110.8	106.8	95.1	90.2	84.2	82.2	76.9	68.1	65.7	57.7	55.7	50.1	44.5	38.4	36	32.7
West Harefield	128.2	118.8	114.8	103.1	98.2	92.2	90.2	84.9	76.1	73.7	65.7	63.7	58.1	52.5	46.4	44	40.7
Moor Park	135.8	126.4	122.4	110.7	105.8	99.8	97.8	92.5	83.7	81.3	73.3	71.3	65.7	60.1	54	51.6	48.3
Hatch End	141.8	132.4	128.4	116.7	111.8	105.8	103.8	98.5	89.7	87.3	79.3	77.3	71.7	66.1	60	57.6	54.3
Stanmore Hill	149.4	140	136	124.3	119.4	113.4	111.4	106.1	97.3	94.9	86.9	84.9	79.3	73.7	67.6	65.2	61.9
Elstree & B'wood	155.9	146.5	142.5	130.8	125.9	119.9	117.9	112.6	103.8	101.4	93.4	91.4	85.8	80.2	74.1	71.7	68.4
Great North Rd	168	158.6	154.6	142.9	138	132	130	124.7	115.9	113.5	105.5	103.5	97.9	92.3	86.2	83.8	80.5
Cockfosters	173.6	164.2	160.2	148.5	143.6	137.6	135.6	130.3	121.5	119.1	111.1	109.1	103.5	97.9	91.8	89.4	86.1
Turkey Street	186.1	176.7	172.7	161	156.1	150.1	148.1	142.8	134	131.6	123.6	121.6	116	110.4	104.3	101.9	98.6
Enfield Wash/Lock	187.3	177.9	173.9	162.2	157.3	151.3	149.3	144	135.2	132.8	124.8	122.8	117.2	111.6	105.5	103.1	99.8
Chingford	194.9	185.5	181.5	169.8	164.9	158.9	156.9	151.6	142.8	140.4	132.4	130.4	124.8	119.2	113.1	110.7	107.4
Chigwell	201.3	191.9	187.9	176.2	171.3	165.3	163.3	158	149.2	146.8	138.8	136.8	131.2	125.6	119.5	117.1	113.8
Havering-a-Bower	212.6	203.2	199.2	187.5	182.6	176.6	174.6	169.3	160.5	158.1	150.1	148.1	142.5	136.9	130.8	128.4	125.1
Harold Wood	221.1	211.7	207.7	196	191.1	185.1	183.1	177.8	169	166.6	158.6	156.6	151	145.4	139.3	136.9	133.6
Upminster Bridge	227.8	218.4	214.4	202.7	197.8	191.8	189.8	184.5	175.7	173.3	165.3	163.3	157.7	152.1	146	143.6	140.3
Rainham	235	225.6	221.6	209.9	205	199	197	191.7	182.9	180.5	172.5	170.5	164.9	159.3	153.2	150.8	147.5
Purfleet-on-Thames	242.6	233.2	229.2	217.5	212.6	206.6	204.6	199.3	190.5	188.1	180.1	178.1	172.5	166.9	160.8	158.4	155.1

London LOOP
DISTANCE CHART
Erith to Purfleet-on-Thames
(KILOMETRES)

Fulwell High St	A30/Hatton Cross	Cranford	Hayes & Harlington	West Drayton	Uxbridge	West Harefield	Moor Park	Hatch End	Stanmore Hill	Elstree & Borehamwood	Great North Road	Cockfosters	Turkey Street	Enfield Wash & Enfield Lock	Chingford	Chigwell	Havering-atte-Bower	Harold Wood	Upminster Bridge	Rainham	
9.7																					A30/Hatton Cross
10.9	1.2																				Cranford
15.4	5.7	4.5																			Hayes & Harlington
20.2	10.5	9.3	4.8																		West Drayton
27.1	17.4	16.2	11.7	6.9																	Uxbridge
35.1	25.4	24.2	19.7	14.9	8																West Harefield
42.7	33	31.8	27.3	22.5	15.6	7.6															Moor Park
48.7	39	37.8	33.3	28.5	21.6	13.6	6														Hatch End
56.3	46.6	45.4	40.9	36.1	29.2	21.2	13.6	7.6													Stanmore Hill
62.8	53.1	51.9	47.4	42.6	35.7	27.7	20.1	14.1	6.5												Elstree & Borehamwood
74.9	65.2	64	59.5	54.7	47.8	39.8	32.2	26.2	18.6	12.1											Great North Road
80.5	70.8	69.6	65.1	60.3	53.4	45.4	37.8	31.8	24.2	17.7	5.6										Cockfosters
93	83.3	82.1	77.6	72.8	65.9	57.9	50.3	44.3	36.7	30.2	18.1	12.5									Turkey Street
94.2	84.5	83.3	76.8	74	67.1	59.1	51.5	45.5	37.9	31.4	19.3	13.7	1.2								Enfield Wash & Enfield Lock
101.8	92.1	90.9	86.4	81.6	74.7	66.7	59.1	53.1	45.5	39	26.9	21.3	8.8	7.6							Chingford
108.2	98.5	97.3	92.8	88	81.1	73.1	65.5	59.5	51.9	45.4	33.3	27.7	15.2	14	6.4						Chigwell
119.5	109.8	108.6	104.1	99.3	92.4	84.4	76.8	70.8	63.2	56.7	44.6	39	26.5	25.3	17.7	11.3					Havering-atte-Bower
128	118.3	117.1	112.6	107.8	100.9	92.9	85.3	79.3	71.7	65.2	53.1	47.5	35	33.8	26.2	19.8	8.5				Harold Wood
134.7	125	123.8	119.3	114.5	107.6	99.6	92	86	78.4	71.9	59.8	54.2	41.7	40.5	32.9	26.5	15.2	6.7			Upminster Bridge
141.9	132.2	131	126.5	121.7	114.8	106.8	99.2	93.2	85.6	79.1	67	61.4	48.9	47.7	40.1	33.7	22.4	13.9	7.2		Rainham
149.5	139.8	138.6	134.1	129.3	122.4	114.4	106.8	100.8	93.2	86.7	74.6	69	56.5	55.3	47.7	41.3	30	21.5	14.8	7.6	Purfleet-on-Thames

INDEX

Page references in **red** type refer to maps

TRAILBLAZER'S BRITISH WALKING GUIDES

We've applied to destinations which are closer to home Trailblazer's proven formula for publishing definitive practical route guides for adventurous travellers. Britain's network of long-distance trails enables the walker to explore some of the finest landscapes in the country's best walking areas. These are guides that are user-friendly, practical, informative and environmentally sensitive.

'The same attention to detail that distinguishes its other guides has been brought to bear here'.
THE
SUNDAY TIMES

● **Unique mapping features** In many walking guidebooks the reader has to read a route description then try to relate it to the map. Our guides are much easier to use because walking directions, tricky junctions, places to stay and eat, points of interest and walking times are all written onto the maps themselves in the places to which they apply. With their uncluttered clarity, these are not general-purpose maps but fully edited maps drawn by walkers for walkers.

● **Largest-scale walking maps** At a scale of just under 1:20,000 (8cm or 3⅛ inches to one mile) the maps in these guides are bigger than even the most detailed British walking maps currently available in the shops.

● **Not just a trail guide – includes where to stay, where to eat and public transport** Our guidebooks cover the complete walking experience, not just the route. Accommodation options for all budgets are provided (pubs, hotels, B&Bs, campsites, bunkhouses, hostels) as well as places to eat. Detailed public transport information for all access points to each trail means that there are itineraries for all walkers, for hiking the entire route as well as for day or weekend walks.

Cleveland Way *Henry Stedman*, 1st edn, ISBN 978-1-905864-91-1, 240pp, 98 maps

Coast to Coast *Henry Stedman*, 9th edn, ISBN 978-1-912716-11-1, 268pp, 109 maps

Cornwall Coast Path (SW Coast Path Pt 2) *Stedman & Newton*, 6th edn, ISBN 978-1-912716-05-0, 352pp, 142 maps

Cotswold Way *Tricia & Bob Hayne,* 4th edn, ISBN 978-1-912716-04-3, 204pp, 53 maps

Dales Way *Henry Stedman,* 1st edn, ISBN 978-1-905864-78-2, 192pp, 50 maps

Dorset & South Devon (SW Coast Path Pt 3) *Stedman & Newton*, 2nd edn, ISBN 978-1-905864-94-2, 340pp, 97 maps

Exmoor & North Devon (SW Coast Path Pt I) *Stedman & Newton*, 2nd edn, ISBN 978-1-905864-86-7, 224pp, 68 maps

Great Glen Way *Jim Manthorpe,* 2nd edn, ISBN 978-1-912716-10-4, 184pp, 50 maps

Hadrian's Wall Path *Henry Stedman*, 6th edn, ISBN 978-1-912716-12-8, 250pp, 60 maps

London LOOP *Henry Stedman*, 1st edn, ISBN 978-1-912716-21-0, 236pp, 60 maps

Norfolk Coast Path & Peddars Way *Alexander Stewart*, 1st edn, ISBN 978-1-905864-98-0, 224pp, 75 maps

North Downs Way *Henry Stedman*, 2nd edn, ISBN 978-1-905864-90-4, 240pp, 98 maps

Offa's Dyke Path *Keith Carter*, 5th edn, ISBN 978-1-912716-03-6, 268pp, 98 maps

Pembrokeshire Coast Path *Jim Manthorpe*, 6th edn, 978-1-912716-13-5, 236pp, 96 maps

Pennine Way *Stuart Greig*, 5th edn, ISBN 978-1-912716-02-9, 272pp, 138 maps

The Ridgeway *Nick Hill*, 5th edn, ISBN 978-1-912716-20-3, 208pp, 53 maps

South Downs Way *Jim Manthorpe*, 6th edn, ISBN 978-1-905864-93-5, 204pp, 60 maps

Thames Path *Joel Newton*, 2nd edn, ISBN 978-1-905864-97-3, 256pp, 99 maps

West Highland Way *Charlie Loram*, 7th edn, ISBN 978-1-912716-01-2, 218pp, 60 maps

'The Trailblazer series stands head, shoulders, waist and ankles above the rest.
They are particularly strong on mapping ...'
THE SUNDAY TIMES

TRAILBLAZER
British Walking Guides
SEE p220 FOR FULL TITLE LIST

Great Glen WAY

Hadrian's Wall PATH

Coast to Coast PATH

THE Ridgeway

Dorset & South Devon COAST PATH

Thames Path

Orkney

Thurso

Stornoway O

Skye

O Inverness

Scottish Highlands Hillwalking Guide

O Aberdeen

Great Glen Way

Fort William O

SCOTLAND

Mull

West Highland Way

O Milngavie

Edinburgh

O Glasgow

Berwick upon Tweed

Arran

Kirk Yetholm O

Pennine Way

Bowness-on-Solway

Carlisle O

Hadrian's Wall Path

O Wallsend

Newcastle upon Tyne

N. IRELAND

O **Belfast**

Coast to Coast

St Bees O

Bowness-on-Windermere O

Dales Way

Robin Hood's Bay

O Filey

Helmsley O

Cleveland Way

REP. OF IRELAND

Isle of Man

O Ilkley

O York

Pennine Way

O Leeds

Hull O

O **Dublin**

I R I S H   S E A

Liverpool O   Manchester O

Prestatyn O

O Edale

Norfolk Coast Path & Peddars Way

O Lincoln

Anglesey

Bangor O

O Crewe

O Nottingham

Cromer O

ENGLAND

Norwich

Offa's Dyke Path

Birmingham O

Knettishall Heath O

Great Yarmouth

Cardigan O

Cotswold Way

WALES

Chipping Campden

The Ridgeway

Ivinghoe Beacon

London LOOP

Pembrokeshire Coast Path

Amroth O

Kemble O

Chepstow O

Cardiff

Bristol O

Bath O

Overton Hill O

London

Thames Path

Canterbury O

Exmoor & N Devon Coast Path

Minehead O

Winchester O

Farnham O

Dover O

North Downs Way

Bude O

Salisbury O

Exeter O

Portsmouth O

Brighton O

Eastbourne O

South Downs Way

Plymouth O

Poole O

Isle of Wight

Cornwall Coast Path

Isles of Scilly

Dorset & S Devon Coast Path

ENGLISH CHANNEL

| 0 | | 50 | | 100km |
| 0 | 25 | | 50 miles | |

TRAILBLAZER TITLE LIST

Adventure Cycle-Touring Handbook
Adventure Motorcycling Handbook
Australia by Rail
Cleveland Way (British Walking Guide)
Coast to Coast (British Walking Guide)
Cornwall Coast Path (British Walking Guide)
Cotswold Way (British Walking Guide)
The Cyclist's Anthology
Dales Way (British Walking Guide)
Dorset & Sth Devon Coast Path (British Walking Gde)
Exmoor & Nth Devon Coast Path (British Walking Gde)
Great Glen Way (British Walking Guide)
Hadrian's Wall Path (British Walking Guide)
Himalaya by Bike – a route and planning guide
Iceland Hiking – with Reykjavik City Guide
Inca Trail, Cusco & Machu Picchu
Japan by Rail
Kilimanjaro – the trekking guide (includes Mt Meru)
London Loop (British Walking Guide)
Madeira Walks – 37 selected day walks
Moroccan Atlas – The Trekking Guide
Morocco Overland (4x4/motorcycle/mountainbike)
Nepal Trekking & The Great Himalaya Trail
Norfolk Coast Path & Peddars Way (British Walking Gde)
North Downs Way (British Walking Guide)
Offa's Dyke Path (British Walking Guide)
Overlanders' Handbook – worldwide driving guide
Pembrokeshire Coast Path (British Walking Guide)
Pennine Way (British Walking Guide)
Peru's Cordilleras Blanca & Huayhuash – Hiking/Biking
Pilgrim Pathways: 1-2 day walks on Britain's sacred ways
The Railway Anthology
The Ridgeway (British Walking Guide)
Scottish Highlands – Hillwalking Guide
Siberian BAM Guide – rail, rivers & road
The Silk Roads – a route and planning guide
Sinai – the trekking guide
South Downs Way (British Walking Guide)
Thames Path (British Walking Guide)
Tour du Mont Blanc
Trans-Canada Rail Guide
Trans-Siberian Handbook
Trekking in the Everest Region
The Walker's Anthology
The Walker's Anthology – further tales
West Highland Way (British Walking Guide)

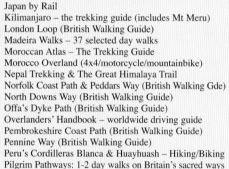

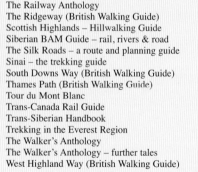

For more information about Trailblazer and our
expanding range of guides, for guidebook updates or
for credit card mail order sales visit our website:

www.trailblazer-guides.com

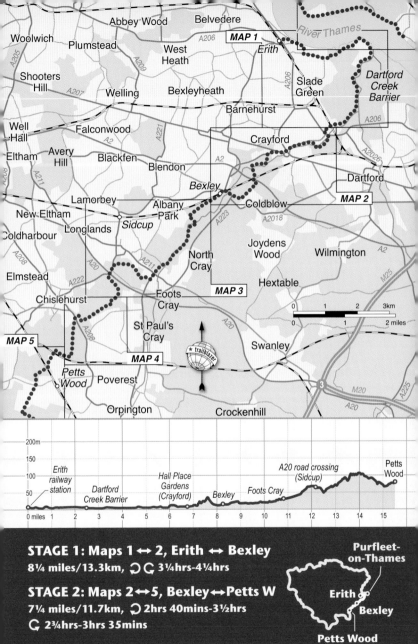

STAGE 1: Maps 1 ↔ 2, Erith ↔ Bexley
8¼ miles/13.3km, ↻ ↺ 3¼hrs-4¼hrs

STAGE 2: Maps 2 ↔ 5, Bexley ↔ Petts W
7¼ miles/11.7km, ↻ 2hrs 40mins-3½hrs
↺ 2¾hrs-3hrs 35mins

NOTE: Add 20-30% to these times to allow for stops

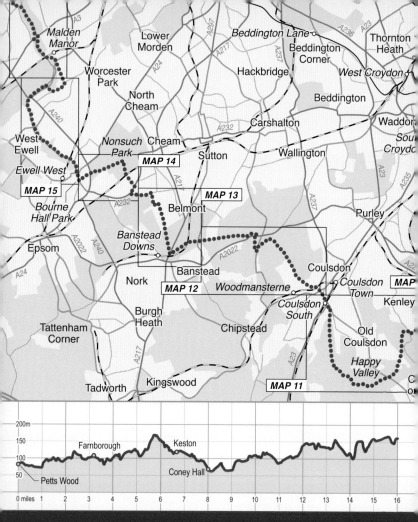

STAGE 3: Maps 5 ↔ 7, Petts Wood ↔ Coney Hall
8 miles/12.9km, ↻ ↺ 2hrs 50mins-3hrs 20mins

STAGE 4: Maps 7 ↔ 10, Coney Hall ↔ Hamsey Green
8¾ miles/14.1km, ↻ ↺ 3hrs 20mins-4hrs

STAGE 5: Maps 10 ↔11, Hamsey Green ↔Coulsdon Sth
6½ miles/10.5km, ↻ 2hrs 10mins-2½hrs, ↺ 2¼hrs-2hrs 35mins

NOTE: Add 20-30% to these times to allow for stops

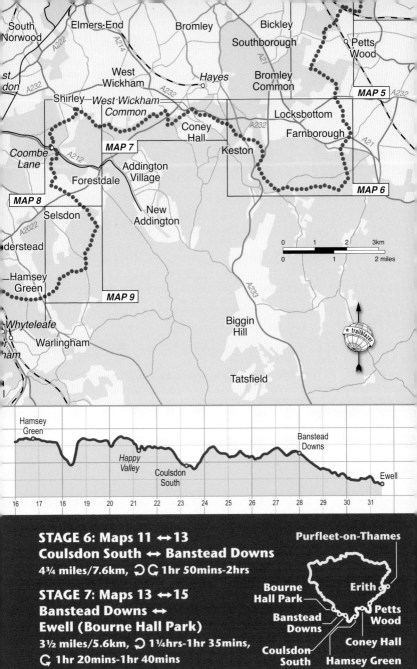

STAGE 6: Maps 11 ↔ 13
Coulsdon South ↔ Banstead Downs
4¾ miles/7.6km, ↻↺ 1hr 50mins-2hrs

STAGE 7: Maps 13 ↔ 15
Banstead Downs ↔
Ewell (Bourne Hall Park)
3½ miles/5.6km, ↻ 1¼hrs-1hr 35mins,
↺ 1hr 20mins-1hr 40mins

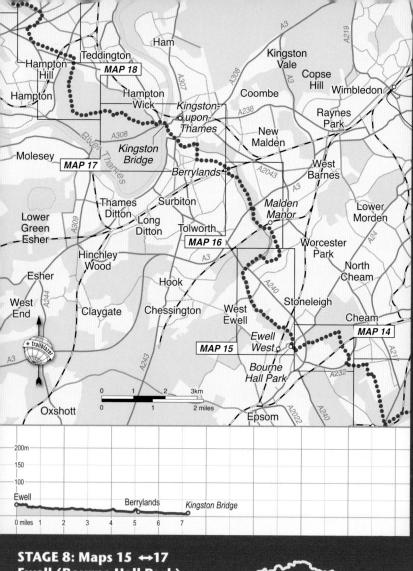

STAGE 8: Maps 15 ↔ 17
Ewell (Bourne Hall Park) ↔
Kingston Bridge

7¼ miles/11.7km, ◔ 2½hrs-3hrs 5mins,
◕ 2hrs 25mins-2hrs 55mins

NOTE: Add 20-30% to these
times to allow for stops

Erith ○—● Purfleet-
on-Thames

Kingston ○
Bridge

Bourne
Hall Park

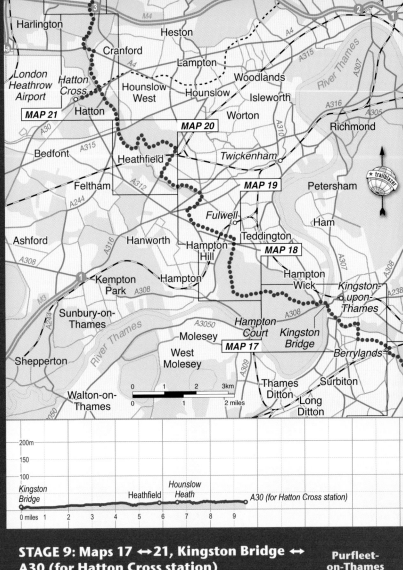

MAP 21

MAP 20

MAP 19

MAP 18

MAP 17

★ trailblazer

STAGE 9: Maps 17 ↔ 21, Kingston Bridge ↔ A30 (for Hatton Cross station)

9½ miles/15.3km, ↻ ↺ 3¼hrs-4hrs
(plus 15-20mins to
Hatton Cross station)

A30 (for
Hatton
Cross
station)

Purfleet-
on-Thames

Erith

Kingston Bridge

NOTE: Add 20-30% to these
times to allow for stops

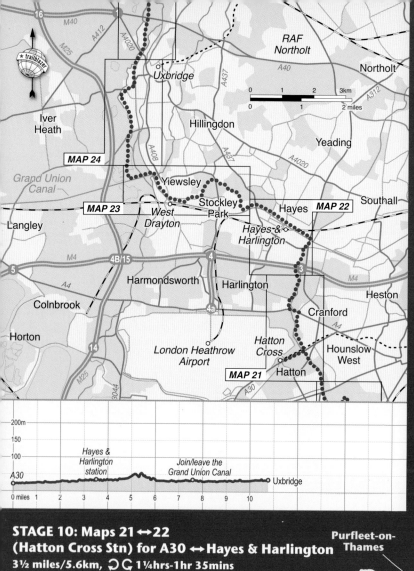

MAP 24

MAP 23

MAP 22

MAP 21

RAF
Northolt

Northolt

Uxbridge

Iver
Heath

Hillingdon

Yeading

*Grand Union
Canal*

Yiewsley

Stockley
Park

Hayes

Southall

Langley

*West
Drayton*

*Hayes &
Harlington*

Harmondsworth

Harlington

Heston

Colnbrook

Cranford

Horton

*London Heathrow
Airport*

*Hatton
Cross*

Hounslow
West

Hatton

200m

150

100

A30

*Hayes &
Harlington
station*

*Join/leave the
Grand Union Canal*

Uxbridge

0 miles 1   2   3   4   5   6   7   8   9   10

STAGE 10: Maps 21 ↔ 22
(Hatton Cross Stn) for A30 ↔ Hayes & Harlington
3½ miles/5.6km, ↺↻ 1¼hrs-1hr 35mins
(plus 15-20mins to navigate the A30)

STAGE 11: Maps 22 ↔ 25
Hayes & Harlington ↔ Uxbridge
7¼ miles/11.7km, ↺↻ 2¾hrs-3hrs 20mins

NOTE: Add 20-30% to these times to allow for stops

**Purfleet-on-
Thames**

Uxbridge

Erith

**Hayes &
Harlington**

**A30 for Hatton
Cross station**

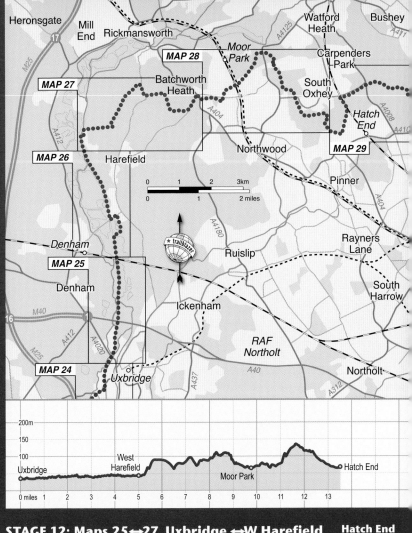

STAGE 12: Maps 25↔27, Uxbridge ↔W Harefield
5 miles/8km, ↻ ↺ 1½hrs-1hr 50mins

STAGE 13: Maps 27↔28, W Harefield ↔M Pk
4¾ miles/7.6km, ↻ 1hr 40mins-2hrs 5mins
↺ 1hr 35mins-2hrs

STAGE 14: Maps 28↔29, Moor Pk↔Hatch E
3¾ miles/6km, ↻ ↺ 1hr 35mins-1hr 55mins

NOTE: Add 20-30% to these times to allow for stops

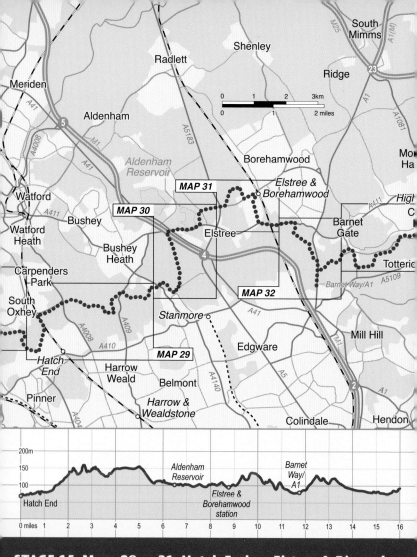

STAGE 15: Maps 29 ↔ 31, Hatch End ↔ Elstree & B'wood
8¾ miles/14.1km, ↻↺ 3hrs 10mins-3hrs 40mins

STAGE 16: Maps 31 ↔ 34, Elstree & B'wood ↔ Cockfosters
11 miles/17.7km, ↺ 4hrs 25mins-5¼hrs ↺ 4½hrs-5hrs 20mins

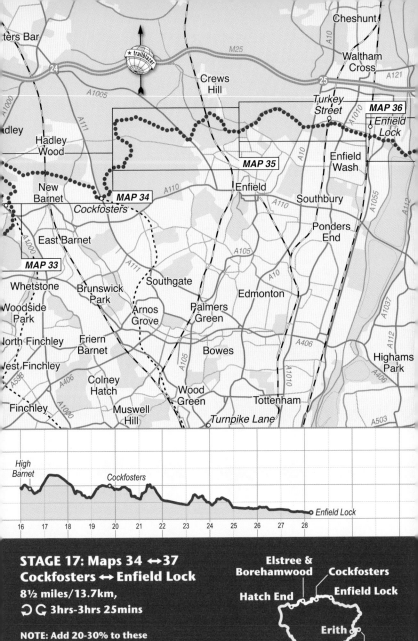

MAP 36

MAP 35

MAP 34

MAP 33

Cockfosters

Enfield Lock

High
Barnet

Cockfosters

Enfield Lock

16   17   18   19   20   21   22   23   24   25   26   27   28

STAGE 17: Maps 34 ⟷ 37
Cockfosters ⟷ Enfield Lock
8½ miles/13.7km,
↻ ↺ 3hrs-3hrs 25mins

**NOTE: Add 20-30% to these
times to allow for stops**

Elstree &
Borehamwood

Cockfosters

Hatch End

Enfield Lock

Erith

Purfleet-
on-Thames

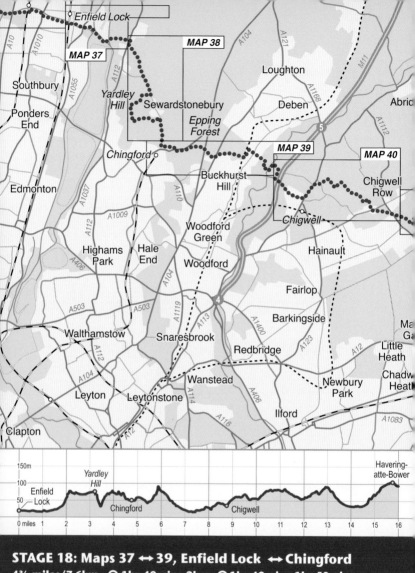

STAGE 18: Maps 37 ↔ 39, Enfield Lock ↔ Chingford
4¾ miles/7.6km, ↻ 1hr 40mins-2hrs, ↺ 1hr 40mins-1hr 50mins

STAGE 19: Maps 39 ↔ 40, Chingford ↔ Chigwell
4 miles/6.4km, ↻ ↺ 1hr 25mins-1hr 40mins

NOTE:
Add 20-30%
to these times to
allow for stops

STAGE 20: Maps 40 ↔ 42, Chigwell ↔ Havering-atte-Bower
7 miles/11.3km, ↻ 2½hrs-2hrs 50mins, ↺ 2hrs 25mins-2¾hrs

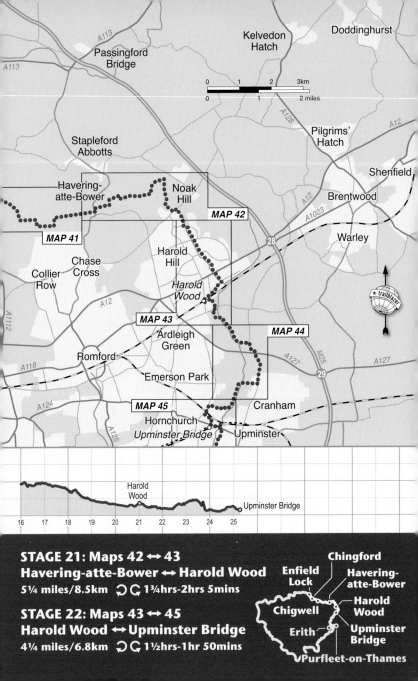

Passingford
Bridge

Kelvedon
Hatch

Doddinghurst

A113

A113

A128

Pilgrims'
Hatch

A12

Stapleford
Abbotts

Shenfield

Havering-
atte-Bower

Noak
Hill

MAP 41

MAP 42

Brentwood

A12

Warley

A1023

28

Chase
Cross

Harold
Hill

Collier
Row

A12

*Harold
Wood*

A1112

MAP 43

MAP 44

Ardleigh
Green

Romford

A118

Emerson Park

A127

M25

A127

29

MAP 45

Cranham

A124

Hornchurch

Upminster Bridge

Upminster

A125

0   1   2   3km
0   1   2 miles

Harold
Wood

Upminster Bridge

16   17   18   19   20   21   22   23   24   25

★ trailblazer

STAGE 21: Maps 42 ↔ 43
Havering-atte-Bower ↔ Harold Wood
5¼ miles/8.5km ↺↻ 1¾hrs-2hrs 5mins

STAGE 22: Maps 43 ↔ 45
Harold Wood ↔ Upminster Bridge
4¼ miles/6.8km ↺↻ 1½hrs-1hr 50mins

Chingford

Enfield
Lock

Havering-
atte-Bower

Chigwell

Harold
Wood

Erith

Upminster
Bridge

Purfleet-on-Thames

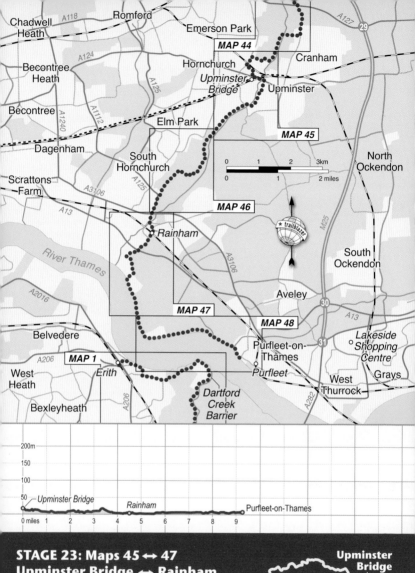

200m
150
100
50 — Upminster Bridge   Rainham   Purfleet-on-Thames

0 miles 1   2   3   4   5   6   7   8   9

STAGE 23: Maps 45 ↔ 47
Upminster Bridge ↔ Rainham
4½ miles/7.3km ↻ ↺ 1½hrs-1hr 50mins

STAGE 24: Maps 47 ↔ 48
Rainham ↔ Purfleet-on-Thames
4¾ miles/7.6km ↻ ↺ 1¾hrs-2¼hrs

Upminster Bridge
Rainham
Erith
Purfleet-on-Thames

**NOTE: Add 20-30% to these
times to allow for stops**

London LOOP
Erith – Purfleet

MAP KEY

0	5 miles
0	10km

home for several species of birds. In addition, the path passes through Rainham Marshes, perhaps the most famous bird-spotting site in the South-East, and the home to a state-of-the-art visitor centre.

For waterfowl, you'll definitely see several species of **ducks** and **swans**, as well as the large, grey, prehistoric-looking **heron**, the more diminutive **little egret** (*Egretta garzetta*) and **little ringed plovers** (*Charadrius dubius*).

Of the several species of geese, the most common are **Canada geese** (*Branta canadensis*). Introduced to the estates of wealthy landowners approximately 300 years ago, the population has exploded since and they're now the most common goose in southern Britain. Large and noisy, they are unmistakeable with their dramatic black and white patterned heads and brown bodies. In contrast to their wild congenitors in North America, which migrate the length of the continent in huge flocks, our Canada geese hardly move at all. Very aggresive, they can even threaten people in the breeding season, charging with an outstretched neck and hissing loudly. They are probably the most recognisable bird on the LOOP, along with the **mute swan** (*Cygnus olor)*.

You may also see (and hear) the **barnacle goose** (*Branta leucopsis*). The birds found here seem to have given up migrating, though those found in other parts of the UK are still migrants, returning to their nesting sites in Scandinavia each spring.

If you're very lucky you may also spot such rarities as the **spotted crake** (*Porzana porzana*) and **bittern** (*Botaurus stellaris*) at either Hornchurch Country Park or Rainham Marshes. This latter site also boasts both **barn owls** (*Tyto alba*) and **short-eared owls** *(Asio flammeus)*.

At home either by marshes and ponds or in the farmer's field, but on the LOOP **lapwings** (*Vanellus vanellus*) are best seen swooping above the marshes of Hornchurch Country Park. Black and white with iridescent green upper parts, the lapwing is approximately the size of a pigeon or tern. Its most distinctive characteristic, however, is the male's tumbling, diving, swooping flight pattern when disturbed, believed to be either a display to attract a female or an attempt to distract predators from its nest, which is built on the ground.

Woodland birds that you may see include the **nuthatch** (*Sitta europaea*), the **treecreeper** (*Corthia familiaris*), and **woodpeckers** of which there are three species: **great spotted** (*Dendrocopos major), **lesser spotted** (*Dendrocopos minor*) and **green** (*Picus viridis*). All of these can be seen to climb the trunks of trees by hopping up them (though only the nuthatch can descend by the same method). They share the woods with species such as the **whitethroat** (*Curruca communis*), **cuckoo** (*Cuculus canorus*; rarely seen but their distinctive 'cuckoo' call is often heard, though their numbers are declining sharply) and owls, in particular the **tawny** (*Strix aluco*) and **little owls** (*Athene noctua*). Hainault Forest is a great place to see most of these species.

In the suburbs it's the usual 'garden' species that dominate: the **great tit** (*Parus major*), **coal tit** (*Parus ater*), **blue tit** (*Parus caeruleus*), **blackbird** (*Turdus merula*), **mistle thrush** (*Turdus philomelos*) and **robin** (*Erithacus rubecula*). The most numerous bird in the town centre, of course, is the

woodpigeon (*Columba palumbus*), that famously thrive in Central London, despite the depredations of their number one enemy, the **sparrowhawk** (*Accipiter nisus*).

TREES

There's lots of woodland on the LOOP. Oak woodland is probably the most prevalent, a diverse habitat that's not exclusively made up of oak. Other trees that flourish here include **downy birch** (*Betula pubescens*), its relative the **silver birch** (*Betula pendula)*, **holly** (*Ilex aquifolium*) and **hazel** (*Corylus avellana*) which has traditionally been used for coppicing (the periodic cutting of small trees for harvesting).

Ash (*Fraxinus excelsior*) also dominates many of the woods along the trail, along with **wych elm** (*Ulmus glabra*), **sycamore** (*Acer pseudoplatanus*) and some **yew** (*Taxus baccata*). The **hawthorn** (*Crataegus monogyna*) also grows along the path, usually in isolated pockets on pasture, or, more commonly, as part of a hedgerow and/or a field boundary. These species are known as 'pioneer species' and they play a vital role in the ecosystem by improving the soil. Without interference from man, these pioneers – the hawthorn and its companion the **rowan** (*Sorbus aucuparia*) – would eventually be succeeded by longer-lived species such as the oak.

In wet, marshy areas and along rivers and streams you are more likely to find **alder** (*Alnus glutinosa*). There's also the **juniper** (*Juniperus communis*), one of only three native British species of conifer, the blue berries of which are used to flavour gin.

One rare species that does well in some of the woodland that you cross is the **wild service tree** (*Sorbus torminalis*), also known as the 'chequers' or 'checker' tree. A species that is part of the same family as the mountain ash, it has a smooth grey bark, though distinctively it flakes away to reveal a darker brown layer. It's a hardwood, and the wood is valuable. The tree requires a lot of light but is often out-competed by other trees. Its presence usually indicates that the woodland is ancient. Bishops Wood (see p144) is one place where it thrives.

Another species that indicates that the woodland is ancient is the **field maple** (*Acer campestre*). On the LOOP you can find it in Churchfield Woods before Bexley and in Crofton & Darrick Woods.

THE ENVIRONMENT & NATURE

Harebell
Campanula rotundifolia

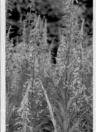

Rosebay Willowherb
Epilobium angustifolium

Himalayan Balsam
Impatiens glandulifera

Early Purple Orchid
Orchis mascula

Rowan (tree)
Sorbus aucuparia

Dog Rose
Rosa canina

Forget-me-not
Myosotis arvensis

Red Campion
Silene dioica

Scarlet Pimpernel
Anagallis arvensis

Bluebell
Hyacinthoides non-scripta

Germander Speedwell
Veronica chamaedrys

Herb-Robert
Geranium robertianum

Ramsons (Wild Garlic)
Allium ursinum

Meadow Cranesbill
Geranium pratense

Common Dog Violet
Viola riviniana

Common Centaury
Centaurium erythraea

Above, clockwise from top left: Grey heron in Bushy Park (© Anna Udagawa), mallard, Egyptian geese, Canada goose, mute swan, greylag goose (all © HS), black-headed gull (© BT).